WHEN FRANCE FELL

WHEN FRANCE FELL

THE VICHY CRISIS AND THE FATE OF THE ANGLO-AMERICAN ALLIANCE

MICHAEL S. NEIBERG

 Harvard University Press

CAMBRIDGE, MASSACHUSETTS

LONDON, ENGLAND | 2021

First printing

Publication of this book has been supported through the generous
provisions of the Maurice and Lula Bradley Smith Memorial Fund.

Library of Congress Cataloging-in-Publication Data
Names: Neiberg, Michael S., author.
Title: When France fell : the Vichy crisis and the fate of the
    Anglo-American alliance / Michael S. Neiberg.
Description: Cambridge, Massachusetts : Harvard University Press,
    2021. | Includes bibliographical references and index.
Identifiers: LCCN 2021010189 | ISBN 9780674258563 (cloth)
Subjects: LCSH: France—History—German occupation, 1940–1945. |
    France—Politics and government—1940–1945. | United States—
    Foreign relations—France. | France—Foreign relations—United
    States. | United States—Foreign relations—Great Britain. | Great
    Britain—Foreign relations—United States. | United States—
    Foreign relations—20th century.
Classification: LCC DC397 .N43 2021 | DDC 940.53/22730944—dc23
LC record available at https://lccn.loc.gov/2021010189

To Geoff Megargee

CONTENTS

Political Division of France after the Armistice of June 22, 1940.

INTRODUCTION

A FIGHT FOR LOVE AND GLORY

SECRETARY OF WAR Henry L. Stimson called it "the most shocking single event of the war."[1] The *New Yorker*'s war correspondent A. J. Liebling said that it had left the entire world in a "complete funk."[2] Veteran diplomat Robert Murphy observed that "never before or since" had one event "so stunned the entire world."[3] William Langer, a Harvard historian hired by the State Department to write a secret study of the American response to the catastrophe, wrote that "history has recorded but few events as cataclysmic." It would, he noted, confront "the United States as well as other nations with a host of new problems, none of which could be ignored or postponed."[4] Harold Ickes, the secretary of the interior, confided to his diary that "there is no doubt in my mind that this country is in the most critical situation since we won our independence."[5] No less a figure than President Franklin Roosevelt said before an emergency joint session of Congress that it represented a major watershed in the history of the world, and one with dire consequences for the security of the United States.[6]

These observers were not talking about the Japanese bombing of Pearl Harbor, the discovery of the horrors of the Holocaust, or the German invasion of the Soviet Union, but the stunning defeat of France in just six weeks in May and June 1940. Although today some Americans tend to treat it as a comedic punch line or the almost inevitable consequence of a

1

combination of French weakness and German boldness, the rapid fall of France absolutely shocked contemporaries. All American and British defense planning had begun from the assumption that the powerful French army, protected by the imposing Maginot Line, would tie the Germans down as the French had done on the western front from 1914 to 1917, giving a new Allied coalition time to organize, mobilize, and join the fight.

The British had counted on the French army almost as much as the Americans had. Lord Halifax wrote in his diary during the campaign for France that "the one firm rock on which everybody had been willing to build" during his tenure as secretary of state for foreign affairs from 1938 to 1940 "was the French Army, and the Germans walked through it like they did the Poles."[7] The collapse of the French army, which in 1937 Winston Churchill had called "the only guarantor of international peace" and in early 1940 "incomparably the strongest military force in Europe," forced the British to recognize that they would soon have to fight the modern, powerful Germans alone.[8]

Normally, historians in the English-speaking world have told the story of the crisis years 1940 to 1944 in Europe almost exclusively in relation to American interactions with the British, a normal response given how close the alliance between the two countries became from 1942 to 1945. The nearly mythic relationship that developed between distant cousins Franklin Roosevelt and Winston Churchill has added a personal touch to the global drama of the Second World War. This book in no way seeks to deny the significance or the long-term importance of the Anglo-American relationship in all of its complexity.[9]

Nevertheless, leaving France out of the picture or moving it to a sideline gives only part of an answer to the infinitely complex problem of understanding the early years of the Second World War in Africa and Europe. Because so few people in the United States or Great Britain could have envisioned the fall of France in 1940, no one had planned for it. When, contrary to all expectations and predictions, it happened anyway, Americans especially panicked. The dramatic redrawing of Europe's borders directly threatened the very security of the United States itself. If the Germans or Italians seized the French fleet or forced France to grant the Axis use of ports in the French empire worldwide, then the United States could find itself in an indefensible position. American strategists worried that German success might also lead to support for pro-Axis operations in Latin America or even fifth column activity inside the United States itself. The basic assumptions that underlay the sense of safety Americans felt from the crises of Europe vanished overnight.[10]

THE WIDESPREAD PANIC throughout the United States following the fall of France had deep and lasting impacts on American society and the way the United States government understood what it had to do to ensure its own security. Never again would it trust so much of its own safety to the military power of a third party. Except for a brief period of demobilization at the end of the Second World War, American strategic plans thereafter centered on large, peacetime appropriations on defense and a standing military of a kind quite unusual in American history. Americans never again wanted to feel the sense of danger and exposure that they felt in the months after June 1940. As this book will show, the United States committed itself in this time period to spending a truly enormous amount of money to build a world-class army and navy that might restore the sense of security once provided indirectly by the French military.

The sense of panic led to fears of spies and traitors at home because Americans assumed that the Germans could not have defeated France so thoroughly and so quickly without inside help. Well before Pearl Harbor, the fall of France led to unfounded questions about the loyalty of immigrants and those with political views outside the mainstream. It convinced President Roosevelt to ignore the Supreme Court on a matter of civil liberties, and it caused a repetition of many of the extralegal acts committed by private groups and local governments during the First World War. America's complex and multilayered relationship with the new French regime also led to the first admission by a senior American official that the United States government knew about the mass murder of Europe's Jews.

At least in hindsight, some Americans claimed to have seen the problems in a rotten Third Republic France.[11] Diplomats like Robert Murphy later wrote that France "exuded gloom" in the late 1930s despite the outward confidence that the French (as well as the British and the Americans) still retained in the French military. Years of political infighting, endless labor strife, the partisan division of French society, and the pressures of trying to remain neutral during the Spanish Civil War had taken their combined toll on the French body politic. French communists drew comfort from the Nazi-Soviet pact of August 1939 that cynically divided

Poland. As long as the pact remained valid, French communists need not see Germany as an enemy, or so they naively convinced themselves into believing. They therefore continued to vote against military readiness programs and focused their hatred on French conservatives.[12] For their part, those conservatives blamed the weak system of parliamentary rule built into the French Third Republic, often openly wishing for a more authoritarian government like the ones found in neighboring Spain, Italy, and Germany.

During the period of the so-called phony war in late 1939 and early 1940, American ambassador to France William Bullitt did what he could to help without committing American power to the conflict. He publicized his meetings with key French officials to send a signal to the Germans of the strength of Franco-American unity. Still, he saw that the deep divisions within French society left France unprepared for war. He described a Paris of "sullen apathy" waiting in "expectation of some dire calamity" to come. Robert Murphy agreed, finding Parisians "just too tired" to face the grim reality of another war and France's leaders "inept and unrealistic." They allowed themselves to believe that their own line of fortifications had forced Germany to look first to Poland in 1939 and then to Norway in 1940, thus sparing France as a battlefield in this war. This kind of wishful strategic thinking proved terribly wrong, as Murphy and Bullitt came to realize, maybe even before most Frenchmen and Frenchwomen themselves did.[13]

Murphy later claimed to have met just one French leader, a well-respected general named Henri Giraud, who seemed fully confident in France's future. The two men met by chance in the Gare du Nord in 1939. That meeting had a dramatic importance for American policy toward France three years later. In May 1940, however, Giraud's confidence was a rare commodity among French leaders. When war broke out, Giraud moved his Seventh Army into the Low Countries a part of France's ill-starred war plan, but Germans tanks surrounded his forces, and he himself became a prisoner of war. The Germans, who accused him of ordering the execution of two German civilians, put him in the high-security prison in the castle at Königstein. That should have ended Giraud's war, but fate took a different turn and placed him back in the spotlight in 1942.

THIS BOOK TELLS the now largely forgotten story of how the United States responded to the fall of France, as stunning an event to contemporaries as any that occurred during the Second World War.[14] This story involves enough espionage, larger-than-life personalities, and even an assassination to make it a thrilling story in its own right. However, looking beyond the good story, it has much to teach us about the past and the present. Examining how the United States dealt with France from 1940 to 1945 fills in some of the empty spaces in American and British understandings of the Second World War. It also provides a case study of statecraft in a rapidly changing environment where long-standing assumptions about the international system often disappeared overnight. This story does not always reflect well on the behavior of the United States government; it therefore tends to run counter to the usual heroic and triumphal stories about the war that normally dominate our memories. To leave America's dealings with France out of the picture, however, leaves that picture terribly incomplete, like a jigsaw puzzle missing some of its most important pieces.

American decisions about France, moreover, caused more friction in the Anglo-American relationship than any other topic in the early years of the war. Thus, taking a closer look at France can help illuminate the limits of the "special relationship" between the United States and Great Britain as well as the tensions in alliances and coalition today. When it came to France, the United States and Britain, allies though they may have been, began from divergent global interests, assumptions, and goals. Those divergences led the two partners to see different problems in France and to look for quite different solutions. On more than one occasion, policy on France threatened to crack the public appearance of Anglo-American unity.

The divergent views about the new France began to emerge even before the French capitulation. The first representative of the new France to come to the United States was a familiar face, a statutory American citizen directly descended from the Marquis de Lafayette and born from an American mother, Clara Longworth. Count René de Chambrun was aristocratic, genteelly conservative, and related by marriage to both the new power broker in France, Pierre Laval, and to the Roosevelts themselves. During an extended visit to the United States that began while France was still fighting for its life, he promised that even in defeat his country would remain pro-American, anti-Nazi, and staunchly anti-communist. That vision of France proved irresistible to Americans trying to make sense of a new and frightening world. A France run by men like Chambrun might be the best that Americans could hope to see emerge out of the tragedy of 1940. It took many of those Americans almost four years to realize how badly they had misread France and how much faith they had unwisely placed in Chambrun's vision of it.

At the same time, the British welcomed the junior-most general in the French army, Charles de Gaulle, to London. Determined to fight for his own vision of France, de Gaulle was one of the few senior French officials to not only reject the Chambrun vision of France but to dedicate himself to its complete and total overthrow. On June 18, while Chambrun was on a speaking tour of the United States, de Gaulle delivered his now-famous radio address from London. Although few heard it on that day, its vision of a France liberating itself with the help of its empire and its global allies gradually took shape and de Gaulle himself became in British eyes the logical, if erratic, leader of a Free France in exile.

Chambrun and de Gaulle represented opposing understandings for how France would deal with the calamity of 1940. Chambrun supported the transfer of the legal trappings and administration of France to a new government based in the small resort town of Vichy, thus ending the Third Republic and making the best out of the new international security environment dominated by Germany. De Gaulle rejected the legitimacy of this new government, arguing that it had no right to dissolve the Third Republic and no authority to speak for France as long as it cooperated with the German occupiers. He charged that French officials like Chambrun and his father-in-law had "ceded to panic, forgotten honor, and delivered the country into servitude." Still, he told his fellow Frenchmen and French-women, all was not lost because in a world war, France could still recover its honor, its freedom, and its grandeur. France had lost a battle, he said, but France had not lost a war.[15]

The Roosevelt administration chose Chambrun's path, the wrong one, as it turned out. Once it recovered from what one diplomat called a shock like a blow to the head, the Roosevelt administration made the controversial decision to recognize the collaborationist Vichy government run by Marshal Henri-Philippe Pétain and Chambrun's father-in-law, Pierre Laval. Roosevelt sent the talented Admiral William Leahy as his ambassador, a symbol of the importance the administration placed on the relationship. The United States also sent limited amounts of money and aid to Vichy. These decisions proved terribly unpopular both in the United States and with America's closest ally, Great Britain. Critics of the administration's decision in London and at home warned that Vichy was nothing more than a Nazi lackey and that, by recognizing it, the United States risked providing direct aid and comfort to the enemy.

Working with Vichy also made it that much more difficult for the United States to claim a moral high ground or to stand on the lofty principles of the Atlantic Charter as articulated by Franklin Roosevelt and Winston Churchill in August 1941.[16] The United States, led by Murphy and Secretary of State Cordell Hull, held stubbornly to the policy of recognition and aid even as the failures of that policy became painfully obvious. Recognizing Vichy meant isolating de Gaulle, whom the Americans disliked in any case. Sharp and intense disagreements over France caused as much division in the Anglo-American relationship as almost any other topic from 1940 to 1944, twice causing Hull to overreact and lash out at his British colleagues, often in petty ways. On at least one occasion he threatened to resign.

After the Anglo-American invasion of French North Africa in November 1942, Vichy broke diplomatic relations with the United States, which might have provided a chance for a fresh start. Instead, the Americans cut a controversial deal with one of the key leaders of that government, a reactionary and power-hungry admiral named Jean-François Darlan. News of the deal sent shock waves of anger through the United States and Great Britain. Once again, the United States government seemed to sacrifice honor and decency for military expediency. Fortuitously for everyone, one Frenchman who hated the deal gave them a way out of it by murdering Darlan outside his own office. But the end of Jean-François Darlan did not solve America's problems with France, which only grew as the anticipated liberation of France neared.

AMERICA'S RELATIONSHIP WITH FRANCE during the Second World War began from a bad policy based on flawed assumptions. American officials had too little understanding of the highly unusual situation in France and too much faith in the flattery of ostensibly pro-American French officials. They took far too long to realize that despite the obnoxious and difficult behavior of Charles de Gaulle, British support of his movement gave the Allies the best option both for winning the war and rebuilding France after it. Instead, the United States dealt with a succession of anti-democratic French officials whose domestic policies directly contradicted the lofty humanitarian goals that American leaders used as the public expression of the Allied war effort. The United States did more than temporarily set human rights aside in the interest of winning the war. Its senior officials lent their immediate and material support to discriminatory and dictatorial policies even after the country had achieved its military aims.

Defenders of American actions during the war and after claimed that the United States had adopted the only course consistent with winning the war. As British policy shows, however, other options certainly existed, and better ones at that. American leaders made decisions in a terrifying period when virtually all of the assumptions the nation had made about its safety and security vanished in six short weeks. The France policy that the Roosevelt administration developed emerged from an atmosphere of deep fear; working with Vichy appeared to some of those officials like a piece of driftwood worth clinging to in stormy seas. Their reflexive dislike of Charles de Gaulle, optimism that they could manipulate successive French leaders, and a suspicion of de Gaulle's links to communists and socialists caused them to hold on to this failed approach, even long after public criticism of it had become almost impossible for the administration to answer.

In 1942 and the beginning of 1943, French North Africa sat at the epicenter of the American and British war efforts in the Atlantic. The North Africa campaign brought together a fascinating combination of future leaders who came to Algiers in those crucial days. They included three future heads of state (Charles de Gaulle, Dwight Eisenhower, and Vincent Auriol), four future prime ministers (Harold Macmillan, René Pleven, René Mayer, and Pierre Mendès-France), two future heads of the Central Intelligence Agency (CIA) (Roscoe Hillenkoetter and Walter Bedell Smith), a future Nobel Peace Prize winner (René Cassin), the so-called father of Europe (Jean Monnet), a future president of the United Nations Security Council (Henri Hoppenot), at least nine future ambassadors to major powers, seven future heads of their nation's or the North Atlantic Treaty Organization's army or navy, and almost a dozen future government ministers. What they did and the lessons they learned in these years had impacts for decades to come.

Moreover, Americans' attitudes toward, and relationship with, France provide a lens into how they saw the world from 1940 to 1943, a time when no one knew for sure who would win the war or what the world would come to look like after it. They also show how American views of the postwar world developed from 1943 to 1945. In this brief period, the United States rose into superpower status despite years of isolationist sentiment and laws enforcing the nation's neutrality.[17] The immediate causes of this transformation pull us back to a battle on the Meuse river in the middle of May 1940 at the fortress city of Sedan, a massive stronghold screened by the Ardennes forest, which most French (and many German) strategists judged too strong ever to fall. As long as it held, the Germans could never conquer France.

But conquer it they did, and with Sedan fell most of the assumptions Americans had made about their own security. The United States had limited military budgets in the 1920s and pursued political isolation in the 1930s in large part because of its faith in the French military. France did not need to be a formal American ally for it to serve as a protective barrier for the United States from the conflicts of the Old World. Working with the Royal Navy to keep the Germans out of the Atlantic and, on land, once again preventing Germany from dominating the continent, the presumption of French strength gave American planners a wide variety of options for a relatively inexpensive defense. As long as France behaved at least as a benign neutral, America could benefit from the protection provided by its power. A budget-conscious nation in need of further domestic spending could therefore reduce its own defense expenditures accordingly. The government could then invest the money saved into the defense of American Pacific possessions such as Hawaii and the Philippines or use it to fund domestic programs.

The United States did not need a formal alliance with France for this strategy to work because the two nations shared common interests. The United States could benefit from French power without having to commit to anything in return. Even while it had fought the war in 1917 and 1918, the United States had rejected all French overtures toward a collective security arrangement or formal alliance. The same attitudes persisted into the postwar period. To the frustration of French officials in the 1920s, Americans knew that they did not need to commit themselves to French defense or for France to cooperate actively with American strategy. Without doing anything, the United States could benefit from French military power because France had its own interests in preventing any major shift in the European balance of power. France also shared the American interest in preventing the German navy from having unfettered access to the Atlantic

Ocean. That overlap of interests permitted the United States to focus its efforts in Latin America in the 1920s and the western Pacific in the 1930s. France provided a kind of insurance policy against the need to return to Europe as long as Americans continued to assume that France had sufficient power to deter or defeat another German invasion. That assumption remained firmly in place until May 1940, informing all American decision making on security.

Of course, few American defense specialists understood their strategy in such explicit terms. They spoke instead of staying away from the hatreds and conflicts of the Old World or they advocated financial and diplomatic solutions that aimed at creating balances of power. Americans helped the Germans refinance their debt, pushed concepts for disarmament, and supported the Kellogg-Briand Pact of 1928 that tried to outlaw war as an instrument of policy.[18] If successful, they all had the benefit of reducing America's need to plan for a return to Europe. None of them would have been an option if Americans had not felt a fundamental sense of safety from the hatreds of the Old World. Europe may not have learned the lessons of 1914–1918, but as long as France held the upper edge, Americans felt themselves protected from the endemic conflicts that Europe seemed to produce.

At least some Europeans understood clearly what the Americans had done and the weakened position in which the United States subsequently found itself in 1940. An insightful report on American defense written for Vichy officials by the Italian journalist and defense analyst Luigi Barzini expounded on the implications of American thinking after the First World War. America, he argued, "had rested on illusions created in the last war. Persuaded that it had won thanks to a decisive push from its marvelous improvised army, considered by Americans to be the world's best, America saw no need to arm" in the postwar years. France, they felt certain, would hold the line in the next war long enough for Americans to improvise another wonderful army if the need arose. As a result, in 1940 the United States found itself with too little money for defense, an industrial base completely ill-suited for war, no doctrine to deal with a war in Europe, and outdated military technology. Its economy, not centrally controlled by the government, retained its built-in bias toward providing the creature comforts of consumers over the vital needs of national defense.

As a result, without France to provide the lion's share of the men, weapons, and ideas, Barzini concluded, "war is an impossibility for America," which consequently "talks loudly, but acts quietly." Less presciently, he predicted that America's limited military power would incentivize it not to try to defeat Germany but to try to "win all that Britain has lost." It made strategic sense, he argued, for America to profit from the war by working with the Germans to achieve the long-term American goal of eliminating the British as a commercial rival. Only thus could the United States turn the negative of its lack of defense planning into a positive. France and Italy, he concluded, therefore had nothing militarily to fear from a United States Army possessing just 500 outdated airplanes and 500 tanks too light for service in Europe.[19]

Barzini, an influential voice among defense officials in the new France, obviously failed to foresee just how well the United States would translate its economic power into military power. Nevertheless, he had correctly diagnosed American overconfidence and unpreparedness. The Washington Conference's Five-Power Treaty of 1921–1922 set international naval tonnage limits to control spending on naval armaments.[20] The treaty seemingly guaranteed that the United States would face no Atlantic threat for the foreseeable future, so the American navy stopped building capital ships altogether. When the treaty expired in 1936, France went on a preplanned and preorganized modernization and growth program, but the United States did not. By 1939, French investments had begun to pay dividends, helping it to outnumber the German navy by seven battleships to six; one aircraft carrier to none; seven heavy cruisers to six; and twelve light cruisers to six. Together with the Royal Navy, the two allies overwhelmed the Germans by twenty-two battleships to six; eight aircraft carriers to zero; twenty-two heavy cruisers to six; and fifty-three light cruisers to six. The United States Navy therefore did not need to play any role at all in balancing the growth of German military power. Moreover, without a navy to transport them, the Germans could never put their army or air forces in a position to harm the United States or its hemispheric allies.

Thanks to French and British naval spending, the United States had the luxury of abiding by the limits built into the Five-Power Treaty well after most of the world's powers abandoned it. Ten of America's fifteen battleships in 1940 were from the First World War. The navy did not resume battleship construction until 1937, when it began work on the two in the USS *North Carolina* class. The completion of those ships in 1940 represented the first addition of capital ships to the American fleet in nineteen years.

By contrast, the French program stood ready to add two battleships, two cruisers, fourteen destroyers, and sixteen submarines.[21] Moreover, the protection provided by France and Britain allowed the United States to send the majority of its ships to the Pacific theater. Of the United States Navy's seventeen battleships, nine were in the Pacific, alongside thirteen of its eighteen heavy cruisers and eleven of its nineteen light cruisers.[22]

Similarly, the United States Army did not increase in size between 1925 and 1935. In 1937, American defense spending still sat at just 1.5 percent of national income in contrast to 5.7 percent in Great Britain, 9.1 percent in France, 23.5 percent in Germany, 26.4 percent in the Soviet Union, and 28.2 percent in Japan.[23] While much of the rest of the world rearmed, the United States maintained hard caps on military spending, and Congress passed a series of neutrality laws designed to insulate itself from the conflicts of Europe rather than prepare to deter or fight them. The more uncertain the international situation became, the stricter the Neutrality Acts became. Even after Italy's conquest of Ethiopia in 1936, Congress extended the Neutrality Act by fourteen more months. Further Neutrality Acts followed in 1937 and 1939. Although many individual Americans abandoned their beliefs in isolation and neutrality in the late 1930s, at the governmental level, neither the German remilitarization of the Rhineland nor the Nazi-Soviet pact nor even Germany's invasion of Poland forced a revision to the grand strategy of depending on France and Britain to act as shields.[24]

In the 1920s and 1930s, therefore, the belief in French power allowed the United States to behave, in the words of political scientists, like a free rider.[25] In effect, American faith in a powerful interwar French army and navy, combined with the British navy's traditional role of keeping open lines of communication, allowed the United States to vastly underspend on defense. Dollars that might have gone into defense instead went into the domestic programs that formed the core of Roosevelt's New Deal. Americans felt protected by more than two vast oceans; they knew (or at least believed) that France and Britain guaranteed their physical security. They therefore felt no direct threat from a rearming Germany.

WITH THE SUDDEN FALL OF FRANCE in May and June 1940, the entire architecture of American grand strategy collapsed. Most American strategists saw for the first time just how much of American security they had in effect outsourced to a foreign country. The resulting national panic over existential security matters led to an unprecedented flurry of defense spending and revolutionary change in American concepts of national security. The rapid and stunning collapse of France shattered American fantasies about its own safety almost overnight. Robert Murphy noted that despite all of the ugliness of world affairs in the 1930s, Americans had held on to a misguided faith in their "power of choice" in world affairs. They clung to a shared "sense of security amazingly possessed by most Americans at that time."[26] France and Britain had effectively underwritten much of that sense of security. But those days had now definitively ended. Looking back, observers like Murphy marveled at America's naive faith in its own safety. Few Americans before May 1940 saw that they had built that sense of security on a foundation of wildly inaccurate assumptions. After May 1940, they realized that their "power of choice" had vanished.

For their part, French officials had warned Americans that they needed to make greater contributions to what the French understood as a common war against dictatorship. French president Albert Lebrun criticized America to Ambassador William Bullitt for the failure of the United States to prepare alongside France for "the battle of all the democracies." Disillusioned by the outcome of the last world war and feeling sure that the Germans could not reach across the Atlantic Ocean to hurt them, Americans remained content to let France bear the full burden of what they should have seen as a common effort to defend democracy against the spread of fascism. Had the Americans done their fair share of the work of deterring and defeating a common enemy, Lebrun implied, France would never have fallen and American security would not be in such dire peril.[27]

The fall of France did more than destroy America's faith in that country; it opened up the real possibility of a German attack on the western hemisphere or on America itself, especially if the Germans managed to get control of the powerful French fleet. An America that one observer had described as "drunk on pacifism" in 1939 quickly became one terrified for its own survival. Military planners like Army Chief of Staff General George Marshall became fixated on fears that the Germans had plans to infiltrate or even seize parts of Latin America to use as a base for attacking the United States.[28] The army's War Plans Division shared that fear and wanted to prioritize the defense of the western hemisphere over that of the Pacific.

There now seemed nothing that could stop the Germans from posing a direct threat to America's core interests.

American defenses sat in such a parlous state in relation to the new threat environment that some influential observers looked to nonmilitary solutions as the only way to rescue the country from its own failures. A remarkable report from the Council on Foreign Relations, with future CIA director Allen Dulles listed as rapporteur, found its way to the army's War Plans Division. The report began from the assumption that "the utter collapse of the French Republic furnishes a vivid illustration of the necessity for ideological conviction as a basis for successful military action." In this view, America's lack of a military instrument of power could, paradoxically, form a cornerstone of the nation's strength. Military power as "the ultimate raison d'être of the state" and war as "a natural and ennobling process in the international struggle for existence" were characteristics of the totalitarian regimes of Germany, Italy, Japan, and the Soviet Union. Not having a military capable of fighting war, the paper suggested, showed that America operated under loftier, higher principles than those of the totalitarian states of Europe.

In contrast to the dictatorships, America stood in a position to lead the world into a brighter future "in which military power is regarded as a necessary attribute, but not a primary goal, of national sovereignty—a philosophy which considers *war as an aberration from what should be the peaceful norm of human development*." In the view of this report, American ideals, not the nation's military prosecution of war, had produced the great triumph of 1918. Not American soldiers but "the ideology of international democracy invaded the very camps of Hapsburg and Hohenzollern." The answer to the crisis of 1940, then, lay primarily not in building arms but in convincing the peoples of the world to adopt an American-style ideology along Wilsonian lines. "If we fail to produce an alternative to the use of force in the totalitarian philosophy, if we fail to demonstrate that our international society hold [*sic*] more hope for a peaceful and profitable future than theirs, then the United States (and other like-minded nations) will be forced into a defensive type of attitude which makes no converts and holds no friends."[29]

This view strikes the modern reader as remarkable in large part because it appears to us as hopelessly naive. We also know now that the United States did not follow anything like this blueprint from 1941 to 1945 or in the subsequent years of the Cold War. By the time Allen Dulles became head of the CIA and his brother John Foster became secretary of state in 1953, the United States had already committed to the massive investment in military spending envisioned in the Truman administration's NSC-68 plan of three years earlier and the country had committed to fighting a war in distant Korea. But in 1940, the Council on Foreign Relations memo offered a way to think outside the box by turning the negative of military unpreparedness into the positive of a higher American set of ideals. In the panicked moments of 1940, it seemed that almost any idea was worth exploring, even apparently paradoxical ones that emphasized nonmilitary strategies for winning wars.

Most Americans disagreed with the peaceful, nonmilitary approach suggested in the Council on Foreign Relations report. Almost unanimously, the newfound fear they felt led them to put military solutions front and center; with that shift in attitudes came a desire to spend almost anything in order to recover some sense of security in a rapidly deteriorating world. South Carolina senator and Roosevelt confidant James Byrnes provides a case in point. Until 1940, he had concerned himself with domestic issues such as supporting the New Deal, getting federal funding for internal waterway improvements for his state, and blocking attempts to pass a federal anti-lynching law. Suddenly in June 1940, he found himself worrying almost exclusively about foreign and defense matters. He began adding massive amounts of money to a pending naval appropriations bill that just weeks before had gotten stuck in committee due to congressional opposition to its enormous price tag. The newer, much larger bill passed after just three hours of debate.[30] In the spring of 1945, Byrnes's friend and sometime rival Harry Truman named him secretary of state, where he presided over diplomacy for the most powerful military the world had ever seen. The change in those five years had its initial spark in the loss of France as an indirect protector of American security.

FINALLY, TAKING A FRESH LOOK at Vichy's place in the international system can help to illuminate some of the most crucial questions in our own time. First, how do individuals, governments, and societies react when assumptions about their safety and security vanish? Just as COVID-19 has overturned assumptions about our world as I write in 2020, the events of May and June 1940 shattered long-standing beliefs that Americans had held dear—namely, that they need not concern themselves with the periodic firestorms of the Old World and that they would have time to organize another army and navy if the need ever arose. To isolationists, the failure of the peace process of 1919 only confirmed those beliefs, whereas to internationalists, the supposed strength of France and Britain plus the Atlantic and Pacific Oceans could at least give the United States that most precious resource of all—time. When that world and its guiding assumptions disappeared, the United States struggled to find a new one consistent with both its interests and its stated values.

American and British relations with Vichy, and with each other, also offer us a case study of great power rivalry in a time of rapid change. Pooling resources between London and Washington eventually emerged as a key to defeating the Nazi menace. But American and British interests did not overlap when it came to France, which in 1940 still had global responsibilities and influence despite its defeat. As in all great power competitions, events in seemingly faraway places like Chad, Iraq, and Indochina shifted power dynamics and changed the nature of the conversation.

The Vichy case study also allows us to ask questions about historical memory. America's Second World War really began not on December 7, 1941, but in the critical weeks of May and June 1940. The decisions American leaders made in the wake of those events shaped the remainder of the war and lasted well into the postwar years as well. Taking France out of this story, as too many histories of this period do, produces not only an incomplete history of the war but also an inaccurate, even a misleading, one. We can learn a great deal by taking a fresh look at Vichy and how the Anglo-American alliance treated it. Even on its own, however, the story is a fascinating one. It starts on the streets of Paris just before the German invasion of France in May, a time when few Americans envisioned that their own sense of security would soon vanish in a flash.

1

WE'LL ALWAYS HAVE PARIS

The Nazis March In

"THE WAR, OF COURSE, was not called off," wrote the *New Yorker* correspondent A. J. Liebling in spring 1940, "but there were few indications that it was on." In the previous weeks and months, Liebling had toured Paris and the front lines, finding a strange calm as Frenchmen and Frenchwomen went about their daily lives despite the mobilization of millions of young men and the reality that the killing and dying of a second world war in as many generations could begin at any minute. The nearsighted, out-of-shape, and distinctly unsoldierly Liebling crawled deep inside the vaunted Maginot Line, talking with confident French officers who told him that the massive concrete structures of the line would suffice to buy time for the British and Americans to mobilize and join the common fight once again. He also talked to French generals, including the commander of the French army General Maurice Gamelin, who told him that France did not depend on the Maginot Line alone. Having learned the lessons of modern war, the French had built anti-tank ditches and trained pilots to conduct tactical missions to control the skies. The Maginot Line did not strike Liebling as outdated but rather as one part of a dynamic French system under, on, and above the ground. The line would anchor French defenses in the center and right while the main Allied strike force on the left advanced into the Low Countries then across the Rhine and into Germany. All that remained now was to determine the timing.

Liebling's American readers followed his adventures in French cafés, government offices, and even brothels through the odd and unusually cold winter of 1939–1940 to gauge the reaction of the French people to a war that was not yet quite a war. He described a France both febrile with the activity of war and dulled by the lack of actual combat. This war seemed like a different kind of contest from the last one. This time, patience rather hurried and bloody offensives might win the day. Instead of wasting lives on pointless attacks by massed infantry, French forces would either block German attacks on the Maginot Line or maneuver around the line to hit the Germans in flank. One Frenchman Liebling spoke to compared France in this war to a peasant able to relax in his slippers because the strong wall he has built to protect his farmhouse keeps the neighborhood marauders away.[1]

The analogy seemed apt for the first few months of 1940. The French, alongside their British ally, had technically been at war since Germany's invasion of Poland in September 1939, but for months the two sides had simply glared at each other with daggers drawn. Or, to borrow the Frenchman's metaphor, the French people had hunkered down behind their walls, pushing the problems of Poland and the threat posed by marauding neighbors from their minds. Riven by internal divisions, few Frenchmen wanted another war for unclear political goals, let alone one to rescue a faraway country about which few people cared.

In this strange new world, France had declared war to rescue a Poland that no longer existed. Quickly divided between Germany and the Soviet Union, France could have done little to save the Poles even if the government had had the political will to do so. Still, even though it may have been true (as the saying went) that few people in France wanted to die for Danzig, Americans like Liebling had no doubt that they would rally and fight for France as they had in the last war.[2] In any case, as status quo powers, the French and British had no territory they coveted and therefore no incentive to attack before they were fully ready to do so.[3]

Most of the interest that Americans had in the war in September 1939 had largely faded by the following spring, even if the articles written by Liebling and others still had a loyal readership. The inaction and inactivity over the winter led isolationist Idaho senator William Borah to downplay the conflict as a "phony war" that had nothing to do with the United States.

His countrymen agreed. *Time* called it "a queer sort of world war—unreal and unconvincing."[4] Americans, the British ambassador reported back to London, displayed feelings of "boredom that the tremendous drama of un-limited aerial war in Europe which they had been educated to expect is apparently not going to come off."[5] Some in the Washington foreign policy elite even thought that an Anglo-French victory might prove as damaging to American interests as a German one because the former might lead to an extension of the British and French Empires, which tended to exclude American trade.[6]

The long period of mobilization without action convinced many in the United States that the diplomats would work out a solution before the war spread to France. There seemed no reason to contemplate the need to send American troops back to Europe for the second time in as many genera-tions. This time, the United States could play the role of arbiter, helping to negotiate a peace before the war spread any further. Surely, now that they had conquered half of Poland and settled matters with the Soviet Union through the Ribbentrop-Molotov Pact, even the vengeful Germans would see the wisdom in negotiating rather than repeating the mass slaughter of 1914–1918.

A poorly organized Anglo-French effort to assist Norway in April and May 1940 failed miserably, but even it did not shatter the aura of calm in the United States. Liebling did not mention Norway in his dispatches home, nor did a Paris-based American embassy employee named Marie-Louise Dilkes in her detailed diary. Almost no one saw in it a preview of the power of the German military to conduct quick campaigns of intense ferocity and localized matériel superiority.[7] Still less did they see the role that a handful of willing Norwegian collaborators played in assisting the German con-quest. Fighting closer to home and with the advantage of fortifications and support from the Royal Air Force, the French and the British would surely do better than the Norwegians and easily deter or defeat any German attempt to invade France.

Or so it seemed from the safety and security of the United States. Amer-ican newspapers featured maps and photo essays of the "impenetrable" bulwark of the Maginot Line complete with its specially trained soldiers, atmospherically controlled bunkers to safeguard troops against poison gas, and retractable turrets to allow the French to protect their artillery pieces.[8] One newsreel shown in theaters across the United States claimed that "the

French have built this great defense of their country, for never again will they run the risk of having their fair land destroyed by the enemy."[9] The French had spent more money on the Maginot Line than the United States and Great Britain together had spent on their fleets. France, every public indication suggested, had prepared for whatever the Germans tried to throw at it. American ambassador to France William Bullitt thought that the British shared that confidence, thus explaining what in retrospect came to look like a woefully insufficient commitment to the defense of France.[10]

Looking back from several decades of distance, it is easy to see how much people, especially in the United States, relied on hope and faith rather than reason. American armchair strategists assured people that the German string of success would surely stop if the German army tried to attack the French line of defenses; perhaps the Germans had avoided attacking in the west because they, too, grasped this essential truth. From his seat in the United States Senate, future American secretary of state James Byrnes recalled that "notwithstanding the success of the Nazis in Poland, a large portion of the American public still was not aware of the danger confronting us. In the absence of action on the western front people began referring to the 'phony war.' The feeling was as widespread as the phrase and was reflected in Congress." Byrnes wanted the United States to play a role not on the battlefield but in the peace negotiations that would end the war before it spread any farther. Just weeks after the fall of France, however, Byrnes found himself playing a different role, hurrying emergency defense spending through a Congress that had seen no need for it before May 1940.[11]

THE WORLD CHANGED not just for France but also for the United States on May 10. German forces invaded Belgium and the Netherlands, overwhelming those two small countries in a matter of days and shattering the phony war's false calm. French forces, confused by the speed of the German attack and partly immobilized inside the Maginot Line, reacted poorly. On May 12, German forces struck at the critical fortress city of Sedan, targeting an understrength French Second Army. Within just a few days, the Germans had torn open a hole almost fifty miles wide in the French line, and panic had set in among Allied forces. The mechanized

German spearhead then had what German armies had sought in France since 1914, exposed enemy flanks that they could rapidly exploit for decisive strategic gain.[12]

British and French forces moved northeast to block the Germans' presumed next move, an advance through Flanders to outflank the static defenses of the Maginot Line from the north and west. The Germans, however, had another surprise in store. Known as the "sickle cut" maneuver, German forces, led by seven Panzer divisions, advanced west then north from the general area of Sedan, exploiting their victory and trapping tens of thousands of Allied troops in a pocket against the North Sea based around the seaside town of Dunkirk. Within days, German forces reached the English Channel and seemed poised to annihilate the pocket.[13]

American ambassador to France William Bullitt was with the recently replaced prime minister Édouard Daladier when Gamelin delivered the "positively shocking" news of the defeat at Sedan. "No one, not even the most pessimistic, had expected the crisis to come so quickly," Bullitt wrote. The ambassador saw the defeatism starting to spread not just among the French but also the British officers remaining in Paris. "It seems obvious that unless God grants a miracle as at the time of the battle of the Marne [in 1914]," Bullitt wrote, "the French Army will be crushed utterly."[14] Unfortunately for the French, miracles like that at the Marne are rare indeed. This time, fortune favored the Germans at almost every step. The Germans seemed no less surprised than the French. The commander of the operation, General Heinz Guderian, used the word *miracle* to describe his army's unexpectedly easy triumph at Sedan.[15]

Back in the United States, Americans did not immediately perceive the magnitude of the disaster. Secretary of the Interior Harold Ickes remarked on the German attack at Sedan in his diary, but he wrote that France and Britain "have rushed troops and supplies so that it looks as if a vigorous resistance will be made." He found only one person then convinced of an imminent German victory, Chicago *Daily News* publisher and recent Republican vice-presidential nominee, Frank Knox, whom President Franklin Roosevelt had just summoned to Washington to discuss the rapidly changing European situation. With the Soviet Union and Nazi Germany in a nonaggression pact, the possibility existed of the two totalitarian powers essentially dividing Europe between them, giving the Germans a free hand to look overseas. Knox told Ickes that Germany would soon take what it wanted in Europe, then turn its eyes to setting up puppet regimes in South America. "We will have our work cut out for us in this country," he warned.[16]

Most American media reports, however, gave cause for optimism. Headlines on May 12 and 13, by which time the Germans had already experienced their first success near Sedan, read, "French Halt Germans; Essen Is Bombed," "British Flyers Hurl Destruction on Advancing Nazi Columns," and "Nazi Drive Halted."[17] The misguided early optimism of such reports made the final collapse of French forces all the more stunning. Not until May 20, five full days after the end of the Sedan battle, did newspaper reports begin to indicate the extent of the French defeat. Even on that day, however, reports wrongly suggested that Paris remained out of danger and that the arrival of French general Maxime Weygand from Syria had lifted the morale of French soldiers and civilians alike.

Americans in France, on the other hand, had little doubt about the magnitude of the French defeat. Marie-Louise Dilkes wrote, "It is the end of an era. It is the beginning of changes that will affect the whole world for generations to come."[18] Just four days after the attack on Sedan began, the French Foreign Office told senior American embassy officials that they would begin burning sensitive papers to keep them out of German hands; they urged the Americans to burn their own sensitive papers because the French army could not guarantee how much longer it could keep the Germans out of Paris. American diplomat Robert Murphy, destined to sit at the center of America's French policy for the next three years, went to the foreign ministry building to get a better sense of the evolving crisis. He arrived on the Quai d'Orsay in time to witness the terrifying spectacle of French diplomatic staff hurling bundles of papers out of windows so staffers could hustle them out of Paris on commandeered city buses. Other papers went directly into a bonfire.[19] The smoke from the fire, visible throughout central Paris, contributed to the growing panic in the capital.[20] If Murphy needed any final proof of the disaster happening to the east, he now had it right before his eyes.

The collapse of France came with shocking speed. Throughout June, 558,032 British and French troops evacuated from Dunkirk and western France to England. Although the British celebrated the rescue operations as a great national success, to the French, they meant the end of the campaign and the need to face the grim reality of a crushing defeat.[21] The Maginot Line had failed to do its job, and it seemed that nothing could stop the advancing Germans. Harold Ickes, now fully awake to the danger to France, recalled in his diary on June 12 that he had been in Paris in 1914 when the Germans had advanced to their closest point to the French capital. "But it must be much worse now because the hope that they can be turned back must be less than it was then."[22]

THE ROOSEVELT ADMINISTRATION PONDERED ITS OPTIONS, but events moved far too quickly for the United States to have an effect. Hastily cobbled schemes to rush American airplanes or warships to Europe melted away as the situation deteriorated by the day. French officials and American diplomats in Europe urged Roosevelt to send whatever he could, but the Roosevelt cabinet feared that any military action might prove unpopular at home. More importantly, specialists argued against sending supplies on logistical grounds because no one had ever thought it necessary to plan such operations. Moreover, the United States could not afford to lose any of its military hardware or its personnel on a risky symbolic gesture far from home.

With the French collapse becoming evident for all to see, "everything was confusion and contradiction" in Washington, leaving the United States with no good choices. As Harvard historian William Langer wrote, American leaders "had relied on the Maginot Line, the French army and the British navy, backed by American industrial power, to stave off the evil day."[23] But now, the evil day had suddenly arrived and no one in Washington had any idea how to react to it. On June 14, diplomat Anthony Biddle urged Roosevelt to make a symbolic declaration of war on Germany, but the president doubted that he would have the backing of the American people and he knew that symbols alone would not help France. He told Biddle that the United States would not recognize any German territorial gains made at French expense, but otherwise, his administration gave Biddle precious little guidance.[24] Roosevelt also dismissed a suggestion to parade military vehicles through Washington as part of an effort to reassure the American people. Ickes wrote in his diary that Roosevelt worried that whatever paltry display the army could arrange might reveal America's weakness rather than display its strength.[25]

The fear in Washington permeated all levels as the fall of France laid bare the basic errors in America's assumptions about Europe and, more immediately, its own security. Ickes observed that "all of us have had the sneaking hope that the façade of Germany was a false one behind which the economy would sooner or later break down and destroy the social structure that Hitler had built up." Instead, Germany was marching triumphant everywhere and, Ickes gravely noted, "with the wholehearted support of the German people." Even in the anti-intervention Midwest, the collapse of French power had forced a change of attitudes. "They are beginning to see," the Chicagoan Frank Knox told Ickes and Roosevelt, "that if Germany can beat all of western Europe to its knees in record time, we are not any too safe over here." Ickes wrote in his diary after a cabinet meeting on May 18 ("the longest cabinet meeting that I can remember") that "the problem now is to throw everything into high gear and prepare as fast as we can" for a suddenly uncertain future.[26] Ickes and Knox could only hope that America had not woken up too late; the fall of France gave a vivid warning of what horrors might await the nation if it had.

American officials in Paris, most importantly Ambassadors Bullitt and Biddle, saw the power of the new Germany up close. They watched helplessly as the France that they loved, and on which Americans had indirectly based so much of their defense planning, unraveled before their eyes. Marie-Louise Dilkes, who had first come to France to help refugees in the last world war, described the scene in a letter to her family in Philadelphia: "There were old men and women falling from exhaustion, having walked miles and miles from their homes fleeing the German army, seeking shelter in a foreign country. Young men and girls were supporting the old people; babies and small children unconscious of danger were sitting wide-eyed and still or sleeping in corners against the station pillars, near their baggage, suitcases, small trunks—their all."[27]

Senior American officials watched in horror as the British and French turned on each other. Ambassador Biddle recounted one heated exchange in which the new British prime minister Winston Churchill tried to stiffen French resolve by telling French marshal and newly named deputy prime minister Henri-Philippe Pétain that they had had tough times in 1918 as well but had won by holding the alliance together. Pétain snapped at Churchill: "In '18 I gave you forty divisions to save the British Army. Where are your forty divisions now?" Pétain did not need to remind Churchill of the other critical difference between 1940 and 1918: there were no American troops in France to provide a critical margin of manpower this time around. American diplomats watched a saddened General Maxime Weygand tell the French cabinet, "You want to hold out to the end. Well, you are at the end."[28]

The news grew more despondent as the disaster continued to unfold. American reporters in France sent back horrifying stories of the uncertain fates of millions of panicked, terrified refugees fleeing in "lurching, groaning, backfiring" vehicles. William Shirer, an American journalist who entered Paris with the Germans, reported that more than four million Parisians had joined a refugee exodus that had grown to an estimated eight million people in all. Fewer than 700,000 people remained in a Paris of shuttered shops wracked by a sense of complete fear. Unlike 1914, the French government had not kept the capital well informed; the approach of the Germans toward the city thus "fed on mounting rumor" that only grew more frightening.[29] Overcrowded railway stations moved what traffic they could, but they could handle only a fraction of the people trying to leave. Those with cars hit the road as quickly as possible, often without packing sufficient food or water for long, slow journeys on packed roads. The flow of refugees quickly turned into a desperate and uncontrollable flood.

Veteran war correspondent Virginia Cowles, who had previously witnessed refugee crises in Spain and Czechoslovakia, wrote that this one struck her as more tragic because it represented the first "mechanized evacuation in history." The terrible contrast of modern technology and the timeless human misery of war created an especially poignant juxtaposition. She saw hearses transporting children, unnervingly mixing images of youth and death. She also described a particular fear in the eyes of refugees whose cars had broken down or run out of fuel. Other refugees, desperate that stopped cars not block their own flight, had simply pushed the immobile vehicles into ditches, leaving their owners to fend for themselves as best they could. "In that world of terror," she wrote, "it was difficult to believe that these were citizens of Paris," the civilized City of Light to which so many Americans over the years had looked as a shining example of the best that humanity had to offer.

That France had disappeared in a flash. "The dam had begun to crumble," Cowles wrote. "Hysteria, a trickle at first, had grown into a torrent." France,

she told her readers, "was doomed."[30] In the *New York Herald-Tribune,*
Sonia Tomara described a France rendered hopeless after "weeks of horror
and misery." Writing from Bordeaux, a city now overwhelmed by tens of
thousands of refugees, she watched as a shocked French people wept while
they came to terms with the realization that their army and air force had
suffered a total and complete defeat. "There were no gestures, no words of
rebellion" in the people she met, only a numb acceptance that "they have
to go on living" amid nearly complete uncertainty about their own futures.[31]
A proud nation stared out at an unknown, and terrifying, future.

From the now "dead city" of Paris, Pulitzer Prize–winning foreign correspondent Louis Lochner wrote about the sad demise of the once "teeming,
gay, noisy metropolis" that so many Americans loved. Lochner walked by
the Hôtel Crillon on the place de la Concorde, a majestic building that
Woodrow Wilson had used as his base during the Paris Peace Conference.
The empty streets and the absence of the usual crowds on the nearby avenue
des Champs Élysées told a story of national tragedy. A swastika flew from
the balcony of President Wilson's former room, "where once the stars and
stripes had been in the days of 1919 when Wilson received the cheers of
French crowds."[32]

American officials watched the panic spread with their own eyes. With
great sadness, they recognized that their country lacked the resources to
ease the suffering and that a civil war could break out at any minute. On
May 28, Ambassador Bullitt reported that the French army, unable to win
the campaign against the German army, had begun to look for internal
enemies. Some of its leaders warned of "a communist uprising and butch-
eries in the city of Paris and other industrial centers as the German Army
draws near. The Paris police have no weapons except antiquated single shot
rifles." Even as the Germans approached the capital, the French army
hoarded ammunition in the event that they needed it to put down an
internal uprising.[33] A *Life* magazine correspondent in Paris noted that
"if ever there was a country ripe for revolution, it is France today." One
French soldier he talked with railed against the French middle class's
selfishness and called them "ripe for paving bricks," a reference to the
barricades the French construct in times of revolution.[34] Memories of
the Paris Commune of 1871, in which as many as 20,000 Frenchmen
died in a civil war in Paris after another defeat at the hands of a German

force, haunted imaginations in 1940. The sight of Paris's middle class fleeing the city in their private cars, leaving those without means to take their chances, multiplied the anger.

AS THE CRISIS BUILT, the remnants of the French government followed the flood of refugees, first to Tours, then to Bordeaux. Some members of that government, led by the Jewish and socialist former prime minister Léon Blum and the recently named prime minister Paul Reynaud, wanted to continue the war from the French colonies in North Africa. They and twenty-five members of the French parliament boarded a ship with the intention of going to Algeria and continuing the war with the French fleet and whatever army units they could rally to their cause. They were on board the ship during the final denouement of the French army, rendering their defiance courageous but ultimately futile. Reynaud, advised by his profascist mistress, the Comtesse Hélène de Portes, had by then lost his will to keep fighting. H. Freeman Matthews, the American chargé d'affaires in France, watched it all happen. "If ever a confident, courageous little man lost his nerve, it was Reynaud. He turned literally ashen grey in public."[35] As Reynaud and Blum surely knew, the battle had, in any case, ended. Reynaud's loss of nerve symbolized the collapsed of an entire country in a matter of a few short weeks. France with no leaders and no allies was left, in the words of one Franco-American journalist, "amputated, headless, nearly formless."[36]

As the dust began to settle, most Frenchmen, stunned by the military collapse, argued that France had no choice but to sue for peace and make the best out of the military and political catastrophe. They were led by an aging hero of the last war, Marshal Henri-Philippe Pétain, who returned from his post as ambassador to Spain to become deputy prime minister on May 18. A larger-than-life figure beloved or at least respected by almost everyone in France, the eighty-four-year-old Pétain was one of the last surviving members of the great generation of senior commanders from the First World War. In 1917, he had taken over command of the French army in the midst of mutinies and crises. He had reformed it, modernized it, and led it to victory a year later. If France's greatest living icon, and a soldier above all, said that France had lost the war, then there really seemed no point in continuing the struggle. Even so proud a Frenchman as René de Chambrun, a direct descendant of the Marquis de Lafayette, recalled that "when we learned of [Pétain's] decision to ask for an armistice, we knew that any further resistance had become impossible."[37]

Only Pétain had the requisite authority and reputation to rally the nation and keep it together amid such a complete collapse and fears of civil war. His legendary womanizing, steely blue eyes, and eventual marriage in 1920 at age sixty-four gave him an aura of vigor and vitality that contrasted with the worries of population decline and decay in interwar France, although Pétain himself never had children. A strong critic of the government's defense policies in the 1930s, in 1940 he returned to France in its hour of greatest need. The cult of personality that developed around him depicted him as a man sacrificing his last years to shield France as well as he could from the traumas of occupation and a military defeat that the nation would never have suffered if its incompetent and venal politicians had only listened to his sage advice.[38] The pro-Pétain writer Céline called Pétain "Philippe le Dernier," King Phillip the Last. In him, the French invested much of the trappings of absolute monarchy, "the stature, the majesty, everything! And he believed in it all."[39] So, too, did his countrymen, desperate to find any light in the darkness and hopeful that the marshal would prove, once more, "capable of a miracle."[40]

Pétain also symbolized for his countrymen a France that had stood alone at the titanic Battle of Verdun in 1916, where the French army suffered an astonishing 379,000 casualties. It became the emblematic battle of the war for France in the interwar years, a life-or-death struggle against Germany that France had endured and survived through the patriotism of its brave men. Verdun launched the careers of several important French writers, many of whom played instrumental roles in the memorialization of the battle as a critical moment of national unity in the face of overwhelming odds. Verdun made Pétain's career as well. Before Verdun, he had a reputation as a general whose pessimistic views on the futility of offensive war placed him out of step with his superiors. In 1916, desperate for someone with the defensive mindset that Pétain possessed, the French government gave him command over the Verdun sector, then command over the entire French army. His efforts at Verdun made him nothing less than a savior of the state and the nation.[41]

A cult of personality dominated the new Vichy state, as seen
in this massive portrait of its chief of state, Henri-Philippe
Pétain. Many Americans bought in as well.

In 1940 as in 1916, France seemed once again to stand alone and in need
of a savior with the proper understanding of a changing world. France's
main coalition partner from the First World War, Great Britain, had limited
its commitments to France, then evacuated its men through Dunkirk;
Russia (now the Soviet Union) had a nonaggression pact with the Germans;
and the United States held firmly to neutrality. It fell once again to Pétain
to pick up the pieces and save France from destruction in its moment of
anguish. As the country's morale evaporated, he emerged as the most obvious, perhaps the only, man able to bear this burden.

Pétain's rise calmed fears, especially among the French middle class, that the collapse of the French army would lead, as it had in 1870–1871, to a communist uprising or a class-based civil war. *Life* wrote that if the French people "had not lost faith in democracy they had certainly lost faith in the kind of democratic system France had and the kind of politicians it raised to power." The French people may have had "very little to say about what happened" in May and June, but they would not object to a more authoritarian government because in times of such instability and chaos, they sought, above all, "some strong power to restore order in the land."[42] Pétain, whom Léon Blum called "the most human of our soldiers," fit that bill perfectly.[43] Indeed, he may have been the only man in France who could have, putting his "genuine gift for the dramatic word or gesture to good use" in order to rally the French to support the new order.[44] The cult of personality that surrounded him made the new France an extension of Pétain himself. Frenchmen and Frenchwomen often called him Le Maréchal, an honorific like Il Duce or Der Führer, but one that suggested that Pétain was not merely a demagogue but also a war hero and a leader with a decades-long record of great success.

Many of those who knew him well, however, knew that, in the words of American historian Robert Paxton, "the flesh and blood Pétain was less interesting than the myths surrounding him."[45] He had far less political acumen than people assumed, and he had both a pessimistic view of human nature and a generally defeatist mindset. He also looked and acted every bit like a tired man in his declining years. A *Life* reporter who knew him called him "a prime anachronism in the world of 1940."[46] In June of that year, however, a humiliated and defeated French people needed myths and anachronisms more than they needed flesh and blood. Pétain the myth served their needs better than Pétain the man.

NOT EVEN PÉTAIN COULD STOP the military collapse, however. On June 11, the French government declared Paris an open city in order to save it from an air and ground assault; the Nazis marched in three days later, parading down the avenue des Champs Élysées to signal their triumph. Pétain took over the government in Bordeaux on June 16 in the midst of the greatest crisis that had ever befallen France. It had taken just one month for France, one of the most powerful nations in the world, to become a conquered and humiliated one. The Germans compounded the humiliation by summoning their French counterparts to the same forest clearing where Marshal Ferdinand Foch and General Maxime Weygand had imposed armistice conditions on Germany in November 1918. The symbolism did not bode well for France. As the German official history noted, the conquerors wanted "to make it clear to the vanquished that the results of the First World War were about to be reversed."[47]

Even amid the collapse, however, the French still retained some power to influence events. The Germans, surprised by their own rapid success, had made no plans to govern or occupy as large and complicated a place as France, especially one that still had the potential for mass resistance, civil war, or a communist uprising. They wanted to exploit French resources, but they did not believe that they needed a complete occupation to achieve those ends. Nor did they want to risk the possibility of the French continuing the war from their empire in Africa and the Middle East. A pliant administration under Pétain's firm control could give them much of what they wanted and at a small price.

The French also had full control of their powerful fleet, which they had modernized and increased in the 1930s despite the global economic crisis and the attendant pressures for more social spending. In 1940, it was one of the best in the world, with eight battleships, an aircraft carrier, twenty cruisers, seventy destroyers, and seventy-eight submarines. Its morale had not broken. Its bases in Toulon and North Africa kept it away from the German onslaught and gave it a prime position to control shipping lanes through the Mediterranean. Although the navy could not help France avoid the catastrophe at Sedan, it did leave France in a position to negotiate something out of the defeat.

The armistice gave a broken France more than one might have expected in the wake of such a complete military defeat. Still, it was devastating. The English Channel and Atlantic coastlines, the industrial northeast, and the major cities of Paris, Bordeaux, and Lille came under direct German occupation. Most Frenchmen and Frenchwomen had to leave the coastal areas, which became a German military zone, and Italy took for itself a slice of southeastern France that included the Alpine defenses and the city of Nice. Most of the remainder of France, including the Mediterranean coast, the naval base at Toulon, and the cities of Marseilles and Lyon, formed an unoccupied zone governed by a new French regime officially called l'État français but more commonly called Vichy France after the quiet spa town that soon served as its capital.[48] The new French government technically maintained control over most domestic matters in the occupied zone as well, but all of its decisions there remained subject to German approval and a German-patrolled line of demarcation restricted the movement of people and goods between the two zones. On June 22, the two parties signed an armistice in the same railway carriage Foch and Weygand had used in 1918 to impose armistice terms on Germany; the conquerors took the railway carriage back to Germany as a trophy. They then destroyed the glade's anti-German memorial, symbolically erasing the past and ushering in the new Europe. The Germans left the statue of Ferdinand Foch intact so that the victor of 1918 would thereafter stand guard over nothing.[49]

PÉTAIN MOVED WHAT REMAINED of the French government to Vichy, an odd choice for a government seat. Before 1940, Europeans knew Vichy for its spas, famous since the Romans had used them. Medical experts advised that Vichy's waters contained high concentrations of the same chemicals found in human blood, thus drinking or bathing in them naturally strengthened the body's own defense mechanisms. The waters had a reputation for curing all manner of health problems from joint pain to liver and digestive ailments. The largest of the town's eleven main springs could produce as much as 140,000 liters of water per day, making it an ideal place to build an enclave for France's rich, powerful, and hypochondriac. Mme. de Sévigné, Napoleon's mother, King Charles X, and Emperor Napoleon III became frequent famous guests over the years. Entrepreneurs and government officials added an opera house, a casino, modern hotels, elegant parks, and dance halls, as well as hiking and riding tours of Vichy's beautiful hinterland. In a typical season, the town of 14,000 permanent residents might welcome as many as 130,000 visitors. Those who could afford it, from members of the old aristocracy to the nouveau riche of the rising middle class, spent entire summers there.

A guidebook published in 1936 described Vichy as "one of the prettiest spa towns in France," with a picturesque setting between verdant mineral-rich cliffs.[50] By the 1930s, modern medicine had begun to replace thermal spas, but the wealthy continued to come to Vichy anyway.[51] Some said they came in hopes of finding relief from sexually transmitted diseases and other maladies that they were too embarrassed to discuss, even with their own doctors. Others came for the entertainment and luxury of a season that lasted from the beginning of April to mid-October. By the late 1930s, Vichy remained a playground of France's rich and powerful, a place where they could get away from the chaos of Paris, relax, sip champagne, see, and be seen.[52]

Vichy's conservative aura suited Pétain perfectly, especially when contrasted to the chaos of 1930s Paris.[53] He and the elite who assembled in Vichy blamed the defeat of 1940 not on the French army they so adored but on the corrupt and ineffectual politicians of the Third Republic. Their venality and inability to put country before partisanship had, Vichy apologists argued, put France in an impossible position. With the nation now freed from the corruption of those politicians, Pétain aimed for nothing less than a national revolution that would wipe France clean of the Third Republic's atheism, self-indulgence, labor activism, and chaotic parliamentary democracy. In their place would come a return of eternal French institutions such as patriarchal families, the Catholic Church, and an economy based on the hardworking and honest peasant farmer. Out of the sins of the 1930s, most importantly the Third Republic's flirtation with socialism and communism, would come redemption.

PARADOXICAL THOUGH IT MIGHT SEEM, this man who had decided to give up the fight had an enthusiastic following in France's darkest hour. Acting as a kind of father figure to the nation, Pétain had seemingly saved a great deal for France out of the defeat and promised to put an end to what *Life* magazine called France's "sorry mess of scandal and backbiting."[54] Senior leaders in Vichy had a long list of domestic enemies they blamed for the defeat of 1940. Vichy would punish those enemies and bear the burden of defeat while a new vanguard of leaders rebuilt France. Pétain blamed unpatriotic schoolteachers, selfish women who had pursued pleasure rather than motherhood, socialists, trade unions, and immigrants. To hear Vichy officials speak, the German army appeared almost incidental to French defeat. The real causes of French rot, they contended, were internal, and now Vichy

A 1930s tourism poster advertises Vichy as a playground for the elite. The Vichy Opera House can be seen at the base of the "V" to the woman's left.

would look inward to find the solution. Pétain ally and writer Jacques Benoist-Méchin borrowed from the medicinal metaphor when he pledged that Pétain and Vichy would bring a "cure of purity" to French society.[55]

The new government would be small, efficient, and answerable directly to Pétain. He summoned the remaining members of the National Assembly to the ornate Vichy Opera House, where they voted themselves out of existence and transferred all power to the new État français. Almost the entirety of the government moved into an art deco hotel in Vichy's most fashionable district, alongside the pastoral Allier River and near the elegant, tree-lined boulevard des États-Unis. Vichy lawyers claimed that by the act of transferring power, the National Assembly had bestowed on Vichy all of the legitimacy and power of France. Resistance to it, therefore, became treason.

The Vichy regime jettisoned the French Republic's motto of *Liberté, Égalité, Fraternité* in favor of *Travail, Famille, Patrie* (Work, Family, Fatherland). Gone, too, were birth control, trade unions, "La Marseillaise" as the French national anthem, and Bastille Day as the national holiday. The new government would represent tradition and stability, not scandal and disunity. It would await Germany's inevitable defeat of Great Britain, then look to play a leading, if not quite equal, role in the new world order that a subsequent peace treaty would create. It was, Vichy officials argued, the best that France could hope for given the disaster of May and June.

Most Frenchmen and Frenchwomen accepted the new regime, if only because the defeat had left them stunned and powerless to resist the hurricane of recent events. As one socialist deputy later described it, the French people were "dazed, dismayed, incapable of judgment, and trusted the Marshal blindly."[56] Yves Bouthillier, Vichy's first minister of finance, defended his support of Pétain as the "best path to safeguard the future of France." In his view, and that of millions of his fellow Frenchmen and Frenchwomen in 1940, the traditional values now expressed as "*le maréchalisme*" offered a third way between the two greatest threats of the age, bolshevism and fascism, neither of which, Bouthillier argued, suited France.[57]

Beginning life under the duress of defeat and occupation proved a tall order for the new state. It had few economic resources and many of those that it did possess found their way to Germany either to pay the costs of the occupation or through trade terms that greatly advantaged the conqueror. Politically, it seemed to belong more to the nineteenth century than the twentieth. An American visitor described Vichy France as "a project of constructing a medieval authoritarian state on the ruins of a modern democracy." Another visitor with a sharper wit called it a banana republic with no bananas.[58]

Nevertheless, some Frenchmen and Frenchwomen, mostly on the right, viewed the ascent of Pétain as a "divine surprise" and his National Revolution as the only possible silver lining that could have emerged from the defeat.[59] The French middle class saw in it an end to the threat from the left's desire for a redistribution of wealth, and the Catholic Church saw it as protection from the atheist Third Republic governments that had rigorously enforced the separation of church and state in the 1930s.[60] Even most French communists reluctantly accepted the new order because Germany and the Soviet Union then had a nonaggression pact between them. Moscow did not want French communists upsetting the deal by actively opposing the German conquest. After the armistice, most of the French soldiers evacuated to Britain returned to France and demobilized, convinced that the war was, for their country, over.

Not everyone bought in, however. Charles de Gaulle eventually emerged as Vichy's most prominent opponent. Just shy of his fiftieth birthday, de Gaulle was then an obscure career soldier who had developed a keen political instinct as he rose through the ranks. He spent most of the First World War in a German prisoner of war camp learning the language of his captors and developing his ideas about war. He became an influential thinker on modern warfare, arguing for more mechanization and better training for French infantrymen. De Gaulle did not oppose the Maginot Line per se, but having seen the limits of fixed defenses firsthand at Verdun, he argued that France should not place its faith entirely on fortifications.[61] He became a key defense adviser to Prime Minister Paul Reynaud starting in 1935.

In large part because of that connection, de Gaulle received a promotion to brigadier general and assumed the post of undersecretary of state for defense in the first days of June 1940. Although he had no way to stop the collapse of the French army or stiffen Reynaud's spine, he did develop a relationship with the new British prime minister, Winston Churchill, meeting with him three times.[62] Rejecting what he saw as the French government's cowardice, he made the difficult decision to head to England on an airplane with the British liaison officer Edward Spears on June 17. As de Gaulle himself later recalled it, "I felt that a life was ending, a life that I had lived in the framework of a solid France and an indivisible army."[63]

Indeed, a life had ended and a new one had just begun. The same could be said of France itself. Once in London, de Gaulle developed a strong anti-Pétain vision of a reborn France that would emerge from the ashes of defeat and return to glory. He tried to offer the French people an alternative to Vichy with his now-famous radio appeal on the BBC on June 18, but few people in France heard it and even fewer yet knew who he was.[64] Still, even at this early date, he had laid out a vision of a renewed France with himself as its savior: "This is not a Franco-German war to be decided by a single battle. This is a world war. . . . Honor, common sense, and the interests of the country require that all free Frenchmen, wherever they be, should continue the fight as best they may. . . . I, General de Gaulle, am undertaking this national task here in England."[65] He sought nothing less than the formation of a French government in exile with himself as its (unelected and unappointed) head.

A few French soldiers, sailors, and airmen made their way to London to join de Gaulle, and a small number of resistance cells began to organize inside France itself, but at this early stage, they had no effect on German or Vichy power in France.[66] Although de Gaulle was still a minor actor in a rapidly unfolding drama, in August, he and Winston Churchill signed a memorandum of agreement solidifying de Gaulle as head of a Free French movement in exile.[67] For the time being, however, the vast majority of French citizens accepted Pétain, if only because they saw no viable choice. For its part, Vichy excoriated de Gaulle, once one of Pétain's most trusted subordinates, for abandoning France in a moment of such existential crisis. The new government revoked de Gaulle's French citizenship, seized his property, and sentenced him to death in absentia for treason, setting up a contest between differing definitions of France itself.[68]

AMERICAN AMBASSADOR WILLIAM BULLITT MET with the senior leaders of the new French government in June, and despite their public confidence, he found them a demoralized and deeply despondent group. Vichy leaders saw France as "so completely crushed and so without hope for the future that they are likely to say or do almost anything." The utter failure of French leadership in the 1920s and 1930s spurred a desire on their part to rebuild France by first destroying the old system root and branch. "French leaders desire to cut loose from all that France has represented during the past two generations," he observed. "Their physical and moral defeat has been so absolute that they have accepted completely for France the fate of becoming a province of Nazi Germany." Absolving themselves of any responsibility whatsoever for that defeat, their only hope lay in a quick German defeat of Britain followed by France becoming "Germany's favorite province" in the new Europe.[69]

American diplomats certainly recognized the level of optimism (or perhaps delusion) required of French officials to believe in a benign future for France under German leadership. H. Freeman Matthews reported that Vichy officials repeated their belief that "this unhappy period will soon be transformed by the resurgence of a strong new France. . . . While it is difficult to pin them down to any logical basis for this confidence—they point vaguely to France's glorious past—the belief here is real. The alternative they say is communism or chaos." After a few unpleasant years, they believed, France "will somehow again be in the driver's seat" as it took advantage of a stalemate between Germany, Europe's great land power, and Britain, its great sea power.[70] Vichy officials continually expressed amazement that Americans could not see the problem from the French viewpoint. France, they argued, was not doing Germany's bidding but doing its part to prevent a communist takeover of Europe. Some of them blamed expatriate French Jews for spreading calumnies about the new France in the United States and Britain.[71]

Bullitt, Matthews, and others found the depth of Vichy's hatred for its former British allies deeply concerning. That animosity did not bode well for a United States anxious to help the British survive the expected German attack to come. Admiral Jean-François Darlan, the head of Vichy armed forces, pledged that he would never allow the French fleet to sail to England for disarming and safekeeping and, more worryingly, said that he feared a British victory in the war as much as he feared a German one. German domination of Europe, Darlan told American officials, would not last forever, but even if lasted for years, "it had to be faced." He saw a Germany-centered Europe as preferable to a continent run on British terms. Pétain raged against the British as well, telling Bullitt that they "had scarcely participated in [the] decisive battle of the war," content instead to watch the

French suffer defeat at Sedan. "Their troops had run," Pétain bitterly complained, and their air force had only committed five of its forty fighter squadrons to the battle for France. Similarly, Darlan complained about British "premeditation to pull everything out of the north without advising us of it," a sardonic and deeply insulting reference to the Dunkirk operation in which the British took such great pride.[72]

Pétain told Churchill that Britain would have its neck wrung like a chicken's in three weeks.[73] Darlan gave the British slightly longer, expecting the British to last around five weeks once the Germans turned their full attention to an invasion or an air assault of the Home Islands. In the peace treaty to come, Vichy officials thought that Germany would likely take Ireland, Glasgow, Liverpool, and Cardiff to ensure that they could strangle British commerce as Britain had previously tried to strangle German commerce. Darlan, Bullitt noted, hated the British so much that he "seemed to regard this prospect with considerable pleasure."[74]

Supporters of the regime inside France understood that France would have to pay a price for the failures of the Third Republic. The Germans would keep Alsace and probably most of Lorraine, but they would presumably release all two million French prisoners of war in German camps and return full sovereignty over the remainder of France. The French government could then return to Paris or to the calmer environment of Versailles and continue to implement the National Revolution across the entire country. Overseas, France would probably have to accept the loss of Morocco, but Pétain believed that France would find a way to keep Algeria, where tens of thousands of Frenchmen and Frenchwomen lived and enjoyed the full rights of French citizenship.[75]

In the end, Vichy's rulers managed to convince themselves that France might even emerge stronger thanks to the cleansing of its corrupt prewar political class. The move from Paris, the "City of Pleasure," to Vichy, now styled by government propagandists as the "City of Work," would begin a national renewal that would eventually make France a world power once again.[76] Americans in France and Algeria watching it all unfold were baffled. When he heard the news, Robert Murphy wondered if moving the government to Vichy hadn't been "a bit of Gallic humor" to deal psychologically with the reality of defeat. It struck him and other Americans as "wryly appropriate that the government of defeated France should choose a place hitherto celebrated only for its rather disagreeable medicinal waters used to treat unpleasant but not necessarily fatal diseases."[77]

AMERICANS FROM WASHINGTON TO VICHY quickly saw that the French defeat could prove fatal not just to British interests but to American interests as well. "I suppose it comes hard to realize that the foundations of the order of things as you know it may have ceased to exist," wrote Assistant Secretary of State Adolph Berle. Or as Army Chief of Intelligence General Sherman Miles said in a public address on June 14, "Everything preceding the 10th of May last is ancient history."[78] Parts of the globe that American planners had once barely bothered to consider such as Senegal, Martinique, and Morocco now figured prominently in American assessments of the new situation. Once safely part of the benevolent French Empire, now they sat under the control of the new and unknown Vichy French leadership. Their fates suddenly became central to American security planning.

An American intelligence report prepared in September emphasized the importance of the French Empire in North Africa to American interests. Although the empire technically remained part of Vichy France and therefore inaccessible to the Germans under the terms of the armistice, the authors of the report had no faith at all that the French could resist German demands for the use of its natural resources, ports, and airfields. The African colonies of France in particular could form a key part of an Axis strategy for "destroying the greater Carthage which is the English-speaking commonwealths," including the United States. "The Axis powers," the report bluntly warned, "have now the opportunity to establish submarine bases [in Morocco and Senegal] off the routes between England and South Africa and South America." This situation posed a direct threat to the United States that demanded immediate action. "In a deteriorating and neglected situation, borrowed time, if not used, favors the totalitarian powers."[79] Analysts like the authors of this report worried that the fall of France would directly destabilize the security of the United States, which had paid far too little attention to events in Europe, let alone Africa, in the 1930s.

American officials in Washington lost several crucial weeks of time when panicked American consular officials in Tunis and Algiers burned their code books on hearing of the French defeat. After the reestablishment of secure communications, American consuls described French North Africa as "tense, depressed, unstable." Young French officers tended to express more pro-British sentiments than their senior officers. Some even claimed a willingness to fly their planes or sail their ships to Gibraltar to keep them out of German hands. Senior officers, however, "are the purest convention-alists who will probably follow whatever orders they get, even to fighting for Hitler." Most of the senior French administrators in North Africa were active and retired naval officers handpicked and promoted by Darlan. They would not take any step he did not approve. They were terrified for the safety of their families back in metropolitan France, confused by the new political atmosphere, and acted "just as Hitler would have [them] act," in the words of a senior American official in Algiers. "In short," wrote American consul Herbert Goold from the Moroccan port city of Casablanca, "the spectacle here is that of human nature at its worst."[80]

Still, not all seemed lost. Americans, too, had faith in Pétain. Bullitt told reporters on his return from France in July that the marshal was "doing his best to bring order out of desperate disorder." Bullitt also rejected a re-porter's claim that the new France had fascist tendencies. Most impor-tantly, Pétain professed a desire to keep positive relations with the United States. In Vichy, Pétain told a visiting American journalist that France "must be integrated within the Continental System" but that he saw no reason to expect any change in Franco-American relations. He even ex-pressed a desire to peg the franc to the US dollar.[81] At least for the first few weeks, it appeared that the new French leader could see France through the chaos without breaking its traditional friendship with the United States, giving a glimmer of hope to those Americans who wanted to believe that the new world order need not necessarily threaten American interests.

The bizarre political arrangements in Vichy did not help Americans un-derstand the new France and its potential political leanings. Pétain's cult of personality dominated both occupied and unoccupied France, although a small number of people vied with him for power in the new system. The best known was Pierre Laval, an unfailingly ambitious son of a butcher who had grown up not far away from Vichy. He had clawed his way up the so-cial and financial ladder, eventually buying the château in his hometown and developing reputations for both bureaucratic efficiency and an abso-lutely unbridled obsession with power. He had familial links to the United States and won *Time* magazine's Man of the Year for 1931 for negotiating an ultimately unsuccessful moratorium of debt payments with President Herbert Hoover. He served twice as French prime minister in the 1930s where he developed a reputation, ironically enough, as one of the leading anti-German voices in the French cabinet.[82]

If he had once seemed like an ideal politician on paper, especially to conservative Americans who shared his hatred of socialism and communism, Laval played less well in person. A notoriously slippery character, he had begun his political career as a socialist before declaring his independence among the shifting political sands of 1930s France. He then drifted increasingly to the right, trading his influence where he could for power, although he kept himself at arm's length from most of the genuine French fascist movements that sprang up in the decade.[83] With his reputation as a cynical politician of the worst kind and his slick mannerisms, he became easy fodder for his enemies. *PM* magazine's political cartoonist Theodore Geisel, better known today as Dr. Seuss, liked to draw Laval as a rat.

Robert Murphy had known Laval longer than any other American politician in France. He described Laval as "the shrewdest, most forceful personality in Vichy," a "ruthlessly ambitious man" who had full faith in his own abilities to steer France through any crisis, even this one. Murphy also noted that only Laval and Pétain seemed to have a plan amid the chaos of June 1940, even if Laval's mostly involved co-opting German power to increase his own. The Germans saw him as a reliable ally, a man willing to do their bidding for the minimal price of guaranteeing him a share of whatever power they chose to cede.

Laval's vision for France shared many of the same enemies and same goals as Pétain's.[84] In the words of the great historian of Vichy Robert Paxton, for Laval, the new world order meant "taking advantage of a foreign army to carry out major changes in the way Frenchmen were governed, schooled, and employed."[85] In return for Nazi support he proved willing to carry out Germany's wishes, including later in the war, facilitating the dispatch of French Jews to German camps. If Germany demanded the persecution of French Jews as the price Laval would have to pay to remain in its good graces, then he would surely pay it.[86]

Murphy, the most senior American official with regular access to the new elite, marveled at the confusion and novelty of it all. "In those first few weeks at Vichy," he wrote, "I think most of us felt as if we had been knocked on the head and were slowly recovering our senses. History has rarely, if ever, moved with such dizzying speed as in that summer."[87] When American officials did awaken, they found themselves in a new and puzzling world. Nothing seemed familiar and no one could read Vichy with any reliability. The new French leadership clearly reviled the British and feared the Germans, but they professed admiration for the United States and argued that nothing that had happened in the past few months should alter the traditional friendship between the two countries. The Vichy government, the legal government of France, could continue to work with the United States just as France always had.

LAVAL PROMISED MURPHY that he could rebuild France and lead it back to greatness. He also pledged to make friendship with the United States a cornerstone of the new government. His half-American son-in-law, the aristocratic René de Chambrun, descended directly from the Marquis de Lafayette and had been a friendly face among the American elite for many years. His mother was the sister of Ohio politician Nicholas Longworth, former Speaker of the House of Representatives and husband of Alice Roosevelt, Theodore's daughter. Chambrun had dual citizenship and in 1935 had opened a Franco-American cultural center in New York City. He was the perfect man to make the case in Washington that the fall of France did not necessarily mean that France and the United States had to drift apart.

Laval rushed Chambrun to the United States to explain the reasons for the French defeat to President Roosevelt, with whom he spent part of the weekend of June 15–16 on the presidential yacht. He then remained in the United States for several months, basing himself in Washington's Mayflower Hotel and speaking to a wide variety of audiences. Chambrun presented a pro-Laval and pro-Vichy version of events to Americans in Washington, New York, and the Midwest. He urged Americans to maintain their country's traditional friendship toward France and to rush aid to France as Americans had during the last war.[88] He also hurriedly published a largely self-serving book with an American publisher titled *I Saw France Fall* that presented the events of 1940 in a manner favorable to Laval to a wider public. The book cited Chambrun's own unsolicited report to the French army, which blamed the collapse of France on well-organized fifth columns and extensive communist propaganda among French soldiers.[89]

Through President Roosevelt, Chambrun met members of the American left, including the leaders of the major trade unions. Through the Longworths, notably including his influential aunt Alice, he met key conservatives. To all of these audiences, he shared his faith in France to survive the storm. Chambrun thought he had largely succeeded in presenting to American reporters and members of the political elite a sympathetic view of France and its new Vichy government.[90]

While Chambrun tried to persuade Washington elites of the merits of the new Vichy regime, Murphy was reporting to the State Department on Laval's supreme confidence that he could outfox Germany and keep the Germans from crippling France in the postwar peace conference to come. Laval blamed the hypocritical and dishonest British for missteps throughout the 1920s and 1930s that had pushed Europe into an unnecessary war. Germany, Laval believed, "contemplates a European Federation of States in which France will play an important role compatible with its dignity and tradition." He hoped that the Germans would soon beat the British on the battlefield and impose the same legal obligation for starting this war that the Allies had unjustly imposed on Germany after the last war through the Treaty of Versailles's infamous war guilt clause. Laval implored Murphy to convince his fellow Americans to send food and other aid to France and support the new anti-communist European order that France and Germany would build together.[91]

Murphy remained skeptical. In a mid-August telegram, he warned Secretary of State Cordell Hull that regardless of Laval's posturing, Germany had no intention of treating France fairly after the war. The Germans, he thought, wanted to eliminate France as a rival in Europe without stirring up unnecessary French animosity for the future. The Nazi regime had concluded that a minimally independent France "under the benevolent leadership of Germany" served its interests better than a vengeful France that might look to upturn the continental order at some point in the future.

An American visitor to Vichy who had lived for most of his life in France perceptively concluded that the proud and nationalist Vichy leaders simply could not grasp the reality that the Germans did not care what happened to France. They did not see France as a partner or even an adversary but just another in a long line of vanquished foes for Germany to eliminate when and how it desired. The French had instead deluded themselves into believing that control over the empire and the independence of the French navy meant that they still mattered in global affairs.[92] All evidence to the contrary notwithstanding, they believed that a peace conference would make France influential and powerful once more. Vichy leaders like Laval could not, or would not, see that France was no longer the great nation that had been a leader on the continent and around the world for centuries. Instead, France was nothing more than another Poland and its people reduced to "hewers of wood and drawers of water" for their German masters. Although they did not realize it, Laval and Pétain could do nothing to materially change that situation.[93]

Under such confused and uncertain circumstances, Vichy leaders might do anything to stay in Germany's good graces. All the more important, then, Murphy concluded, for the United States to develop a productive policy for dealing with the new France. Germany had defeated France on the battlefield, and its new political leadership, regardless of how it had come to power, claimed to want America's friendship. Murphy and Hull wanted to give it if for no other reason than that no alternative seemed better. For the first few months, at any rate, officials in the United States took a fairly positive view of the new French government notwithstanding the voices of concern from American officials in Vichy itself. Even if most Americans mistrusted or despised Laval, Pétain remained a widely respected figure in the United States and a man whose leadership seemed worth backing. Unlike the British, therefore, Americans argued that Vichy had the strongest claim to legitimacy in France. Americans, no less than the French themselves, seemed willing to put their faith in the hero of Verdun and hope beyond hope that he could create a France willing to do what they needed it to do.

TWO RIVAL OFFICERS, one from the army and one from the navy, shared military power in the new state. The more pro-American of the two, General Maxime Weygand, was an almost stereotypical martinet of a soldier. He had served as a young, energetic chief of staff to Pétain's colleague and rival Ferdinand Foch. Having personally delivered the terms of the armistice to the Germans in the railway car at Compiègne in November 1918, he loathed the idea of surrendering to them in 1940, but like Pétain, he believed that the failures of the left-leaning politicians of the now-disgraced Third Republic had given the French little choice but to seek an armistice.

Having worked with the Americans so closely in 1918, he knew many senior American officials, most of whom found him an odd character but a supremely competent and capable officer. Others saw him as just another superannuated French hero in a long line of old men out of their depth in the modern world. J. R. M. Butler, one of the British military's chief advisers on France, called Pétain and Weygand "two ghosts of the ancient glories of France."[94]

Darlan, the longtime head of the French navy, had ancestors who had served France in and out of uniform for generations. One had died at Trafalgar and his godfather had served as the French minister of the marine for seven years. His career skyrocketed after the First World War as he built a modern, powerful French fleet in the face of parliamentary parsimony. In the process, he acquired enormous prestige and power as well as the skills of a seasoned political infighter. Darlan made many enemies along the way, and almost no one in the French political system, least of all Laval, fully trusted him, but he instantly became one of Vichy's leading figures.[95] He commanded enormous influence in Africa through the French navy, whose senior officers held many of the most important administrative jobs there. The governors-general of Morocco, Tunisia, and Senegal were all Darlan protégés. Although he had not had a shipboard assignment in many years, he had the navy so deeply ingrained in his soul that American intelligence officers code-named him Popeye. One observer called him a "stuffy, unimaginative, infinitely ambitious" political operative with no friends but plenty of "yes-men and side boys" around him at all times.[96] He, too, had hated surrendering to the Germans but had seen no choice.

Darlan recognized the magnitude of the French army's defeat, but he also knew that his fleet remained intact and far from Germany's clutches in its Mediterranean bases. He told France's senior military envoy to the armistice negotiations not to sign any document that would force France to give away a single ship, and he told both the Germans and Winston Churchill that he would order the fleet to scuttle itself before he would see it commanded by anyone not French. He gave orders to that effect to his entire fleet and directed that those orders could not be revoked, even if they came in written form with his own signature. The French army may have capitulated, but as long as the fleet remained, Darlan argued, France could remain a world power able to control the resources of its far-flung empire. The navy would also give France a way to protect against further Italian aggression in the Mediterranean and deter the Germans from violating the terms of the armistice.[97]

Even amid all this upheaval, the calm, summertime environment of Vichy lent an odd air of normalcy to a very unusual situation. Pétain prevented most of France's fascist ideologues and violent troublemakers from coming to Vichy; he wanted nothing to do with fascism's modernism and corporatist economics, nor did he want to reform France along German or Italian lines. Instead, he would return France to its traditional models of Catholicism, pastoralism, and patriotism while France waited for Germany to force the British to a peace conference. His domestic model had more in common with the Portugal of António de Oliveira Salazar than the Futurist visions of Benito Mussolini's Italy.[98] Italian desires to expand at French expense, moreover, naturally put Pétain and senior Vichy officials in no mood to model Italy. Instead, Pétain sometimes spoke of forming a neutral "Latin bloc" with Spain and Portugal.[99]

As to dealing with Germany, Pétain may not have shared Laval's swagger, but he, too, assumed that France would help to shape the direction of the negotiations that would end the war and send the occupying German forces back home. Then, just as if it were the end of the tourist season, the French government would leave Vichy and return to Paris cured of its ills. Vichy officials did not even bother to install central heating in the buildings the government had requisitioned. They had managed to convince themselves that they would be back in Paris long before the weather turned cold.[100]

OBSERVANT AMERICANS IN THE SPRING of 1940 harbored far fewer illusions. They knew that the collapse of France suddenly made the war in Europe America's war as well. A public opinion survey in *Fortune* magazine showed two in three Americans believing that after the fall of France and Britain, the United States would become Germany's next target. "If you could have asked millions of Americans what single moment made the war real to them," wrote the historian and future *American Heritage* publisher Richard Ketchum, "many would have answered that it was the day the Germans marched into Paris."[101] On that day, Americans began to realize the price they would have to pay for their years of military parsimony and neglect of foreign affairs.

The professionals were no less stunned than the amateurs. No American military planner before that spring had thought it necessary to question the assumption of French strength. Now that the fall of France had suddenly rendered it invalid, the United States had no viable plan for defending itself or its allies. Future army chief of staff Matthew Ridgway, then a senior strategist in the War Plans Division, wrote a memorandum on May 22, 1940, warning that the fall of France and the retrenchment of Great Britain to home defense could lead to German military operations in the Caribbean, Brazil, or Mexico. Once logistically unthinkable, the Germans could now conduct offensive operations in Latin America with French assistance from Dakar, which sat just a few hours' flying time to Brazil astride the main Allied shipping routes from South America. If successful, such operations might inspire large German populations and fifth columnists in several Latin American states to attempt pro-Nazi coups throughout the region. Ridgway saw the threat as so ominous that his memorandum suggested abandoning Guam and maybe even the Philippines in order to shift resources to existential crises much closer to home. Ridgway's colleagues in the United States Navy also began to plan to transfer warships from the Pacific to the Caribbean and Atlantic. The war had now come home.

And it had come home with shocking speed. As late as March, Ridgway had written that the phony war in Europe did not require the United States to make any changes in its defense policies. His division's only recommendations to the army involved building more underground storage facilities for aviation fuel and gaining access to more modern airfields in South America. Less than two months later, however, he wrote that German success had laid bare the reality that without France in the picture, the American military could not conduct sufficient operations to defend the western hemisphere for at least one year. Possible Axis next moves, he warned, included:

a. Nazi-inspired revolution in Brazil;
b. Widespread disorders with attacks on US citizens in Mexico and raids along our southern border;
c. Japanese hostilities against the United States in the Far East;
d. Decisive Allied defeat, followed by German aggression in the Western Hemisphere;
e. All combined.

In their weakened state, American forces could not meet "a combination of any two of these areas without dangerous dispersion of force." Ridgway urged a focus on defending Latin America. "This appears to be the maximum effort of which we are capable today." Americans, he warned, would have to accept the reality that the nation must decide now "what we are not going to do" and "what we must prepare to do."[102] Army Chief of Staff General George Marshall bluntly warned President Roosevelt the day after Ridgway wrote his memo that "the time had now come to stop being afraid and to take positive action while there was still time."[103] As we will see, President Roosevelt needed little convincing. He, too, understood how fundamentally the world had changed; without France in the war, Americans suddenly realized that they could not defend themselves, their hemispheric allies, or their core interests in their own backyard. American foreign policy elites spoke of defending only a "quarter sphere," extending from Canada to the Brazilian bulge into the Atlantic Ocean. The nation, they argued, lacked the resources to contemplate doing anything more.[104]

At about the same time, Secretary of the Interior and Roosevelt confidant Harold Ickes had a meeting with a family friend serving as an officer in the army who wanted to share his anxiety over the new situation. The officer told Ickes that "nothing would be safe in America" if Hitler gained access to the French or British fleets. "We would be in real jeopardy," the officer warned him. He wanted Ickes to make sure that Roosevelt understood the dangers. Ickes met with the president the next day who told Ickes that he "had been doing some worrying about this same matter."[105] Ickes wrote in his diary that "we are looking into a pretty dark future indeed."[106]

These fears went far beyond government and military officials with a professional duty to foresee trouble and plan for it. *Time* magazine showed a map of Latin America with the caption, "The 90 million [Latin] Americans who may go to work for Hitler." The magazine noted that German agents already crawled around the region "like beetles nibbling at morale. They promise to put Uncle Sam on perhaps the hottest spot of his career." The French base at Dakar jutted menacingly out on the map toward Brazil. If it fell into German hands, the western hemisphere would be dangerously exposed, just as Ridgway's memo had warned. The ensuing battle for America's own backyard, the magazine warned, would be "as crucial to the U.S. as Saratoga or Gettysburg." And the nation was completely unprepared to fight it.[107] The dark future Ickes had predicted had become the present.

2

A HILL OF BEANS IN THIS CRAZY WORLD
America's New Insecurity

IN MAY 1939, WARNER BROTHERS studio released *Confessions of a Nazi Spy,* starring legendary Hollywood tough guy Edward G. Robinson as Federal Bureau of Investigation (FBI) agent Ed Renard. The plot revolves around Renard's efforts to disrupt a plot led by the fiendish Dr. Karl Kassell, played by veteran actor Paul Lukas. Dr. Kassell hates the "uncultured" Americans, their misguided Constitution, and their "fanatical faith" in the obsolete notion of democracy. He plans a coup, using German Americans as his agents, to replace the pluralistic American system with a nation of racial purity led by Nazis and America-born Nazi sympathizers.[1]

The film loosely followed the real-life Rumrich case, the FBI's first major international espionage investigation. A spy ring led by a naturalized American citizen named Guenther Rumrich tried to obtain genuine American passports to enable the German government to smuggle agents into the United States undetected.[2] They would then form what we would today call a sleeper cell, ready to wreak havoc on American industry and infrastructure if so ordered by their masters in Berlin. FBI agents infiltrated the ring in 1938, and Rumrich gave the bureau information on some of the other plotters in exchange for a lighter sentence. American agents then broke up the group, arresting four German spies. Ten spies, however, got away, causing a major scandal at the FBI that led to more invasive methods of investigation and increased surveillance of other suspected aliens in the United States.

Despite the national attention that the Rumrich case generated, the film's fictionalized account flopped at the box office. Its life did not end, however, with that initial failure. Warner Brothers rereleased it soon after the fall of France, not only making it profitable but also gaining the studio praise for shedding light on a critical issue of national security. Similarly, a book by *New York World-Telegram* reporter George Britt titled *The Fifth Column Is Here* became a surprise best seller amid the new mood of 1940. It claimed that the Germans had already placed almost one million spies inside the United States. The fall of France also boosted the sales of *Why England Slept,* published in July and based on the senior thesis of a Harvard graduate named John F. Kennedy.[3]

Their gains were America's collective loss in a time of fear, paranoia, and deep national uncertainty. The fall of France vaulted into public discourse the most important question of the second half of 1940 and the early part of 1941: how could the United States best ensure its security from enemies both within and without after the collapse of all of the fundamental assumptions underlying American safety? As had happened in the early months of 1917, the shocking events of summer 1940 revealed that neutrality and isolation as strategies had made the nation less safe, not more.[4] How, then, should America react? The American people and their elected officials responded with radical, unprecedented changes to the ways they thought about themselves, their alliances, and their national grand strategy. As they did so, they began to diverge from their future British allies on several items of national security, none more important than the vital question of how to handle the new France.

THE INTELLECTUAL AND POLITICAL TRANSFORMATIONS necessary to transition from regional power to superpower began in 1940 when the American people and their government for the first time in history recognized two basic truths. First, that they could no longer depend on the assistance or benign indifference of another country, like France, to ensure their own security, and second, that they faced clear and present safety and security threats from across the Atlantic Ocean. If the world war of

1917–1918 put these issues temporarily into the national psyche, the events of 1940 moved them to center stage. The ideas, hopes, and fears that had fed neutrality and isolation disappeared, replaced by a new mood that demanded an active, not passive, defense. It also demanded weapons and trained manpower instead of the security normally provided to Americans by two great oceans.[5]

We know now that a close alliance with Great Britain would form a critical part of the American answer to the question of how to solve this dilemma. In summer 1940, however, many Americans, including some with influential voices, thought that Britain could not possibly survive a German onslaught once the Nazis turned their seemingly unstoppable military power against the British Isles. Writing in June to Lord Lothian, the British ambassador to Washington, the always witty and acerbic Winston Churchill criticized the dominant anti-British approach of American officials to the crisis sparked by the fall of France. "Up till April, [Americans] were so sure that the Allies would win that they did not think help necessary," he wrote. "Now they are so sure we shall lose that they do not think it possible."[6]

The collapse of France did indeed invalidate American assumptions about both itself and its allies. It also put the United States in an almost impossible strategic position. The American military suddenly found itself with precious few resources and myriad calls upon the use of those resources. As Ambassador William Bullitt said in Philadelphia upon his return from France, "America is in danger. It is my conviction, drawn from my own experience and from the information in the hands of our government in Washington that the United States is in as great a peril today as France a year ago. And I believe that unless we act now, decisively, to meet the threat, we shall be too late."[7]

With France defeated, voices quickly rose demanding active assistance to the British, but many prominent people argued that helping the British would only waste precious resources on a lost cause. Worse yet, if and when the Germans did conquer the British, the Germans might use American supplies given to the British in good faith to help prepare an attack on the United States or Latin America. In other words, having lost the security guarantees and assurances indirectly provided by the French, the United States could not, and should not, then rely on similar assurances from Great Britain. The United States would have to take a much more active role in its own defense as well as that of the entire western hemisphere.[8]

The fear that the British might not survive had spread not just among the elites but also across the country. In one public opinion poll, only 30 percent of respondents thought a British victory over the Germans possible.[9] In London, Ambassador Joseph Kennedy felt certain that the British would not survive even a relatively small German attack. In an interview with the *Chicago Tribune,* the American media's main isolationist standard bearer, he described Britain and its empire as "irredeemably lost."[10] British historian Sir John Wheeler-Bennett came to lecture in 1939 at the University of Virginia, then remained in the country to open the British Information Service in New York City. He wryly noted that Americans "had already written us off as defeated, albeit gallantly, and spoke to me in those hushed tones which are customarily used for the lately bereaved."[11] Similarly, Lord Lothian wrote that Americans "were really terrified that we would go the same way as France."[12]

THE CRISIS REACHED ITS ZENITH at the same time as the 1940 political conventions, vaulting questions of national defense into the forefront of political discussions for the first time in decades. The Republican Party convened in Philadelphia from June 24 to 28, less than two weeks after German troops marched into Paris. Using language that recalled the Declaration of Independence's list of grievances against King George III, the Republican platform accused Roosevelt of having allowed the nation to find itself in such a state of peril. "Instead of Providing for the Common Defense," it alleged, "the Administration, notwithstanding the expenditure of billions of our dollars, has left the Nation unprepared to resist foreign attack."[13] Despite their new rhetoric on defense and preparedness, the Republicans had led much of the isolationist movement, although even its key leaders, most notably the presumptive presidential nominee, Ohio senator Robert Taft, began to call for vastly increased spending on defense.

The mood had changed and the delegates in Philadelphia grasped for answers just like the rest of the country. Because of the crisis in France, the Republican convention took an unexpected turn. Events in Europe launched the dark horse internationalist candidate Wendell Willkie out of obscurity and to the Republican nomination over his more established and more isolationist rivals. Willkie fully supported providing all aid short of war to Great Britain and agreed with Roosevelt on the need to begin a massive rearmament program. The other Republican front-runners, Taft, Thomas Dewey, and Arthur Vandenberg, did not change their public messages, even if in private they began to share many of Willkie's views. One of Willkie's closest advisers went as far as to say that "Adolf Hitler nominated Willkie. With the fall of France and the Low Countries, American popular opinion shifted overnight—and that was responsible for Willkie's nomination."[14] As a result, Willkie, who had polled in the single digits just weeks earlier, became the nominee, assuring that the Republicans would present no major partisan disagreements over American defense policy on the campaign trail.

The crisis impacted the Democrats as well. At the time of the German invasion of France, a tired Franklin Roosevelt had not yet announced whether he would run for an unprecedented third term in office. He appears to have definitively made up his mind only on June 10 as the defeat of France became inevitable. While in Charlottesville, Virginia, for his son's graduation from law school, news arrived of Italy's declaration of war on France. An angry Roosevelt gave a fiery speech that pledged American power to the defeat of "the philosophy of force." To continue to exist under the assumption that the war would pass America by, he said, was now "an obvious delusion."[15] Although he played his cards close to his vest, he likely made up his mind in Charlottesville to run for another term and to shake up his national security team as well.[16]

The fall of France created some strange political bedfellows and some even stranger ideas. Journalist Dorothy Thompson proposed that Roosevelt and Willkie should run together on a national unity ticket, thereby burying the bitter partisanship in recent years over the New Deal and Roosevelt's attempt to add seats to the Supreme Court.[17] Her extraordinary plan never had a chance of succeeding, although Roosevelt realized the need to make changes in order to form a kind of national unity government on his own terms.

Almost everyone in Washington wanted to get rid of Secretary of War Harry Woodring, one of the few Americans whose views seemed not have changed as a result of the crisis in France. Secretary of the Interior Harold Ickes approached the president with a plan to have the entire cabinet offer their resignations on the pretense that he needed a reshuffle for the upcoming presidential campaign; then Roosevelt could accept only Woodring's.

Roosevelt disliked Ickes's plan and preferred to keep cabinet members in their place for long periods but told Ickes that he, too, wanted to be rid of his "cautious, provincial, and strongly isolationist" secretary of war.[18]

Roosevelt probably decided around the time of his Charlottesville speech to replace Woodring with a prominent Republican, both to project an image of unity and to undercut the remaining power of that party's isolationist wing. He thought of nominating New York City mayor Fiorella La Guardia, but confidants convinced the president that the popular and effective mayor might prove more useful in wartime as leader of the nation's largest city. On June 19, Roosevelt called his second (or, by some accounts, his third) choice, veteran Republican Washington insider and supporter of increased defense spending, Henry Stimson, to ask if he would replace Woodring. Stimson, who had served as secretary of war under William Howard Taft and as secretary of state under Herbert Hoover, recalled that Roosevelt "thought I would be a stabilizing factor in whom both the Army and the public would have confidence."[19] One British woman who met him during the war certainly thought so, describing Stimson as "a rock-like and benevolent old man who might have stepped out of the *Mayflower,* so shining was he in his integrity."[20]

Roosevelt told Stimson that another Republican would become secretary of the navy, a post near and dear to the president's heart.[21] One-time Rough Rider, newspaper publisher, and 1936 vice-presidential candidate Frank Knox had agreed to replace Thomas Edison's son, Charles, whom the White House had convinced to run for governor of New Jersey, in part to put someone else in his job. Knox could provide an internationally minded and media-savvy midwestern voice to counter the isolationist and incurably anti-Roosevelt Robert McCormick, the owner of the *Chicago Tribune.* Roosevelt announced the appointments together the next day, just one week before the Republican convention opened. In his confirmation hearings, Stimson bluntly announced his new policy: "I do not believe that the United States can be safely protected by a purely passive or defensive defense. I do not believe that we shall be safe from invasion if we sit down and wait for the enemy to attack our shores."[22] The new cabinet members both favored peacetime conscription, large-scale aid to Great Britain, and an aggressive military appropriations program. Their appointments sent an unmistakable message that in its response to the fall of France, the country

Republican stalwarts Frank Knox and Henry Stimson (seen here holding a paper) joined President Roosevelt's cabinet after the fall of France to project an image of unity in the face of a national crisis.

would make major changes in the ways it thought about the world and America's place within it.

PRESIDENT ROOSEVELT HAD TESTED THE IDEA of a massive military appropriation program with the American people weeks before and found no opposition. On May 16, less than a week after the German invasion of France began, the president asked for an eye-popping $1.2 billion addition to a crash rearmament program that included $100 million for a presidential emergency fund controlled exclusively by Roosevelt. The request represented in the starkest terms how much the atmosphere of fear had come to permeate the nation. As recently as April 3, the House Appropriations Committee had approved a measure cutting the defense budget by 10 percent. Roosevelt now demanded unprecedented peacetime spending on national defense, tens of millions of dollars of which would sit outside congressional oversight. "No old defense is so strong that it requires no further strengthening, and no attack is so unlikely or impossible that it may be ignored," Roosevelt warned. "Let us examine, without self-deception, the dangers which confront us. Let us measure our strength and our defense without self-delusion. The clear fact is that the American people must recast their thinking about national protection."[23] Desperate times called for desperate measures.

Harold Ickes thought Roosevelt's speech "magnificent" and one of the best he had given in years. The American people added their acclaim; telegrams to the White House were 80 percent in favor, another indication of the changing national mood. A usually hostile Congress, Ickes noted, gave an energized Roosevelt "the finest reception that he has been accorded by a joint session of Congress for five or six years." Although a small number of isolationist "diehards" refused to clap for the president, Ickes confided to his diary that "the Republicans will have to go along with this program because the country is for it, and they dare not do otherwise."[24] With Willkie emerging as their nominee and leader, the chances of organized Republican opposition to rearmament dwindled.

The days of free riding on the French military had clearly and definitively ceased; a sense of panic in the United States now pervaded American life. Politicians and ordinary Americans once willing to see Germany as primarily France's problem suddenly backed massive new defense appropriations. As early as June 14, the day German troops entered Paris, Congress passed the Naval Expansion Act and a National Defense Tax Bill that promised to raise $1 billion per year via taxation. Congress also added another $3 billion to the federal debt limit. Much more legislation and much more money quickly followed as Congress realized that even these huge steps might not sufficiently address the problems at hand.

A small core of noninterventionists, led by Robert Taft and Charles Lindbergh, still had a loyal following, but the national mood had definitively shifted. Old arguments that preparation for war made intervention more likely suddenly had no purchase with the American people, who now saw those preparations as protection rather than provocation. The French embassy staff in Washington warned their new bosses in Vichy that although Lindbergh and his coterie still opposed war with Germany or massive aid to Great Britain, even they had come around on the need to increase American defense spending by almost any amount the president requested. The embassy passed along a survey conducted in August by *Time* that showed 84 percent of Americans anxious for their country to contribute to the defeat of the Nazis—and any country allied to them.[25]

All of a sudden, the government and the American people showed their willingness to spend anything. In early 1940, before the fall of France, Congress had begun debating an authorization of $4 billion for new warships, an enormous amount that almost everyone involved thought would prove more than sufficient to meet American defense needs. As James Byrnes saw firsthand, enough senators thought the amount so high that they tried to delay the authorization's passage. The fall of France radically changed the thinking of both the navy and Congress, leading to demands for much larger sums. On the day of the armistice that ended the war between Germany and France, the House of Representatives supplemented the Naval Expansion Act by unanimously passing the Two-Ocean Navy Act after less than one hour of debate. The act more than doubled the initial sum requested, authorizing more than $8.5 billion for the navy. Without a single voice in opposition, a frightened Congress broke the bank and provided money for building an astonishing fleet of 7 battleships, 18 aircraft carriers, 33 cruisers, 115 destroyers, 43 submarines, and 15,000 sea-based airplanes. Then the largest peacetime defense appropriation in American history, it could never have passed as long as Americans had assumed that France would do most of the early fighting. After the fall of France, it passed with barely a whisper of opposition.[26]

The United States Army, kept small and badly underfunded in the interwar years, also received unprecedented new resources. As late as April 1940, Congress had balked at army requests to authorize increases to the 280,000-soldier ceiling imposed in 1920 and strictly maintained thereafter. On June 6, however, Congress began discussions to triple funding for the ground and air forces. A week later, the army finalized a hurried plan to build a 4,000,000-man force and a 36,000 plane air corps in less than two years. President Roosevelt and Army Chief of Staff General George Marshall pared down the plan to 2,000,000 men, although most observers thought that Congress would easily have approved the higher number if the president had asked for it. Opinion polls showed public approval for the 2,000,000-man army at 66 percent, and the bill passed the Senate by a lopsided vote of seventy-one to seven.[27] Roosevelt also ordered all members of the National Guard to undertake a full year of rigorous training, taking the unprecedented peacetime step of pulling them out of their civilian jobs to meet that goal. With the new army authorizations came four billion more dollars from a once-parsimonious Congress. At a time when the total expenditures for the entire federal government barely exceeded $9 billion (only 20 percent of which went to defense), Congress committed an extraordinary $12 billion to the army and navy in the blink of an eye.

To man this new army, Congress took the previously unthinkable step of imposing conscription in peacetime. As quickly as early August, a bipartisan group had drafted, debated, and passed the Burke-Wadsworth Selective Training and Service Act by the comfortable margins of 58–31 in the Senate and 263–149 in the House. It authorized, for the first time in American history, peacetime compulsory military service. The law required all men between eighteen and thirty-five to register; by October, the first of a theoretical maximum of 900,000 draftees had joined. The lightning speed with which Congress drafted, debated, and passed a law with such historic implications gives an indication of how fundamentally the fall of France shook America's collective sense of security to its core.[28] Opinion polls showed a consistent two-thirds to three-fourths of the American people in favor.[29]

Americans also jettisoned the Neutrality Laws that complicated providing military assistance to countries at war. New British prime minister Winston Churchill's first cable to President Roosevelt, sent just hours after the Germans broke through the French line at Sedan on May 15, requested that the United States send Britain forty to fifty destroyers, hundreds of airplanes, anti-aircraft guns, and ammunition. "The scene has darkened swiftly," Churchill warned. "The voice and force of the United States may count for nothing if they are withheld too long."[30] With what one observer called thunderclap suddenness, the two governments worked out the Destroyers-for-Bases Agreement, giving the Royal Navy fifty American destroyers and the United States basing rights in a half dozen British possessions in the western hemisphere. The agreement, called by one popular magazine "the most important defense measure since the Louisiana Purchase of 1803," represented a major shift in hemispheric power to the United States that it has never yielded, as well as the precedent for the ensuing Lend-Lease agreements.[31] Wendell Willkie, Henry Luce, and John Pershing all expressed their immediate and wholehearted support for the measure.

Even anti-interventionist newspapers like McCormick's *Chicago Tribune* voiced approval.[32]

In truth, the Americans wanted the bases far more than the British wanted the old, leaky destroyers. The British saw the agreement's value as largely symbolic. British intelligence officer and adviser on France J. R. M. Butler recognized that the ships could do little to solve the Royal Navy's operational problems. Nevertheless, it "would have made a long step towards [the United States] coming into the war on our side. To sell destroyers to a belligerent was certainly not a neutral act."[33] For the Americans, by contrast, access to the British bases provided a way to keep a close eye on potentially hostile French possessions in the western hemisphere. President Roosevelt's May 16 address reminded the American people that their attempts to remain neutral in the latest European conflict had failed. "These are ominous days—days whose swift and shocking developments force every neutral nation to look to its defenses in the light of new factors," he warned. "The clear fact is that the American people must recast their thinking about national protection." Roosevelt noted the new "motorized armies" that could move 200 miles in a single day and airplanes that could drop paratroopers behind enemy lines. These new technological changes would revolutionize the battlefield and require the United States to adapt and invest in new generations of weapons. The president then highlighted the fact that an enemy warplane operating out of a base in the Caribbean (such as the French island of Martinique) could now reach Florida in just over three hours. A string of new American bases in the western hemisphere could help neutralize that threat and the threat to Latin America that so obsessed senior military figures like Generals Marshall and Ridgway.

French officials based in Washington thought that Americans both in and out of government did not really want to help a British government that many of them still distrusted but that the fall of France had "simplified" the war in American eyes. Whereas before the fall of France Americans had seen the British as a commercial and military rival, after the fall Americans came to see the British as their new bulwark—if they survived. As French diplomats reported, when the "world's best army" (France's own) collapsed in June, Americans reluctantly came to see that supporting their British "cousins" offered the best method to keep the war stalemated and across the ocean. Accordingly, the report concluded (correctly, as it turned out) that no matter how much material aid the Americans gave to the

British, the United States would not send an expeditionary force to Europe in the immediate future, even if they could somehow manage to raise one. Despite the crisis, Americans still had no desire to see their "children leave once again for the trenches of Europe."[34]

In the eyes of the Vichy leadership, these calculations meant that the Americans could not possibly provide enough help to ensure a British victory. American assistance would therefore unnecessarily prolong the war by giving the British just enough help to stay alive but not nearly enough to defeat Germany.[35] American destroyers and other aid, however generous they appeared from a public relations perspective, thus only had the effect of replacing British losses. American policy, Vichy presumed, aimed at enriching the United States by taking British assets in the western hemisphere without materially improving Britain's parlous military situation. This strategy would produce an extended stalemate that would unnecessarily prolong the conclusion of a final peace agreement and, consequently, potentially put Vichy in the advantageous position of mediator between the British and the Germans.[36] The Americans, they concluded, might prove unwittingly useful to French designs after all.

THE FRENCH HAD HALF OF THE ARGUMENT RIGHT: in 1940, the United States lacked a military strong enough to protect itself, let alone rescue Britain at the same time. In the absence of military power, the Americans tried diplomacy as a means to protect their hemispheric interests. In late July, Pan-American foreign ministers met in Havana to discuss security for the western hemisphere. More than two dozen officials pondered the fate of the "orphaned" Dutch islands of Aruba, Bonaire, and Curaçao, then clinging loyally to the London-based Dutch government in exile, as well as the British colonies whose contact with the mother country had suddenly become less regular. The elephants in the room were the threats of Axis coups aimed at existing Latin American governments and the possibility of the French possessions of Martinique, Guadeloupe, and Saint-Pierre and Miquelon coming under Nazi influence or being transferred to German control in a final peace agreement. If any of those islands became German, the United States and its hemispheric allies could find their already parlous strategic situation deteriorating even further.[37]

Fear for the safety of the hemisphere had certainly increased and not only among the diplomats meeting in Havana. Earlier that month the *New York Herald Tribune* reported that European, especially French, territories in the Americas sat "on the point of being used by the Nazis as naval bases."[38] If the Germans won the war in Europe, they might force the British to abrogate the Destroyers-for-Bases Agreement and maybe take any or all of Europe's western hemisphere islands and colonies as spoils of war. In that case, the United States could not hope to defend Latin America and might even have difficulty defending itself. This risk further argued for limiting American commitments to a Britain that might or might not survive the war intact.

In Havana, the United States expressed its firm opposition to any transfer of sovereignty for European possessions in the western hemisphere notwith-standing its own recent possession of basing rights in British territories in the region. As the final declaration argued, the United States and its allies could not risk European colonies and territories turning into Axis "stra-tegic centers of aggression" against American interests such as the Panama Canal or American allies in Latin America. Diplomats from the United States floated a much more aggressive plan to put all European possessions in the hemisphere under an American-dominated international trusteeship until the end of the war. That plan had some support but smacked too much of old-style imperialism, so the United States backed away from it, although Washington officials did not officially renounce it.[39]

The United States instead settled on a radical redefinition of the Monroe Doctrine. Hereafter, it would serve as the justification for the adoption of a collective security arrangement whereby "any attempt on the part of a non-American state against the integrity or inviolability of the territory, the sovereignty, or the political independence of an American state shall be considered as an act of aggression against the states which sign this dec-laration."[40] In effect, lacking the military power to prevent Axis aggres-sion in Latin America, the United States looked for ways to unite the states of the western hemisphere into a common defense structure based on concepts rooted in collective security. If it worked, then the Germans would face a war with the entire hemisphere if it challenged the independence of any single part thereof. The United States also invested more than $2 billion to tie the economies of Latin America even more closely to the United States and to ensure that the end of trade with Europe did not lead to an economic crisis that could force a collapse of their governments or give them an incentive to reach out to Germany.[41]

The United States further declared in Havana that all European possessions in the Americas should have the right to self-determination after the war, a statement to which the French, British, and Dutch governments all objected. The Vichy government "vigorously" opposed any implication that the United States might play a role in determining the postwar status of French possessions. America had no right, it argued, to "question the independence and the sovereignty of the French government, despite the partial occupation of its land."[42] The United States, however, had already determined that securing its own interests close to home took precedence over acknowledging the legal fine points of the highly unusual political situation in France. Threatening to support independence also gave the United States a nonmilitary method to deter officials in Vichy from using their regional possessions in any way that might undermine American security. Leaders on both sides of the Atlantic clearly understood the message the Americans were sending: if Vichy gave the Germans the use of Martinique, then the United States would respond by helping it gain its independence.[43]

The fate of the French navy formed a fundamental part of all discussions about the future of the relationship between the United States and France. Any use of the French fleet by the Axis powers could pose an existential threat to American interests. French envoy René de Chambrun, in Washington with President Roosevelt on the day the Germans entered Paris, warned in a cable to Prime Minister Paul Reynaud on that same day that France must keep control of the fleet if it had any hope of maintaining positive relations with the Americans.[44] Roosevelt later followed up by sending diplomat Anthony Biddle to Vichy to warn Admiral Darlan that the "friendship and goodwill of the Government of the United States" depended entirely on the French fleet remaining out of German hands.[45] To make the point as clearly as he could, Roosevelt followed that meeting with a public speech to the same effect. He wanted to take no chances that the Germans might add French ships to their own fleet.

THE DANGERS AMERICANS SAW CAME not only from without but within as well. Americans assumed that a country as powerful as France could not have fallen as quickly and completely as it had unless the Germans had had inside help. Roosevelt shared this belief. The fundamental cause of the fall of France, the president said in his major address on the topic, was not technological, but internal: "We have seen the treacherous use of the 'fifth column' by which persons supposed to be peaceful visitors were actually a part of an enemy unit of occupation. Lightning attacks capable of destroying airplane factories and munitions works hundreds of miles behind the lines are part of the new technique of modern war." Roosevelt drew links between the two methods of modern war, the fifth columnists preparing the ground with propaganda and sabotage in order to clear the way for the conventional weapons of infantry, armor, and aviation.[46]

The actual evidence for the existence of fifth columnists remained thin, but that hardly mattered to a country feeling the anxieties the United States felt in the summer of 1940. Fifth column fears played on existing anxieties, as expressed in films like *Confessions of a Nazi Spy*. They allowed observers to pass blame for the collapse of France on groups they already hated. The staunchly anti-communist American ambassador to France, William Bullitt, told Roosevelt that "nearly all the French heavy tanks were manned by Communist workmen from the Renault works in the outskirts of Paris. When they were given the order to advance against the German tanks they did not move." Bullitt concluded his long missive on the "serious fifth column problem" with the words, "Please, for the sake of the future, nail every Communist or Communist sympathizer in our Army, Navy, and Air Force." Bullitt's information appears to have come either from French politicians looking to shift the blame of defeat to someone else or from panicked Frenchmen seeing ghosts and demons around every corner as the magnitude of the defeat became clear. Although they had little basis in evidence, Bullitt's allegations undoubtedly influenced Roosevelt's speech.[47]

The American media played up the same themes. One French journalist who had made it to Lisbon wrote for an American magazine, "Treason! The word jumps from man to man, group to group as the only plausible explanation" for the quick defeat.[48] In the hysterical weeks after the fall of France, President Roosevelt sent William Donovan to report on the fifth column problem in Europe. On his return, he wrote a widely syndicated four-part series of alarmist newspaper articles blaming "sympathizers in the victim countries" for the shocking defeat. The articles came with the notation that Secretary of the Navy Frank Knox had approved their release "as part of the national defense program," giving the impression that the government was sharing sensitive information with the American people.[49]

As the successful rerelease of *Confessions of a Nazi Spy* showed, paranoia about potential fifth columnists at home pervaded national discourse. Under the headline "5th Column in Action: How It Worked in Fall of Paris," the *New York Post* informed its readers that the French people "paid slight attention to the new elevator operator. He was a little Alsatian, very subdued, unfailingly polite, and adept in the handling of his lift. In Paris he was as small a cog as the city's wheels had—until it fell." Other fifth columnists, the paper alleged, included "butchers and teachers and doctors; men about town and sewer rats; ditch diggers and druggists." German agents lurked everywhere, smiling at their neighbors and opening doors for ladies while quietly plotting to aid the enemy. "Nobody ever realized how effective the fifth column was, in the countries whose downfall it assisted, until it was too late to do anything about it."[50] Donovan shared these fears. He worried about "a German-American colony of several million strong" that included "thousands of domestic workers and waiters" living and operating in virtually every community in the United States.[51]

In a nation growing more hysterical by the week, those who had argued Germany's case became increasingly suspect. Senator James Byrnes took to the radio on May 23 to attack one of America's most famous celebrities, the pro-German Charles Lindbergh. Byrnes reminded his listeners of the medal Lindbergh had accepted from the Nazis and issued a powerful warning: "Fifth columns are already active in America. And those who consciously or unconsciously retard the efforts of this government to provide for the defense of the American people are the fifth column's most effective fellow travelers." Days later in a fireside chat, Roosevelt warned the country about active foreign agents who were "weakening [the] nation at its very roots" and spreading "undiluted poison."[52]

"PARANOIA," WARNED ASSISTANT SECRETARY OF State Adolph Berle, "can be catching."[53] It became an obsession in the wake of the fall of France. Attorney General Robert Jackson worried that the mania over fifth columnists had already gotten out of hand. At a cabinet meeting on May 26, as the Allies retreated to Dunkirk and the British arrested their own fascist leaders Oswald Mosley and Diana Mitford, Jackson expressed concern about hypervigilance on the part of local authorities and private groups.

He feared a "spy hunt" on the model of the First World War that could get quickly out of hand, putting innocent people under unwarranted suspicion and maybe even in jail or lynched by self-styled patriot vigilantes. "Anyone you don't like is a member of the fifth column," Jackson warned. He noted that the governor of Georgia had already begun "hunting down every alien" in his state on the justification that he needed to control enemy espionage. Harold Ickes, who attended the meeting with Jackson, wrote that "America isn't going to be any too comfortable a place to live in during the immediate future, and some of us are going to be ashamed of the excesses that will be committed against innocent people." He decried a congressional plan to limit the number of noncitizens who could work in defense plants, confiding to his diary that "some of our superpatriots are simply going crazy."[54] Other excesses of the type that Jackson and Ickes feared quickly followed. First Lady Eleanor Roosevelt, in an article published on June 21, denounced mobs that dragged two Jehovah's Witnesses from their home in Wyoming and forced them to swear allegiance to the flag. "Are we going to be swept away from our traditional attitude toward civil liberties by hysteria about 'fifth columnists?'" she asked.[55]

Little did Roosevelt, Jackson, and Ickes know how deep such sentiments ran. Fears of a fifth column had important consequences, both in stoking American anxiety for the security of Latin America and setting the stage for the search for internal enemies. The obsession with fifth columnists had grave consequences across the country, although in this war not predominantly against Germans. After Pearl Harbor, a report by Supreme Court Justice Owen J. Roberts alleged (on no evidence) that Japanese Americans had helped to guide and give intelligence to Admiral Chūichi Nagumo's strike force. General John DeWitt then made the absurd argument that the lack of evidence to prove the charge only showed the sophistication of the Japanese fifth column and what a danger it posed to American security. The paranoia over Japanese Americans would surely have been much less acute if not for France's stunning collapse and the explanations of it emanating from the White House on down.

The world had suddenly changed and with it came a new relationship between security and civil liberties. The right of citizens to maintain their privacy in the face of new technologies available to the government was then a hot topic both in the courts and among the public more generally. In 1937 and 1939, the Supreme Court heard the same wiretapping case twice. In the process of rendering its decision, the court threw out a revenue fraud conviction based on evidence collected in a wiretap, which the majority ruled violated Fourth Amendment protections.[56] The attorney general banned all use of wiretaps as a result.

But on May 21, 1940, just a week after the German breakthrough against the French at Sedan, President Roosevelt signed a secret executive order authorizing wiretaps, even though he acknowledged that "it is almost bound to lead to abuse of civil rights." The president argued that the court's rulings in a domestic criminal case could not have foreseen the "grave matters involving the defense of the nation" that the government now faced. Roosevelt told the attorney general that "it is too late to do anything about it after sabotage, assassinations and 'fifth column' activities are completed. You are, therefore, authorized and directed in such cases as you may approve . . . to secure information by listening devices direct to the conversation or other communications of persons suspected of subversive activities against the Government of the United States, including suspected spies."[57] Roosevelt hoped that the Justice Department would focus its surveillance exclusively on aliens from potential enemy countries, but he had to have known that in the frightened days after the fall of France, he had just given officials of his own government the tools to pry open a Pandora's box involving one of the great issues in a democracy in wartime: the balance between safety and liberty.

WIRETAPS MIGHT HELP THE GOVERNMENT root out spies, but they could not stop the rapid deterioration of the geopolitical situation. In early July, British apprehensions about the fate of the French fleet reached a crisis point. The British government argued that owing to the German occupation, Vichy lacked the freedom and independence of a sovereign state; therefore, it had no legitimate right to govern France or command its military forces. Secretary of State for Foreign Affairs Lord Halifax called Vichy "the most teasing problem I have ever had to deal with. None of the jig-saw pieces fit." In his private diary he wrote that "it is really maddening being in this kind of twilight between friendship and the reverse" with France. "By all the rules, they ought to declare war on us." He heard of rumors from "many quarters" that a German invasion of the British Home Islands

might be just days away, possibly executed with French help. In such febrile circumstances, he wrote about the French fleet, "one thing I think
stands out above all the rest, which is that if it can be humanly prevented,
the Germans must not get it."[58]

The most immediate concern for the British centered on the modern
French flotilla anchored at Mers-el-Kébir adjacent to Oran in Algeria.
Churchill, Halifax, and others worried that it might join the German navy or
take anti-British action on its own against Gibraltar, Malta, or Suez. Halifax
expressed his concern that the ships might act against the British "under
orders from the French government, themselves no doubt under orders
from the German government."[59] Admiral Darlan had steadfastly refused
British demands to send French warships to a British port to be disarmed
and interned for the duration of the war. He had, however, given the
British a promise that the French navy would never come under German or
Italian control. Still, Darlan's word did not count for much in the days
immediately after Dunkirk, when Great Britain sat in fear of a German
invasion.

Given the lack of faith the British had in Vichy's leaders and the vital
importance of Suez, Malta, and Gibraltar to British survival, Churchill believed that he "could not afford to rely on the word of Admiral Darlan."[60]
Churchill sent a naval task force to Mers-el-Kébir to give the French four
choices: join Britain in the war against the Germans, sail their ships to
British ports for internment until the end of the war, sail for the West Indies for the duration of the war, or scuttle themselves. The French admiral
Marcel Gensoul told a commission after the war that in his view, "it was
absolutely inadmissible that I accept any term of this ultimatum under such
pressure."[61] He decided instead to stall for time and sent out a message
asking nearby French forces to send airplanes and submarines to his aid.

British ships intercepted Gensoul's message and responded by laying
mines outside the harbor, effectively trapping the French ships. Gensoul's
messages, moreover, arrived in a Vichy still in the process of moving its
offices from Bordeaux. The government had only officially opened its doors
two days before. The new state had insufficient radio communications and
some French officials wanted Vichy to share the texts of the messages with
the Germans before responding. As a result, confusion reigned among the
French. Around 6:00 p.m. on July 3, 1940, the commanding British officer on the scene reluctantly carried out his orders to attack. That assault

killed 1,300 French sailors and destroyed or damaged three French battleships and four destroyers. Another operation struck the *Richelieu,* considered among the world's finest battleships, while it was undergoing maintenance in Dakar. Future British prime minister Harold Macmillan, then serving as a parliamentary secretary, called the attack on the *Richelieu* "one of the most unhappy episodes of the war" and one likely to poison Anglo-French relations for years.[62] Lord Halifax wrote in his diary that night, "It is a very tragic situation and, whether we call it so or not, the French and ourselves are now in a condition of something like war."[63]

The French fleet that Darlan had spent the 1930s painstakingly building was damaged but still the second largest in Europe, behind only Britain's own. A series of retaliatory French air raids on Gibraltar raised fears that Vichy might provide even more help for German war aims in return for the acquisition of large parts of the British Empire in the final peace treaty that the Germans would dictate after Britain's expected capitulation. France might even declare war on the British if the Germans incentivized them to do so. American diplomat H. Freeman Matthews told Cordell Hull that as a result of Mers-el-Kébir, Pierre Laval was inclined to deliver to the Nazis "complete acquiescence in Germany's wishes and an active pro-German policy."[64] Vichy leaders knew that Hitler had already discussed giving Corsica, Tunisia, and Nice to Benito Mussolini's Italy.[65] British colonies therefore offered France the most obvious compensation for those expected losses, plus the inevitable loss of Alsace and / or Lorraine and whatever else the Germans chose to take.

For weeks after Mers-el-Kébir, Vichy leaders spoke openly of declaring war against the British, and Vichy-British relations remained at a boiling point for months. Posters throughout France read, "Remember, and Never Forget, Mers-el-Kébir." Both Vichy and German propagandists depicted the British as France's true enemy and Churchill as an ogre anxious to destroy a France that merely wanted to remain neutral in a war that no longer concerned the French people. They spread rumors that the Royal Air Force planned to bomb Paris on Bastille Day (July 14) and also blamed the increasing lack of food on the hostility of the British and their ever-intensifying blockade.[66]

A Vichy war against Great Britain seemed entirely possible in the tense weeks and months after the raid. Some Vichy officials spoke openly of "chasing the English from Africa" in exchange for the Germans giving

Vichy poster listing parts of France and the French Empire attacked by British forces. Most senior Vichy leaders reserved their deepest hatreds for the British, not the Germans. The text reads "We Will Remember."

France large sections of British imperial territory at the peace conference to come. The obvious inability of a weakened French military to put such a plan into action, however, led the Germans to ignore these schemes. They wanted France isolated and neutral. They did not want France to start new fronts in Morocco, Algeria, Gibraltar, and sub-Saharan Africa. The Germans sought from France "docility, loot, and perhaps bases" but surely not the "cooperation among equals" that Laval and others envisioned.[67]

Laval saw the same problem. He had even warned American diplomats that "if Germany decides to take such bases what can we do to stop her? For the present we can do nothing."[68] For the moment, however, the Germans demanded nothing. Instead, they read the French response to the attack as justifying their faith that the French would prove pliant and reliably pro-German. As a gesture of gratitude for standing up to the British, they suspended Article 8 of the 1940 armistice, which required the French fleet to stay in ports designated by the Germans.[69] The French navy then dispatched six more capital ships to Dakar to defend against a rumored Gaullist coup de main there. The French also sent the powerful battleship *Jean Bart* to Casablanca. The French even briefly considered inviting Italian ships to form a joint Franco-Italian defense of Algiers.[70] These decisions showed Vichy's inclination to view the British and Charles de Gaulle as their main adversaries, exactly as the Germans had hoped.

THE MERS-EL-KÉBIR ATTACK AND THE suspension of Article 8 had the unintended consequence of increasing the chances of the war spreading to the western hemisphere and further stoking the uncertainty that Americans felt. Shortly after he learned about the attack, a furious French ambassador to the United States, Comte René Doynel de St. Quentin, met with a "visibly shaken" ("*ébranlé*") Roosevelt for thirty minutes. Roosevelt worried that the attack would force the French fleet in Martinique, which included France's lone aircraft carrier, to go on full alert. That decision could in turn spark anxiety among American officials worried about the security of the Panama Canal. Vichy might also give the Germans access to bases in Senegal or Morocco.

The arrogant and aloof St. Quentin, whom the president quickly came to dislike, found Roosevelt unwilling to criticize the British decision to launch what St. Quentin called an "unjustified attack" on the ships of neutral France at Mers-el-Kébir. Roosevelt even told St. Quentin that he would have given the same order if he had been in Churchill's position. Roosevelt did not offer material or even diplomatic support to France, the victim of what America should, in St. Quentin's view, have seen as unprovoked British aggression.[71]

American reactions to the Mers-el-Kébir raid supported St. Quentin's pessimism. The French embassy in Washington reported to Vichy that the American media, including normally Anglophobic journalists, almost unanimously supported the British. One British survey of American opinion concluded that the incident had forced Americans to choose sides and they had chosen Britain. Whereas the American people had once shown a willingness to give Vichy a chance, now they "assert that there is no essential difference between the aims of the Vichy government and those of Nazi Germany."[72] Any Vichy military move against Britain could change American moods enough to lead the United States to declare war.

French officials complained that the British had successfully sold the attack to American reporters by spreading false rumors that the French planned to hand the fleet to the Germans for use against the United States. They alleged that British propagandists had even convinced some American officials that the British had secret intelligence that proved the imminence of such an agreement. The whole sordid episode, the French complained, would damage American attitudes toward France and bind the British even more closely to the Americans. It also seemingly proved the effectiveness of British propaganda in the United States.[73]

The British narrative of Mers-el-Kébir struck a welcome chord in the United States not only because of the superior effectiveness of British propaganda but because so few Americans felt sympathetic toward Vichy. American newspapers largely followed the British version of events. Churchill called the attack "a Greek tragedy, but no act was ever more necessary for the life of Britain." The House of Commons erupted in applause so great that it moved Churchill to tears. American media outlets reported it all in fawning and admiring terms. An aggressive attack on a neutral French fleet ironically helped to convince Roosevelt and the American people of British determination to fight Germany to the end if necessary, an indirect indication of the closeness Americans saw between Germany and Vichy.

Churchill tried to soothe the French by promising to "restore the greatness and territory of France" after the war, but he could not possibly have believed that the French would come away from Mers-el-Kébir favorably disposed to Great Britain.[74] They did not, of course. According to one British intelligence report, even many French officers in the Vichy military once willing to consider working with the British "were swung around" to the German side as a result of the attack. Most had become "actively hostile" toward the British.[75] It went without saying that the already Anglophobic senior officers in Vichy, most notably Pétain, Laval, and Darlan, were white with rage at the British. Their hatred of Great Britain, and of Churchill personally, gave them another incentive to move closer to the Germans.[76]

EVEN AS THIS LATEST CRISIS brought them closer together, policy toward France soon became the single biggest point of contention between the Americans and the British. Mers-el-Kébir and the stirring broadcasts of American journalists in London like Edward R. Murrow helped to convince Americans to see the British not as a doomed nation but as a pugnacious ally in desperate need of American help.[77] The ease with which the Destroyers-for-Bases Agreement and later the Lend-Lease agreement passed through a once-Anglophobic Congress gives an indication of how warm the relations quickly became and how much confidence the United States had gained in the British they had so recently written off as beaten. Problems undoubtedly remained, and the British realized that the war might well result in the Americans replacing them as the world's commercial and maritime hegemon, but from 1940 to 1945 the two sides needed each other. In a world of fascism on one side and communism on the other, the two shared a critical common political and cultural outlook.[78]

Yet it was because of France that the new Anglo-American relationship became, in the words of British Foreign Secretary Anthony Eden's biographer, "most strained."[79] Eden, an aristocrat of the old landed gentry and a strong opponent of appeasement, had initially decided that after France's collapse in 1940, it had no right to return to the ranks of the world's great powers after the war's end. He envisioned postwar France as something more akin to a middle power like Italy, stripped of its overseas possessions and largely excluded from leadership roles in any postwar multilateral organizations. The continued venality and craven pro-German behavior of Vichy officials only confirmed those beliefs in his mind. Eden thought that the Americans did not really understand Europe, nor could they fully comprehend the threat that Vichy's continued existence posed to Britain and to the postwar order. He also suspected that after the war, the Americans might try to use Vichy France as a client state, much as the Germans were then doing, keeping the same leaders in place but orienting them toward the United States.

His hatred of Vichy France and its leaders notwithstanding, however, Eden came to realize that a friendly postwar France was, in his words, "a geographical necessity" for British security.[80] A postwar Britain could not afford for France to remain hostile or subservient to its neighbors Germany and Italy. Moreover, it would make no sense to win the war against the Germans and the Italians only to see a quasi-fascist French state emerge as a rival in the Atlantic, Mediterranean, and across the empire. Britain might even need help from France to balance the Soviet Union's power. Consequently, Eden, like most other senior British officials, saw little choice but to back Charles de Gaulle as the best of the anti-German French leaders. He had few illusions about de Gaulle, whom he had mistrusted and loathed from their first meeting in June, when de Gaulle, then simply a renegade brigadier general who refused to accept Vichy's legality, had insisted on being seated next to Winston Churchill as if he were already the head of the French government.[81]

Despite his manifest flaws, de Gaulle proved useful for the British, and not just because of the thin hope that his speeches on the BBC might one day inspire a French resistance movement. More immediately, the British needed his allies in the French Equatorial African province of Chad. A Vichy French invasion out of Chad into British-controlled Sudan, possibly supported by Italian forces in Abyssinia (Ethiopia), would threaten British lines of communication along the Nile River and, in a worst-case scenario, stir up anti-British sentiment among the Sudanese. Loss of Sudan would mean exposure of Egypt from the south and a loss of part of the Red Sea coast.

Fortunately for the British, this strategic nightmare never materialized because of the Gaullist sentiment of Chad's governor, Félix Éboué. Born in Guiana and the first non-White French governor of a colonial possession, Éboué secretly reached out to British officials in Nigeria to tell them that he wanted to declare Chad loyal to de Gaulle. Such a coup, from the British perspective, would secure Sudan's western frontier, but de Gaulle and the British would have to move quickly and quietly lest Vichy get wind of Éboué's plans and replace him with someone more pliable, as they planned to do in French Somaliland.[82]

The British and Free French worked together to dispatch a high-level team to Chad that included future marshal of France Philippe Leclerc and future prime minister René Pleven. They met with Éboué to pledge their support in August. Within a matter of a few days, he declared Chad the first major part of the French Empire to pledge its loyalty to de Gaulle. For de Gaulle and his team, the events in Chad showed the power of the Gaullist idea to offer an alternative to Vichy. French Cameroon, French Congo, and Ubangi-Chari (today's Central African Republic) quickly followed Éboué's lead.[83]

The British and de Gaulle understood that they needed each other because they had many African interests in common. For the British, Gaullist control of French Equatorial Africa meant one less critical military theater to defend. As the war progressed, the two sides realized that they could profitably conduct joint operations against the Italian power base of Ethiopia. Free French and British Commonwealth forces then worked together (unsuccessfully) to seize Dakar and (more successfully) to retake Somaliland from the Italians who captured it in August 1940.[84] De Gaulle's pledge that he would ensure that the entire empire remained in French hands after the war gave him a significant advantage over the Vichy government, which, knowing that it would have to deal with postwar German and Italian demands for French territory, had a much more difficult time making such promises.[85]

From the beginning, therefore, de Gaulle had a strategic importance to the British in Africa and the Middle East that he did not have for the Americans. The British recognized that a productive strategic relationship with de Gaulle meant having to suffer through the frequent bouts of pride and arrogance that the Frenchman could display. The 1940 and 1941 campaigns in Africa thus set a foundation of mutual interests that the British and de Gaulle built upon for the remainder of the war.[86]

De Gaulle proved an important ally but also an incredibly difficult one. At one point, Eden (and others in Westminster) worried that he might be insane. Still, personalities aside, Eden and the British quickly realized that de Gaulle offered them the best chance at restoring France and the French Empire on favorable terms, especially as it became increasingly obvious that the new Vichy government had no intention of putting up any kind of resistance to the Axis.[87] As a result, Eden, supported by Churchill, pushed for a policy of recognizing de Gaulle as the head of a French government in exile. British officials had to bear "with what patience and understanding they could the storms that [de Gaulle] let loose upon them," observed

William Strang, Eden's key adviser on French matters. They may have hated de Gaulle, but they saw little choice other than to welcome him "in every sense [as] an ally."[88] British diplomat Harold Nicolson even up-braided Churchill, bluntly telling the prime minister that he had to stop "administering any snub [to de Gaulle] which ingenuity can devise and ill manners perpetrate."[89]

Churchill took the advice to heart. The British government recognized de Gaulle as "the leader of all Free Frenchmen, wherever they may be, who rally to him in support of the Allied cause."[90] In doing so, they symbolically transferred to de Gaulle the guardianship of French territories, traditions, and governance. They also agreed to provide Free France with weapons and other war matériel in exchange for de Gaulle's agreement to serve under an overall British command structure.

THIS EVOLUTION OF POLICY put the British at odds with the Americans who hated de Gaulle's arrogance and conceit from the start. The United States, moreover, did not have an empire in Africa to protect, so it did not think that it needed de Gaulle's help as the British did. American officials feared that the British might try to set de Gaulle up as puppet and a Gaullist France as a kind of postwar British client state. The Americans thus saw a closer relationship with Vichy as in its best interests. To Secretary of State Cordell Hull, Vichy had all the legal trappings of the government of France. He therefore saw no diplomatic justification on which to recognize de Gaulle as the head of a Free French movement, much less as the head of a state in exile.

For his part, de Gaulle did himself few favors in the United States. He selected as his first representative in the United States a friend and perfume salesman already based in New York City named Jacques de Sieyès, who proved supremely unsuited to the task. He managed to fill Carnegie Hall for a "France Forever" rally, but he also gossiped too much about the private lives of American officials and had few resources with which to convince Americans to take a chance on de Gaulle.[91] Sieyès's competent and experienced replacement, René Pleven, came to America to try to repair the damage. He brought with him continental charm, his perfect command of English, and the prestige that came from his role in having helped Chad declare its loyalty to de Gaulle. Pleven arrived in Washington with a plan to bring the entire French Empire in sub-Saharan Africa into the war on the Allied side, create a "revival of French fighting spirit," and make de Gaulle's movement a "magnet" for all Frenchmen opposed to Vichy. Although at least the first two of those goals would have matched American aims, Roosevelt nevertheless told the State Department not to deal with Pleven and to keep him away from the White House, leading de Gaulle to complain about the "almost belligerent attitude of the United States" against his movement.[92]

In order to avoid offending Vichy, de Gaulle and his accredited representatives had effectively become personae non gratae in the United States. Nor did the United States recognize de Gaulle's control of Chad or other territories that declared their loyalty to him. By contrast, American officials had granted Pierre Laval's son-in-law, René de Chambrun, privileged access to Roosevelt, even allowing him to spend a weekend on the presidential yacht. They also facilitated his well-publicized tour of the United States and helped him meet prominent Americans across the country. America's desire to reach out to Vichy in 1940 was therefore more than a case of the United States reluctantly getting its hands dirty. Americans in the early stages of the war saw much more that they liked in Vichy than in de Gaulle's Free French, even if that decision caused friction with the British.

However, the decision to move toward Vichy carried with it the risk of further undermining American security. William Bullitt told Cordell Hull that the Mers-el-Kébir attack would surely strengthen the hand of those senior Vichy officials like Laval who wanted to move France into closer strategic alignment with Germany. Such a movement posed obvious problems for America's own safety, especially if it led Vichy to reconsider its policy of not allowing the Germans to use the French fleet or overseas French bases.[93] Although Darlan continued to insist that he would keep the fleet away from the Germans at all costs, others inside Vichy argued that integration with the Germans might offer the best way to protect the rest of the fleet from future British attacks.

To solve that problem, the United States offered on July 8 (just five days after the British attack) to demilitarize and protect any French ships that sailed to the United States for the duration of the war. The French ambassador rejected the idea out of hand, citing French honor and arguing that

Secretary of State Cordell Hull (right) after meeting with a group of senators in July 1940. American leaders in those chaotic days began a frantic search for any policy that might give the nation the sense of the security it had lost.

the Germans might see such a move as a violation of the armistice terms and reinstate Article 8.[94] A week later, Hull all but threatened further military action when he told the French ambassador that he was "getting very impatient and disappointed at the course of the French government in this regard." If the French insisted on continued stubbornness, "the British and this country would presumably take their own respective courses." To the British ambassador, Hull shared his "disgust and disappointment" at the French.[95] Within weeks, he and the United States Navy began to move the issue of French ships and planes in Martinique to the top of their agenda. They worried that, as Hull told the French ambassador, "when the French naval commander at Martinique gets a message from Vichy it might in fact be a message from Berlin in disguise."[96] Yet despite these tensions, Hull still favored a more pro-Vichy policy.

Faith that the Vichy leadership would, in the end, turn anti-German died hard in both Washington and London. Incredibly enough, Churchill still hoped, even after Mers-el-Kébir, to find a way to lure Vichy to the Allied side. In December 1940, he informed American officials of a plan to offer General Weygand six infantry divisions (approximately 90,000 to 100,000 men) as well as air and sea support if his troops in North Africa would join British military operations against Axis forces in Libya. The offer represented yet another long-odds gamble from the mind of Churchill; that he made it at all shows just how unusual a position Vichy forces occupied in 1940. Weygand, however, refused and added that he would only consider cooperation if the British first cut off all contact with de Gaulle.[97]

Vichy continued to behave as though it saw Britain as its main enemy. In October came (false) rumors that Darlan and Laval both favored turning over the port of Toulon and small parts of the French fleet to the Germans as a way to punish the British for Mers-el-Kébir. The British drafted a telegram for King George VI's signature to warn the French against such cooperation. They hoped that President Roosevelt might issue a similar warning. Churchill himself worked on the telegram between trips to air raid shelters. The recent German bombing of the treasury and the constant stress of the blitz had put the British in a confrontational mood. The British dropped the idea of the telegram when they heard the shocking news that Pétain had left Vichy for direct meetings with Hitler in Montoire.[98]

AT ABOUT THE SAME TIME, de Gaulle began to grow into his role. Sir Alexander Cadogan noted in his diary in late November that the Frenchman had become "less pompous and talked rather well, firmly but with restraint." De Gaulle rejected any and all proposals about negotiating with Vichy officials, warning the British that to do so would "offend the mass of the French people." He described Darlan as "the root of evil" and a man "determined to produce a clash with us." Cadogan still disliked and mistrusted de Gaulle, but he saw that they shared a hatred of Vichy and a desire to ensure that Darlan did not bring France into the war on the Axis side.[99] British officials like Harold Macmillan continued to believe in their hearts that Vichy did not represent the interests and mood of the French people and that "there were countless men and women, inside and outside France, who mourned in silence their country's dishonour."[100] If de Gaulle would lead them in a fight for the soul and future of France, then the British would back him, even if the Americans mistrusted him.

During and after the war, apologists for American policy like William Langer and Henry Stimson argued that American relations with Vichy France in 1940 provided a crucial back channel of communications between France and Britain. The risks that came with America getting its hands dirty with Vichy, they contended, kept the British and French talking, even if indirectly. But the British argued the reverse, seeing Vichy as using the United States to act as its "only effective means of pressure" to influence British activity.[101] Rather than the Americans manipulating Vichy, they concluded, Vichy manipulated the Americans. As seen from London, America's flirtations with Vichy only proved how little the United States understood the true security situation in Europe.

Disagreements with the British notwithstanding, the Americans believed that they had found the right path for dealing with France. After Roosevelt won reelection, moreover, they stood in the favorable position of nearly complete agreement on foreign policy. Most of the president's rivals and critics either joined forces with him or went silent in the face of the national emergency. The nation had voted with virtual unanimity to build the weapons and equipment it would need to face the coming storm, and it had a new, much more aggressive leadership team in place to direct those resources. Journalist Dorothy Thompson worried that the flurry of action seemed to promise the American people "more security than it is wise for them to think they can have."[102] Tough decisions still lay ahead for a nation quickly awakening to the risks it faced.

Those decisions now involved questions about the attitudes and policy decisions that the new global crisis sparked by the fall of France would require. Specifically, should the United States continue to recognize Vichy as the legal government of France or designate it an Axis ally and, as the British wanted, recognize Charles de Gaulle's Free French movement instead? Should the United States see Vichy as a collaborationist government or as the neutral state that Vichy's defenders claimed? Within weeks of winning the 1940 election, Roosevelt decided he needed to know more. He called an old friend and one-time political rival to see if he would take a long trip on the government's behalf.

3

NO GOOD AT BEING NOBLE

The Vichy Quandary

ON DECEMBER 6, 1940, a man calling himself Donald Williams boarded a Pan Am Clipper flying boat out of Baltimore headed for Bermuda. After stopping there to refuel, the plane continued its journey across the Atlantic Ocean to the Azores and then to mainland Portugal. The man's paperwork listed Lisbon as his final destination, but the people tracking his movements from Berlin, Paris, and the sleepy spa town of Vichy in unoccupied France did not believe that he had any intention of stopping there. They suspected that he planned to go on to Spain, Greece, the Balkans, or maybe even to parts of the French Empire in North Africa. They also knew that the man calling himself Donald Williams was in fact the legendary William "Wild Bill" Donovan.

It required no brilliant piece of intelligence work to identify the fifty-seven-year-old Donovan, a great American hero of the last war, a celebrity lawyer in the interwar years, and a candidate for several political offices, including governor of New York, in the 1920s and 1930s.[1] His round, avuncular face regularly graced the political pages of the daily newspapers—and frequently the society pages as well. He had a reputation for bravery, intrigue, and mystery perfectly suited to a trip like this one. Moreover, a few newspapers had covered his departure, he had chosen a pretty obvious code name, and "Mr. Williams's" luggage had the initials WJD stamped on it.

Donovan was no ordinary passenger and his trip to Europe no ordinary voyage. As a soldier in the First World War, he had refused to accept a medal until the army gave one to the courageous Jewish sergeant who had fought alongside him. As a lawyer, he had stood up for the rights of his Jewish clients in Europe. Some people close to him even thought that he had considered converting to Judaism for a short period in his youth. Just months before taking this trip, he had narrowly missed out on becoming secretary of war to Henry Stimson.[2] With the nation facing a new crisis, Donovan knew he had to be involved in some way. The trip he had just begun would eventually take him 25,000 miles across Europe, all the way to Palestine, and back to London before returning to the United States.

Shortly after Donovan left the United States, the American media began to speculate about his mission and what it might mean for America and its increasingly tenuous security situation. The *New York Times* guessed that perhaps he would return to England, where he had gone in June on behalf of President Franklin Roosevelt to bolster British morale in the wake of France's stunning defeat. In London, he had delivered a much more positive and helpful message than that coming from American ambassador Joseph Kennedy, who expected the British to sue for peace as the French had. Kennedy therefore wanted the United States to minimize its commitments to a presumably doomed Britain. Donovan's June trip, by contrast, gave the British faith that the United States would stand by them. He also opened a more effective communications channel between British and American leaders than Kennedy had provided. Donovan backed up his words with action, helping Roosevelt rush the Destroyers-for-Bases Agreement through Congress.

The *New York Times* also reported that before leaving Baltimore, Donovan met with Secretary of the Navy Frank Knox. That meeting suggested that Donovan might be traveling as an agent of the government, not in his personal capacity. It also suggested the possibility of some new arrangement between Great Britain and the still-neutral United States, maybe an extensive economic agreement or even an alliance. Such ideas had gained momentum. Around the time of Donovan's trip, his friend and noted journalist Dorothy Thompson proposed a formal Federation of English-Speaking Peoples that would come with security guarantees from the United States to Great Britain.[3] Donovan's hometown newspaper in Buffalo reported that he might have gone to England to explore those ideas as well as the possibility of replacing the "defeatist" Kennedy as ambassador to Great Britain. Or maybe he wanted to learn the military lessons of the 1940 campaign from the British before returning to the United States Army as a general in charge of training. Or maybe President Roosevelt wanted to use him as an unofficial envoy the way that Woodrow Wilson had used Edward House in the last war.[4]

The French and German officials tracking his movements placed great importance on the fact that Donovan, a Republican, had joined forces with his former Democratic rival, President Roosevelt. As previously noted, two other prominent Republicans, Secretary of the Navy Frank Knox and Secretary of War Henry Stimson, joined Roosevelt's cabinet on July 10, just weeks after the fall of France. This new bipartisan spirit served as yet another indication that the crisis in Europe had brought Americans together, rather than pull them apart, as had happened in France. The fall of France had unexpectedly rallied the Americans to a stunning degree. Congress had passed an unprecedented appropriations bill to build a two-ocean navy, authorized peacetime conscription, and drawn closer to the British. Germany's conquest of France thus had the unintended consequence of waking the Americans from their slumber and getting them beyond their own internal divisions.

Whatever his final destination, and whatever name he used, Donovan's departure signaled to German and French officials that something important had shifted in the American approach to the war. German military officers warned French diplomats against giving Donovan a visa to enter unoccupied France or any part of the French Empire. They must have made their case quite convincingly because the French official to whom they delivered the message warned his superiors that the Germans would "hold the French government responsible and would impose unpleasant consequences" in the event that Donovan made his way into any part of the world that France controlled.[5] Vichy French diplomats responded by warning their embassies and consulates not to issue Donovan or "Williams" a visa under any circumstances and to deny him entry into French territory even if he somehow obtained valid paperwork from a French embassy or consulate.

French officials reported to the Germans that Donovan would surely head back to London as soon as possible, but the Germans deduced that he intended to go to the Balkans first. Once there, he would meet with Greek and Bulgarian officials to try to woo them to the Allied side. He might also attempt to obtain a visa in Mr. Williams's falsified passport from an unsuspecting French consular official in a Balkan country. His mission proved to the Germans that the United States had developed an interest in making the Mediterranean and Europe, not East Asia, its main strategic priority.

The Germans had guessed right. Roosevelt's instructions to Donovan asked him "to make a strategic appreciation from an economic, political, and military standpoint of the Mediterranean area."[6] Those instructions show the interest that the United States had developed since the fall of France in exploring all options for becoming further involved in Europe. Donovan's trip, and the emergency defense measures the Americans had put in place, demonstrated a readiness to do more than fulfill Roosevelt's public promise to give the British "all aid short of war." As early as November 1940, the Americans had begun to contemplate operations of their own in the Mediterranean theater if the dire circumstances of war compelled them to do so.[7] Donovan had come to Europe to figure out how best to put such ideas into action.

In the Balkans, Donovan tried to do what he could to help amid growing indications that the next German move would target Greece (which the Italians had invaded in October with only limited success), Bulgaria, and Yugoslavia.[8] In Athens, he saw firsthand the fear of an imminent German attack, which the Greeks expected would come within six weeks. Without massive outside help, the Balkan states had no hope of effective resistance.[9] German agents in Athens soon learned that Donovan told Balkan leaders that they must resist the Axis at all costs and refuse all cooperation with the Germans and Italians. The United States would help by providing enough aid to keep the British, then fighting in North Africa, in the war indefinitely. That aid would include 80 percent of America's 1941 aircraft production, amounting to an astonishing 14,000 airplanes.[10] Congress, then putting the finishing touches on the Lend-Lease Act, would provide Britain with all manner of civilian and military assistance. The Americans, Donovan promised, could and would back the British to the hilt in Europe and Africa, ensuring that they would not only survive but triumph. The US military leadership had also decided that it could focus on Europe for the time being because Japan's deepening war in China rendered it unable to pose an immediate threat to the United States.

The "forceful declaration" Donovan came to deliver to the Balkan countries sent a strong signal. The American minister in Bulgaria reported that Donovan had pledged that "America, exerting all her enormous force will ensure ultimate victory for England." He hoped, futilely as it turned out, that Donovan's mission "may prevent cooperation between Bulgarian and German troops" in the Balkans campaign to come.[11] Finally, Donovan told Balkan leaders that no one should count on America remaining neutral for much longer. As in the last war, if provoked, the United States would enter the war and win it within two years, three at the most. The Mediterranean, he pledged, would play "a capital role" in any American strategy. Unlike 1918, the United States would not seek compromises or a "peace without victory." This time, if America fought, it would fight to the end.[12] Balkan leaders had to choose which side they favored if they wanted to remain in America's good graces.

THE SEEMINGLY IMMINENT EXTENSION of the war to the Balkans explained Donovan's trip to Athens, Belgrade, and Sofia (where German agents broke into his hotel room and rifled through his papers), but what explained his interest in getting a visa to enter French North Africa? The Germans and their allies in unoccupied France could think of only one reason: they assumed that Donovan would try to meet with French general Maxime Weygand. Others drew the same conclusions. Drew Pearson of the *Washington Herald* reported in his popular "Washington Merry-Go-Round" column that Donovan would attempt to "stop in North Africa where he will see his old World War friend, Marshal Weygand, now controlling the large French Army in Africa."[13] Such a meeting, if it resulted in Weygand changing allegiances from Vichy to the Allies, could have profound effects on the course of the war.

The mercurial Weygand held the key to the military future of French North Africa. When the Germans invaded France in May 1940, he had been commanding French forces in Syria. The French government, although mistrustful of his archconservative politics and fearful that he might use the crisis to dissolve the cabinet, recalled him to Paris to take command of the rapidly deteriorating military front. On seeing the collapse unfolding in front of him, he supposedly remarked that if he had

French marshal Maxime Weygand (second from left), seen here before the war with former prime minister Joseph Paul-Boncour and French army commander Maurice Gamelin. Weygand was Vichy's most consistently pro-American voice, but he proved unwilling to translate his words into action.

known the full scale of the disaster that had befallen French forces, he would have stayed in Syria. He also had a furious argument with a newly promoted undersecretary for war named Charles de Gaulle, who wanted to continue the war from the overseas French Empire.[14]

Weygand was a strange and enigmatic figure, exactly the type of man a spy like Donovan would find intriguing. He had risen to prominence as the ever-present and supremely efficient alter ego of French marshal Ferdinand Foch during the First World War, getting to know most of the senior American leadership, including Donovan, in the process. Taciturn and highly disciplined, he had somehow gained an appointment to the French military academy at Saint-Cyr despite having been born in Belgium and despite never knowing the identity of his biological parents. Rumors spread that he was the illegitimate offspring of Empress Carlota of Mexico, King Leopold of Belgium, or (most likely) of a Belgian general named Alfred van der Smissen and his mistress, Melanie Marie Metternich-Zichy, one of the many daughters of the legendary Austrian diplomat Prince Klemens von Metternich. His mysterious parentage only added to the aura of intrigue that followed him as he rose in the ranks. The left-wing French governments of the 1930s feared him and always suspected him of wanting to support, or even lead, a coup d'état. Those fears partly explain why such an experienced and talented military commander languished in near exile in Syria when the battle for France's survival in the west began.

Weygand had reluctantly supported the decision of the French government to ask the Germans for peace terms in June 1940. Like most senior French military leaders, he blamed the failures of the country's left-leaning interwar governments for leaving the country unprepared to meet the German onslaught. An armistice that could at least leave France in control of the empire, the navy, and most internal affairs seemed to him the only reasonable way out the crisis and the only way to save French honor. Weygand became a founding member of the Vichy government, serving as its first minister of national defense. Initially, he agreed with the general consensus that Germany would quickly force the British into an armistice; the Germans, French, and British would then negotiate a final peace treaty that would return France to its rightful place among the great powers.

Weygand was too smart and too experienced to be blinded for long by the unwarranted optimism then prevalent in Vichy. He did not share Pierre Laval's "supreme confidence in his [Laval's] own ability to outsmart the Germans" at a postwar peace conference.[15] Weygand figured out long before Laval and most of his other colleagues did that the Germans had no intention of restoring France to its greatness after its supposedly inevitable defeat of Great Britain. His love of France, moreover, would not allow him to stomach French politicians like Laval jumping like terrified servants at Nazi commands, nor could he sit idly by while theoretically independent unoccupied France suffered under Nazi domination. In a private conversation with American diplomat H. Freeman Matthews, Weygand called Laval "a dog, rolling in the dung of defeat."[16]

As one top-secret American study concluded, Weygand believed that "a definitive German victory would mean slavery for France, and that for an indefinite length of time."[17] Germany's failure to defeat the British also shattered in Weygand's mind the aura of German invincibility. Ironically, this man who probably had no French blood became the first senior Vichy French official to see the grave long-term risks to France of Vichy's cooperation with Germany. Among his other actions in 1940, he insisted on gaining more favorable armistice terms for France, and he assured the transfer of French uranium stocks to the British, a farsighted decision that might have had the most critical of consequences.[18] Weygand did not trust the British, but neither did he share the knee-jerk Anglophobia of Jean-François Darlan, Pierre Laval, and Henri-Philippe Pétain.

American officials like Robert Murphy took notice as Weygand developed a reputation as the most anti-German of the senior Vichy officials. The Germans took notice as well. In September 1940, the German government pressured Vichy to remove him from his job as defense minister and send him out of Europe. Laval, who disliked him in any case, arranged to dispatch Weygand to Algiers in the newly invented post of delegate-general to the North African colonies. Although Vichy intended to put him in a largely ceremonial position, Weygand found ways to rebuild a modicum of French military power, with the goal of defending Morocco, Algeria, and Tunisia from the avaricious eyes of the Germans, British, Italians, Free French, and Spaniards alike.

The Germans initially gave Weygand limited support, even sending him a few old tanks, in hopes that he might use his military force to reconquer those parts of French sub-Saharan Africa that had declared themselves loyal to de Gaulle's Free French movement.[19] They also hoped that his new job might keep him too busy to plot a return to Vichy. He built a force of 100,000 soldiers, mostly Africans, that could easily tip the balance of the war in Africa, even if most of them had outdated equipment and little training. In truth, no one knew what Weygand planned to do, but British and American strategists hoped that they could convince him to flip to their side. In October, Secretary of State for India and Burma Leo Amery wrote to the chief of the imperial general staff, General Sir John Dill, that "I cannot help hoping that Weygand in North Africa will refuse to participate in the further humiliation of France and will turn the corner for us presently."[20] In the United States, *Life* reported that if Weygand, who was "keeping his own counsel," combined his forces with the British and the Greeks, the Allies could win the war in the Mediterranean in a matter of a few weeks.[21]

Although his early collaboration with the Germans and Vichy tainted him both during and after the war, in the difficult days of late 1940, he seemed as likely a Frenchman as any for an American like Donovan to approach in hopes of building strategic partnerships.[22] Weygand's power as a more or less independent military commander explains the intense

German and Vichy interest in blocking Donovan's attempts to get a French visa under a false name. The warnings from Vichy reached Belgrade just in time to deny "Mr. Williams" a visa from the French embassy in Yugoslavia. French officials then reached out to Weygand himself, who promised not to meet with Donovan even if the American did somehow find his way to North Africa. Weygand subsequently wrote to his friend Jules Henri, the French ambassador to Turkey, and asked him to ensure that Donovan had no luck getting a visa anywhere in the Balkans. A Donovan visit to North Africa, Weygand warned, "could not fail to provoke a strong reaction from the Reich" that could harm French interests.[23] Weygand particularly worried about the fate of the two million French prisoners of war still held in German camps as virtual hostages.

Donovan probably tried once more to get a French visa in Madrid, but he failed there, too. The Spanish capital was a hive of spies and wartime subterfuge where he may have thought he could bribe or pressure someone into getting him a visa. He did, however, tell senior officials in the Spanish government of the "gigantic material program now going on in the United States" that would tip "the scales of victory for Britain."[24] In mid-February 1941, French agents spotted him in Gibraltar where he boarded a plane for London before going to Dublin, then returning to Washington.[25]

ALTHOUGH DONOVAN LEFT NO RECORD of what he wanted to discuss with Weygand, the future of the French Empire, and especially the French fleet, must have sat at the top of the list. Senior officials in the United States needed to know what exactly the Vichy government planned to do with the large, modern warships under its control. According to the armistice of 1940, those ships remained under exclusive French command. As noted earlier, Darlan had even issued orders to French crews to scuttle the fleet rather than see it seized by any foreign power. Still, no one in Washington knew how long the French could protect those ships from a German or Italian demand to hand them over, and after the collapse of the French army, no one had any faith that the French could resist an Axis power grab to seize them. On more than one occasion, a worried Secretary of State Cordell Hull described the French fleet as "a cocked gun waiting for Germany to shoot at us."[26]

The proximity of Spain to French North Africa and the attendant threat to Gibraltar kept the possibility of Vichy-Spanish cooperation in American and British minds at all times. Spain had its own possessions in North Africa, including the port city of Tangier, which Spanish troops occupied on the same day that Paris fell to the Germans. Above all, the United States, like Great Britain, wanted to keep Spain neutral in order to ensure that it did not attempt to seize Gibraltar or Malta and thereby endanger Allied shipping through the Mediterranean. Spain could also grant Germany permission to use the Canary Islands as a base from which to plan operations in the North Atlantic. The Spanish, still recovering from the ravages of a terrible civil war, lacked the power to conduct military operations on their own, but they could possibly do so with French assistance. Weygand held the key, as any attack on Gibraltar or Malta would likely rely on the resources he commanded.[27]

Donovan surely wanted to know if Weygand could actually use his army to tip the balance of the war in Africa. The French forces he commanded were large but lacked equipment, training, and officers for operations against Gibraltar or Vichy. On the other hand, the intense hatred of the British then common across the Vichy regime might have incentivized its leaders to plot revenge for Mers-el-Kébir. Most likely, Donovan wanted to travel through North Africa in hopes of gaining information and assessing possible future opportunities with Weygand. He undoubtedly wanted to get a sense of the loyalties of Vichy French officers and their likelihood to join the Americans if the United States found itself conducting operations in Europe or North Africa.

Donovan did not succeed in meeting with Weygand or seeing the confusion of French North Africa for himself, but he had not given up his efforts to learn more. The United States still needed information and connections to potential allies before it could even hope to influence events there. Donovan therefore began to hatch a plan to set up a team of agents in French North Africa to gather intelligence and send it back to London via a network of radios that could transmit to the main British radio tower at Gibraltar. His plan faced both technical and political problems. The unusual geography of Gibraltar made sending and receiving radio signals to and from Algeria difficult, but engineers could overcome that problem if given time and stronger transmitters. Donovan worried more about the hostility that Vichy and the Germans had shown to his attempt merely to enter French North Africa. They would most certainly not look kindly on him or his agents trying to run an intelligence network there.

Donovan solved both problems by basing the scheme in the small slice of Africa around Tangiers that neutral Spain controlled.[28] Having just seized the city, which had been an international zone since 1923, Spain did not have an established police network or system of informers in Tangiers. The idea was inspired. Donovan would soon work with veteran diplomat Robert Murphy, sent to Algiers by Roosevelt in September 1940 to represent American interests in Algeria and Morocco. Murphy, a Francophile who had worked with politicians from across the French political spectrum in the 1930s, knew all of the key players, including Admiral Darlan. He played a critical role in crafting America's North Africa strategy. In 1942, he and Darlan would sit at the center of what Murphy described as the most difficult decision of his long and illustrious diplomatic career. His interactions with Darlan, although controversial, may have saved thousands of American and French lives in the process.[29] All that lay in the future, however.

In 1940, the Americans needed Donovan's intelligence network because no one, not even Murphy, had reliable information on the new French regime, which one American publication called "the barren rump of France."[30] The situation had no precedent in diplomatic history. Even veteran diplomats had no idea how to read the Vichy government or how to deduce what the new arrangement meant for American or British security. Most interested observers worried that France might soon become an American or British enemy, especially after the Mers-el-Kébir attack had riled the French to such anger against the British. With his penchant for understatement, Lord Halifax wrote about Spain and France that "this twilight between peace and war is altogether very tiresome." Two weeks later, he reported that the members of the British cabinet, himself included, "spen[t] an interminable time trying to solve what was evidently quite insoluble."[31]

DESPITE REPEATED VICHY PROTESTATIONS OF NEUTRALITY, the new regime's hatred of Great Britain and obsequious subservience to Germany indicated its true colors to anyone who wanted to see them. Few German officials came into the unoccupied zone, but they didn't need to. Their power over the occupied zone (which, of course, included Paris), the French prisoners of war in German camps, and the Wehrmacht's seeming invincibility on the battlefield cowed the new French regime into doing Germany's bidding. The German Armistice Commission based in Wiesbaden enforced the terms to Germany's advantage and never let the French forget who had won the war. They also increased the rigidity of controls at the demarcation line between occupied and unoccupied France whenever they wished to send a message to the Vichy government. French officials also worried that the Germans might give in to Benito Mussolini's vocal demands to annex Corsica, Algiers, and Tunisia as a reward for Italian loyalty to Germany.

An American journalist who went to Vichy described unoccupied France as "poor and paralyzed." Terrified of the Germans and convinced that Britain would soon fall, a "stagnant" France "waits for Germany to finish the war" and determine France's fate.[32] To secure a prominent role in that future, Vichy might grant Germany access to French bases in the western hemisphere or loan the Germans its warships. Britain and the United States would then find themselves in a defenseless position. France, which only a few months before had acted as a cornerstone of American defense, now appeared as one of the biggest potential threats to its security.

The timing of Donovan's trip and his highly publicized meeting with Secretary of the Navy Frank Knox were hardly coincidental. The Americans learned from French and German media reports that Adolf Hitler had met with Laval in the French town of Montoire on his way to Spain on October 22 and then with Pétain on his way back two days later. Hitler's meeting with Francisco Franco, and the possibility of Spain entering the war on the Axis side, raised enough alarm bells on its own, but the Pétain-Hitler meeting, hastily arranged by Laval, caught the Americans completely by surprise. A week later, Pétain announced in a nationwide radio address that France would "enter into the way of collaboration," coining the term that would come back to haunt him and an entire generation of French officials. In exchange for working with the Germans in the new European order, Pétain told the French people that "the weight of suffering of our country could be lightened, the fate of our prisoners ameliorated, occupation costs reduced, the demarcation line [between occupied and unoccupied France] made more flexible, and the administration and supply of our territory made easier."[33]

We know now that the Germans made no such promises to the French at Montoire, but at the time, American officials responded with genuine alarm over what Pétain must have pledged in return for such uncharacterıstic Nazi generosity. Might they have discussed Vichy entering the war against the British? A joint Spanish-French attack on Gibraltar or Malta? German use of warships and ports in the French Empire? President Roosevelt worried enough to send an unusually stern letter to Pétain warning that any use of the French fleet against the British or Americans would "constitute a flagrant and deliberate breach of faith with the United States Government" that "would most definitely wreck the traditional friendship between the French and American peoples." If Vichy entered the war on the Axis side, Roosevelt warned, the United States would "make no effort when the appropriate time came to exercise its influence to insure France the retention of her overseas possessions."[34] With those words, the Americans bluntly threatened to invalidate all the hard work Vichy officials had done to assure French sovereignty over the empire.

Rumors reached the American chargé d'affaires in Vichy, H. Freeman Matthews, that matters might deteriorate even further. He told Secretary of State Cordell Hull that after the Montoire meetings, the French had come to the conclusion that Britain's hopeless military position required France to accept virtually any final peace terms the Germans demanded. Germany, he reported, had almost settled on a list that included outright control of the major ports of Marseille, Toulon, Bizerte, Oran, and Dakar, the strategic Senegalese port that de Gaulle had tried but failed to capture in September 1940. The Nazis would also demand French inclusion in a German-dominated customs union and operational control of the French fleet for the limited purpose of breaking the British blockade. Laval denied the imminence of any deal with Germany, but Matthews warned Hull to take any and all statements from Laval "with large and numerous grains of salt." Under Laval's direction, he warned, Vichy "is plunging definitely along the road of subservience."[35] Hull did not, apparently, know just how far Laval had already gone along that road. He had offered Germany 200 French pilots symbolically commanded by the Allies' top First World War ace, René Fonck, for use against the British.[36] If such a peace deal came to pass, it would represent a massive increase in German power and an exponential growth of the threat posed to the United States.

AMERICAN ATTITUDES TOWARD FRANCE became increasingly confused in a world that seemed to grow more dangerous almost by the day. Laval's comment that "democracy is dying all across the world" made headlines in the United States, as did French fascist Jacques Doriot's strident critiques of President Roosevelt as a stooge of capitalist, imperialist, and Jewish interests.[37] French subservience to the Germans became more obvious with every passing week. Shortly after his collaboration radio address, Pétain gave another in which he said that France must liberate itself from its "traditional friendships." He privately clarified to H. Freeman Matthews that he meant Poland and Yugoslavia, not the United States, an explanation that did not convince Matthews in the least.[38]

Above all, the French tried, as René de Chambrun had, to convince the Americans that their increasingly warm relationship with Nazi Germany need not negatively impact their traditional friendship with the United States. Writing in *Life*, André Maurois, a Jewish writer and member of the Académie française (Pétain had helped him get his seat in 1938), tried to ease American anger at the French drift toward Germany. Writing from Washington where he had moved in order to rally anti-Nazi sentiment in the United States, Maurois bemoaned the way that Americans saw France in 1940 "not as a victim but as a wicked and guilty nation" for its capitulation to the Nazis. As a result, Americans did not respond to France's hour of need with aid and charity as they had so generously done in 1914. Instead, Americans unsympathetically labeled France, and especially the new ruling class in Vichy, as "entirely subservient to the conqueror." Maurois wanted his American readers to know that Frenchmen of all political views saw working with the Germans as "repugnant" but that France had no choice because the Nazis had a "rope round the neck" of his country.[39] Such views failed to convince most Americans. One reader wrote to Maurois that "the France of today is not the France of the Revolution, of the Republic, of Liberté, Égalité, Fraternité." He accused Vichy French officials in 1940 of acting as "Nazi spokesmen for Nazi France."[40]

Such public attitudes made the government's task of dealing with the new France much harder, but Roosevelt and his leadership team remained determined to try, if only, they argued, to guard American interests in a dangerous world. A series of reports prepared by economist Alexander Sachs and given to Donovan to prepare for his trip may well have influenced the president's thinking. Sachs, then a vice-president of the Lehman Corporation, had close links to the Roosevelts and he certainly had the credentials to be taken seriously at the highest levels of government.[41] In October 1939, he had delivered to Roosevelt a letter from Albert Einstein and Leó Szilárd demanding "quick action on the part of the Administration" because the Germans had begun work on a uranium bomb.[42] The letter led to the creation of the Manhattan Project.

One year later, in September 1940, Sachs's reports on Vichy painted a terrifying picture of "the grave danger to our [western] hemisphere policy" that the weakened state of France and the French Empire posed. Vichy's repeated "duplicity" further revealed a "pattern of the enveloping danger to the United States." The French regime's clearly pro-German orientation indicated, Sachs concluded, an Axis desire to effect "the virtual encirclement of the United States."[43] Sachs urged the United States to lose no more time setting a constructive or, if necessary, confrontational, policy for its dealings with Vichy and the French Empire. "The Fascist powers are bound to exploit the crippled and parasitic political entities of Metropolitan France and the French Colonial Empire for purposes of piracy," he wrote, in order to seek "aggrandizement at the expense of the future and the security of the British Commonwealth of Nations, the United States, and Latin America. The present position of the United States, as is apparent from the map—which should be continuously and vividly before everyone's eyes— is that of threatened strategic envelopment."[44] Every moment lost, he wrote, benefited the totalitarian powers and their ability to exploit the resources of the French Empire from the Caribbean to North Africa to Indochina. Matthews's reports on German plans for a final peace treaty with France seemed to confirm those fears. Sachs argued for placing more pressure on Vichy and warning its leaders of severe consequences if France behaved in ways that threatened the core interests of the United States or Great Britain.

The fate of the Caribbean islands of Martinique and Guadeloupe preoccupied Sachs and several senior American officials in 1940. Home to 1,200 French military personnel, an aircraft carrier with 106 planes, and almost half of the French gold supply, Martinique sat in a position to interfere with Allied shipping from Colombia, Venezuela, and Puerto Rico, as well as trade routes through the Panama Canal.[45] The planes included American-built Curtiss SBC-4 "Helldiver" dive bombers and Brewster "Buffalo" escort fighters. Although not the latest in aviation technology, they still had the potential to support an attack on weakly defended areas like the Panama Canal or Puerto Rico. The State Department had begun to pressure the French governor in Martinique by circulating propaganda, consistent with the Havana meeting of the Organization of the American States, stating that the United States might support independence for French colonies in the Caribbean after the war. It also broadcast and circulated President Roosevelt's speeches on the need to end global empires after the war and give colonized peoples a greater say in their own futures. In doing so, the United States sent an unmistakable message that it might help Martinique get its independence from France if the French used it for military or strategic purposes. Sachs wanted the government to go much further. Senior State Department officials, worried about the security of the Caribbean, pressed for a more forceful policy as well, including direct threats of military action against the island.

Secretary of the Navy Frank Knox agreed and, less than a month after Mers-el-Kébir, sent an American admiral to Martinique, now largely cut off from trade with France by the British blockade, to work out a deal. Instead of threats of military action on the Mers-el-Kébir model, the Americans came offering money. The United States would provide the island with food and oil for its merchant ships and would also release some French funds and lines of credit frozen by the Treasury Department when France fell in June. The war had badly depressed prices for Martinique's principle exports (mainly sugar, rum, and bananas), leaving the governor desperately in need of hard currency and access to American markets. In return, the French promised that the aircraft carrier *Béarn* and the cruiser *Émile Bertin* would not leave Martinique, nor would the French transfer any military assets on the island to a third party. As a goodwill gesture, the French removed the planes from the carrier and allowed visiting American officials to see them lined up and abandoned on the beach where they quickly fell victim to mechanical neglect and the humid, salty Caribbean climate.[46] The French also dropped a plan for fortifying Martinique's harbors and accepted a small American naval mission on the island "to prove the honesty of our intentions."[47]

The talks proceeded on a friendly basis, but the French governor, a Laval ally, refused American requests to send the two ships and the gold reserves to Puerto Rico for the duration of the war. He also refused to give the United States Army Air Corps permission to use the airfield on the island or to return the American-built airplanes. The Americans had broken the French code, so they knew that the French considered the situation "stable" but still characterized by mutual "uneasiness." One report read, "The Americans have always the fear that in spite of our mutual verbal agreements, they may see the officers obeying an order of the French Government which would send the gold and the *Bertin* to Dakar." Once in Dakar, the Germans could transport the gold overland for their own use. For their part, the French worried that the United States might seize upon, or even manufacture, an internal disturbance to justify invading the island.[48]

ABOUT 450 MILES NORTHWEST OF MARTINIQUE, one man in particular in the Caribbean would soon see his whole life changed because of America's confusion over Vichy. On a November morning between the Martinique meetings and Donovan's trip, a courier arrived in San Juan, Puerto Rico, interrupting the breakfast of the American governor-general, retired admiral William Leahy.[49] Seated on the elegant terrace of the sixteenth-century palace known as La Forteleza, Leahy hoped that the message from Washington would order his recall to active service to command one of the new fleets the United States was building as part of the enormous Two-Ocean Navy Act.[50] Leahy wanted to get back to sea as a commander of one of the brand-new battlegroups.

President Roosevelt, whom Leahy had first met during the last world war, had other ideas for him, however. The message asked if Leahy would take on the difficult job of ambassador to Vichy France. Stating that Roosevelt saw Franco-American relations as being in an "increasingly serious situation," the telegram warned that "the French Fleet may be utilized under the control of Germany." Roosevelt wanted Leahy, a military man, to go to Vichy and "talk to Marshal Pétain in language which he would understand and the position which you have held in our own navy would undoubtedly give you great influence with the higher officers of the French navy who are now openly hostile to Great Britain."[51]

Given Pétain's singular importance to the new France, Roosevelt had first reached out to the Vichy leader's friend and fellow First World War general John Pershing. Pershing, however, turned the job down because of poor health. He later wrote a graceful note to Leahy to wish him well and tell him that "a much better man has been chosen for this most difficult duty."[52] Leahy had solved problems for Roosevelt before, most recently as chief of naval operations and in calming tensions in Puerto Rico after the killing of nineteen peaceful protestors in Ponce under the administration of his predecessor. The admiral had gone to the island, gained the trust of its leaders, and overseen badly needed upgrades to its military facilities. Now the future security of the United States might well hinge on whether he could solve the Vichy France problem for Roosevelt as well.[53]

The American media praised President Roosevelt for the "diplomatic coup" he scored in naming so able a man for so challenging a job, but it also noted the grave obstacles Leahy would face in "one of the touchiest missions any U.S. diplomat ever undertook." He would have to "stiffen the spine" of Vichy officials "against the Nazi conqueror" and make clear to the French that the United States would protect its own interests, including guaranteeing the survival of Great Britain and its empire. The job would challenge even a man as capable as Leahy, especially since the Germans, who called Leahy a "warmonger," opposed the whole idea of the United States being diplomatically represented in Vichy.

Leahy carefully orchestrated his departure for France and its attendant symbolism. The new ambassador left for his assignment not on a commercial ship but on a fully armed 10,000-ton heavy cruiser, the USS *Tuscaloosa*. The ship had nine 200 mm guns and eight 130 mm guns. He and his wife came aboard with the full pomp and ceremony usually afforded only to the president. Leahy did not need all that firepower to deter German submarines, which could easily identify the *Tuscaloosa* with its American flag as a neutral warship. They would therefore never dare to fire on it; the ship and its destroyer escorts, moreover, could certainly defend themselves if the need arose. The show of force sent a diplomatic message, namely that Leahy would conduct business in France on American terms. As *Life* magazine noted, "it is unlikely that sensitive Frenchmen will overlook the significance of the big-gunned *Tuscaloosa*."[54] The ship later bombarded Iwo Jima and Okinawa.

Leahy and his francophone wife were initially impressed by Pétain, with whom they had friendly conversations that seemed to augur well for the future. Nevertheless, the new ambassador soon found that Vichy, quiet and dull on the surface, hid a snake pit of political rivalries behind the scenes. Pétain had exiled Weygand to Algiers to please the Germans, but he still had to deal with the cravenly pro-German Laval and his German backers, including the most influential German in France, the cultured but venomous German ambassador Otto Abetz. All senior Vichy leaders hated the British for their attack on the French fleet at Mers-el-Kébir in July, but they claimed to want good relations with the Americans. They hoped that the United States might persuade the British to loosen their blockade on French ports and maybe even sell Vichy food, fuel, and other supplies it desperately needed.

BACK IN WASHINGTON, senior American officials disagreed about what to do with Vichy. States aligned with Germany or anxious to remain in its good graces recognized Vichy as the legal successor to the Third Republic, but the British did not. Instead, they began to intensify their relationship with the anti-Vichy Free French movement led by de Gaulle, effectively recognizing it as the legitimate government of France in exile. President Roosevelt and Secretary of War Henry Stimson instead favored normalizing relations with Vichy and using those relations to try to slowly woo it away from Germany. Stimson also argued for giving Vichy full access to frozen assets belonging to the French government in the United States. Secretary of State Cordell Hull sided with Stimson, but he worried that the decision might backfire and that he might find himself one day facing charges of having aided and abetted a Nazi ally. He therefore invited Harvard historian William Langer to record, in a manner favorable to Hull, what Langer himself called "a far from creditable episode in our diplomacy."[55]

Stimson, Hull, and Roosevelt believed that however distasteful working with Vichy might be and however angrily the British might respond, the United States should nevertheless work with it to try to modify its behavior. American leaders suffered from the same sense of fear, insecurity, and panic that gripped their countrymen. With American security suddenly in jeopardy, they reached for any plan that might buy them time.

American officials gave four rationales for reaching out to Vichy despite an intense American distrust of the new French regime. First and foremost, should the French fleet voluntarily join or be captured by the Germans or the Italians, then the Axis powers would have a world-class navy to supplement their dominant armies. William Bullitt, the former American ambassador in France, bluntly told Roosevelt that "you will be unable to protect the United States from German attack" if Germany absorbed the French fleet. For this reason, American officials condemned the Mers-el-Kébir operation in public, but privately many felt a sense of relief that the raid had reduced the French fleet by seven capital ships. American media and popular opinion also supported the attack.[56]

Second, Vichy controlled the French Empire, most critically to Americans those parts located in the western hemisphere. They included the islands of Saint-Pierre and Miquelon at the mouth of the Saint Lawrence River and Martinique and Guadeloupe in the Caribbean. American strategists worried that the former two could become a dangerous base of operations for Axis ships operating against the American east coast, and the latter two had sufficient military capability to threaten trade routes through the Panama Canal. Despite the agreement with the United States, Martinique still held more than $245 million in French gold reserves (equivalent to about $4.5 billion today). The desire to monitor and, if necessary, fight French forces in these islands motivated the Americans to request access to British bases in the western hemisphere via the Destroyers-for-Bases Agreement. Vichy also controlled a naval base in Dakar, Senegal, that could, as Matthew Ridgway had warned, enable German submarines and surface warships to interfere with cross-Atlantic shipping or, in cooperation with ships and planes in Martinique, support Axis operations toward Latin America.

The fall of France threatened American interests all over the globe. French officials repeatedly pleaded with the Americans to help them bolster their defenses in Indochina, where the Japanese had become ever more aggressive in their demands for the use of key infrastructure. Undersecretary of State Sumner Welles told the French ambassador in Washington that they could expect no such help and that, if he were a French official, he would see no choice but to give in to Japanese demands for greater control of Indochinese ports, resources, and border posts, as well as the right to move Japanese forces through the territory. A September 1940 agreement gave Japan a "preeminent position" in French Indochina that the Japanese used to exert increasing control. The Japanese now had the same kinds of effective vetoes over the actions of French officials in Saigon and Hanoi that the Germans exercised over their counterparts in Paris and Vichy.[57]

Third, the Americans needed information about Vichy and its possible future moves. By recognizing Vichy, the United States hoped that it could open a critical channel of communications not just to France itself but to North Africa as well. The United States could lure Vichy with the carrots of trade, diplomatic support, and help reducing the effects of the British blockade. On the other hand, the Americans could use the stick by making public statements of opposition to France retaining its empire after the war, as Roosevelt sometimes did. Vichy seemed too important to American planners to cut off communication with it. To not recognize it only risked driving it further into Germany's arms, an outcome that clearly worked against American interests.

Fourth, although Americans did not like everything about their Vichy counterparts, the two sides did share a hatred of communism. William Bullitt, a former ambassador to both the Soviet Union and France, noted in July 1940 that Vichy leaders remained haunted by the left-leaning Popular Front governments of the 1930s; they saw the French Army's defeat as "the penalty for its own sins," most notably the acceptance of prominent leftists into the cabinet during the Popular Front government of Léon Blum in 1936–1937. For many Americans, Vichy's doctrinaire anti-communism and anti-socialism was worthy of grudging admiration, even if it came with a pro-German and anti-British attitude.[58]

William Langer, the Harvard historian whom Cordell Hull hired to record his department's policy decisions in a favorable manner, cited other reasons that do not hold up as well today. He argued in notes he prepared for a book he published after the war that the British needed the United States to act as their indirect representation to Vichy. That back channel, Langer argued, helped to advance first British, then American, military interests. Langer also wrote that the Americans had already concluded that the ultimate German war aims lay in the east, therefore the British faced no real threat from Vichy forces. American recognition of Vichy thus did Britain more good than harm. No evidence from the period supports Langer's conclusions. They represent postwar attempts to provide further justification for an American policy that turned out to be deeply unpopular and strategically unwise.[59] The British disagreed quite forcefully with America's decision to recognize Vichy. When necessary, they most often used Spanish diplomats as their backdoor channel.

AMERICAN INSIDERS LIKE ROBERT MURPHY who supported the recognition policy believed that Vichy officials were not anti-American except to the extent that they saw the United States as unwisely keeping the British in a war they could not win. In Vichy's eyes, the Americans thereby only prolonged the inevitable and unnecessarily delayed the day when they might reach a final peace deal with the Germans. To Vichy's great relief, however, the United States had not supported de Gaulle. Although he had British backing, de Gaulle had no legitimate claim to the French government, and French émigré leaders in Washington like former permanent undersecretary of foreign affairs Alexis Leger despised him. Men like Leger, also known as the poet Saint-John Perse, and Chambrun helped to convince American officials to keep themselves at arm's length from de Gaulle.[60]

American leaders thought that they had levers with which to force Vichy into a more pro-American policy. Unoccupied France had to deal with almost six million refugees from the occupied zone and also faced the likelihood of successive bad harvests at the same time that the Germans took as much food as possible out of France. The British blockade further cut into the French food supply, risking a massive famine. Only the United States had the power and the will to help the French by sending food and pressuring the British to relax their blockade. Murphy noted with sadness the probable "starvation of our friends" in France over the winter 1940–1941, but other officials, like Henry Stimson, saw a chance to use food as a lever to ensure that Vichy did not act in a manner contrary to American interests.[61] Roosevelt also saw economics as the key instrument of national power. He responded to a French plea for help in November 1940 by offering to buy France's two powerful battleships, the *Jean Bart* and *Richelieu*. Pétain refused.[62]

The situation had certainly become grim. One report estimated that as many as 22,000,000 people in France and its empire did not have enough to eat. Paris had no coal, "vegetables are non-existent, and butter is very scarce." Darlan blamed the British, arguing that their blockade forced him to "loyally collaborate" with Germany. If the British did not modify its "imbecile" policies, he threatened, he would ask the German armistice commission to give him the power to arm his ships for the purpose of breaking the blockade.[63]

The British and de Gaulle both supported a policy of economic pressure "at its maximum" on Vichy and all pro-Vichy French colonies. They noted that Germany planned to seize 58 percent of French crops grown in the occupied zone, including 80 percent of the wheat. The British undersecretary of state for dominion affairs warned the Americans that as much as 80 percent of their trade with Vichy would likely end up in Germany or Italy. He especially worried about fats and nuts, which the Germans could convert into the raw materials necessary to manufacture explosives. He wanted the Americans to help the British intercept smugglers and French merchant vessels in the Caribbean as part of a get-tough economic policy with Vichy. The Colonial Office in London even blocked a plan to allow limited shipments of American tea and sugar to pass through the blockade to French Morocco.[64]

If the British were right, then American economic assistance to Vichy would indeed directly aid the Axis war effort. One American report agreed, concluding that 80 percent of the trade between North Africa and the port of Marseille had ended up in German hands.[65] Historian J. R. M. Butler, then serving as a senior British strategist on French issues, later wrote that America's Vichy policy represented the leak in the blockade "which caused the most trouble." The Admiralty cited it as the reason why the blockade "had almost completely broken down," in part because of the difficulty of patrolling the expansive French Empire but mostly because of the diplomatic tensions with the United States that came with enforcement.[66] British general Fabian Ware proposed that the Americans negotiate a deal that would require the Germans to give the French in the occupied zone goods from their captured stocks equivalent in value to those the Americans sent to the unoccupied zone. Such a policy would prevent the Germans from using American goods to add to their own stockpiles. The US government never bothered to respond.[67]

In October, a prominent media critic of the American policy of recognition, the *New Republic,* suggested an approach similar to the British one. It noted that although Americans wanted to help feed starving Frenchmen, they could not ignore the fact that Germany, "instead of organizing the distribution [of food] along the lines of need, has drained the resources of conquered countries for the sole profit of its armies and its peoples." Americans should therefore only provide aid to France if Germany agreed not to requisition any part of that aid for its own use, the British allowed aid to go through the blockade, and the French used their own merchant ships to transport it. Otherwise, the United States could not take the risk that the charity it offered to provide would in fact end up fueling the German war effort.[68] Former president Herbert Hoover, widely admired for his efforts to feed starving Europeans during the last war, organized a committee to provide food relief to Norway, the Netherlands, Belgium, and Poland, but he notably excluded France from his efforts because of what he called the "unusual political situation" there.[69] From Paris, American embassy staffer Mary-Louise Dilkes saw the suffering of the French people with her own eyes but nevertheless argued for a full blockade because the Germans, "instead of giving [imported food] to starving French children either send it to Germany or keep it themselves in France."[70]

In the end, President Roosevelt decided on a compromise policy for aiding France. He agreed to send perishable food and medicine intended for children as well as oil for heating and the transportation of food to the major North African cities. He suspended the dispatch of all other goods to France and the French Empire including clothing. All of the aid, moreover, would go through the Red Cross. Handling aid in this manner theoretically limited the risk of supplies materially aiding the Germans and also limited the level of friction with the British. Roosevelt made it clear that if this policy worked as desired, the United States would add more items to the list of goods shipped to France.[71]

American policy had a humanitarian justification, but mostly it served two immediate strategic aims. First, American officials made it clear that the aid would stop if Vichy gave the Germans access to military facilities in Dakar or North Africa. Second, the aid would help Weygand retain a nominal independence from Darlan's controlling hand in Vichy in hopes that he might one day turn his forces to the Allied cause. As with American relations with Vichy more generally, the oil policy came with risks and diplomatic friction. The British saw American oil as a vital military resource that should under no circumstances end up in Vichy (and thus possibly German) hands. The Americans nevertheless forced the British to allow thousands of tons of oil to go to North Africa, privately admitting that they intended it not for civilian relief as publicly stated but in order for Weygand to keep building his military power. The British reluctantly complied but were left baffled by an American policy that materially aided their common enemy.[72]

THE CONTROVERSY OVER AID SYMBOLIZED America's problems with the new France. How could America exert a positive influence without simultaneously helping the Nazis and their allies? Not all Americans thought the Roosevelt administration had the right answer. The *New Republic* and the *Christian Science Monitor* published editorials that argued against recognizing what the latter called France's new fascist government.[73] America's controversial Vichy policy also met with opposition at the highest levels of government. William Donovan, Secretary of the Interior Harold Ickes, Dwight Eisenhower, and George Marshall all favored treating Vichy more like a "Quisling" collaborationist government like those in conquered nations such as Norway.[74] Ickes acknowledged the grim possibility that "literally millions will die of starvation" over the winter in France, but he still argued that "we ought not to send a pound of flour to any country that is controlled by Germany," a direct recognition of the closeness between the Nazis and Vichy and an implicit criticism of the president's policy.[75] Prominent people outside the government, such as Republican presidential candidate Wendell Willkie and influential journalist Walter Lippmann, argued against aid as well because they saw Vichy as illegitimate and an effective ally of Nazi Germany.

Ickes and other American opponents of Vichy worried that any proGerman action by Vichy's leaders, such as the use of the French fleet or colonies to support Axis operations worldwide, could drag the United States into the war at a time not of its own choosing. The Army War Plans Division noted that "date of the loss of the British or French fleets automatically sets the date of our mobilization." In other words, if the Vichy fleet did join the German or Italian fleet, the United States would need to go on a full war footing immediately. Americans similarly warned Vichy officials that a German occupation of Dakar would "bring America actively into the war in Africa."[76] Indications also continued to mount that Vichy officials might conduct operations against the British in Africa or Gibraltar, perhaps in coordination with Spain.[77]

Although the US government recognized Vichy, American leaders wanted their French counterparts to feel pressure. Cordell Hull's memoranda on his meetings with French officials in Washington contain plenty of terse language. He wrote in these memoranda that he interrupted the French ambassador (whom he intensely disliked) and used direct language at every point of disagreement. Hull repeatedly told French officials that American friendship depended "primarily on the disposition of their naval and merchant fleet." He also warned them not to expect much American aid as long as the French fleet could still "possibly fall into the hands of Germany."[78] In September, Hull tested French loyalties by offering to give the French $40 million to $50 million of food aid in exchange for the largely symbolic act of France giving the United States the antiquated airplanes rusting away on the beaches at Martinique. The offer represented a figure many times more than the actual value of the planes. When the French ambassador meekly replied that the Germans might object, Hull responded angrily that the French were willing to see that "this vast amount of money should be thrown into the ash hopper or sink hole" because of their fears of a possible response from a Germany all too willing to enslave France. He warned the French ambassador that collaboration as a policy had no chance of succeeding and that "there is no such thing as appeasing Mr. Hitler any more than a squirrel can appease a boa constrictor." The sooner the French saw matters as the Americans did, the better for both countries.[79] Still, Hull remained unwilling to reverse course on American policy and continued to approve aid shipments to Vichy.

Hull warned the French ambassador in Washington that American leaders loathed Laval and that France "will not get two inches in carrying on its relations" with the United States as long as he remained in power. Hull described Laval as "an extreme partisan of Hitler and Mussolini and very bitter toward Great Britain." When these comments made their way to Laval, he replied to Hull through the American chargé d'affaires that "Hitler offered me collaboration in a spirit rare in a conqueror" while the British bombed French ships and killed French sailors. He blamed the decline in Franco-American relations on "the propaganda of those miserable people who fled France—most of them Jews—who are now conducting such abominable propaganda in the United States."[80]

Hull recognized the tight links between Vichy and Berlin, but he still advocated recognition and building closer ties. At first glance, this circle would seem tough to square. The answer rested with Hull and Leahy's faith in Pétain, a man well-liked by Americans of that era. Anyone old enough to remember the First World War would have recognized his icy blue-eyed stare and admired him as the man who had stepped in to save the French army in 1917 and lead it to victory in 1918. In the interwar years, he became a great hero not just to the French but to many Americans as well; there were hundreds of streets named for him in the 1920s (Petain Streets still exist in at least six states) and the famous Antoine's restaurant in New

Admiral William Leahy, the American ambassador to Vichy (right) meeting with Pétain. Despite ever-mounting evidence to the contrary, Leahy retained faith in Pétain as an eventual American ally.

Orleans once had a dish named after him.[81] Most Americans in 1940 saw him as coming into an impossible situation and trying to do the best he could for what remained of France. H. Freeman Matthews told Hull that despite his failings, Pétain was "the one man who today for all his age can alone speak for France and who alone possesses the prestige and affection of his people. Without him, this Government would not last ten minutes."[82] Astonishingly, Roosevelt even told Leahy that he believed that Vichy behaved as it did because "Marshal Pétain was not cognizant of all the acts of his Vice Premier and Minister for Foreign Affairs, Monsieur Laval."[83]

Pétain therefore seemed the most logical potential American ally in Vichy, even if no one knew just how much actual power he wielded or exactly what kind of future he had planned for the new France. Nevertheless, Leahy's diaries and papers from his time as ambassador to Vichy show his struggles to determine who was really in control in Vichy ("I am a prisoner," Pétain told him twice in the span of one single meeting), how the United States could most effectively influence Vichy's behavior, and how much power the Germans could exert over Vichy's navy. Pétain expressed anti-German and pro-American views, but Leahy could not determine if he actually called the shots. Laval, whom Bullitt called "an outright crook," had Germany's backing, and he certainly had sufficient ambition to seek to force Pétain into a purely symbolic role. Under his guidance, the Americans worried, Vichy would become "Germany's willing slave."[84]

AMID ALL THIS CONFUSION, a sudden event occurred that seemingly proved to Americans that Pétain did, in fact, control affairs in Vichy and that therefore Hull's policy had been correct. In December 1940, Pétain learned about a scheme, masterminded by Laval, to secretly hand over to Germany gold that the Belgians had given to France for safe keeping. Laval had also tried to build support behind Pétain's back for a military operation against Cameroon, a French colony whose leaders had declared their loyalty to de Gaulle. That operation risked civil war and also war with the British, who provided material support to Free French general Philippe Leclerc's operations there. Pétain and Darlan might have hated the British, but they saw no reason to risk a war over faraway Cameroon that would drain Vichy's limited military resources and force Frenchmen to choose sides. Laval, however, wanted to punish Leclerc for his ability to rally French Equatorial Africa to the Free French side. The charismatic and courageous Leclerc, in many ways Laval's polar opposite, gave a withering speech in Cameroon in which he called Vichy "the hook on which men hang their cowardice."[85] Huge crowds greeted Leclerc wherever he went and men joined his Free French units in large numbers.[86]

The success of the Free French revealed the falsehood behind a Vichy article of faith, namely that Frenchmen of the empire wanted to remain loyal to Vichy and saw de Gaulle as nothing more than a puppet to the same British imperial interests that had attacked Mers-el-Kébir. Laval thus wanted to bring Leclerc to justice in order to reestablish Vichy's authority in the empire, but his behind-the-scenes machinations and the attendant risk of war with Britain proved a step too far. Pétain, supported by Darlan, called a cabinet meeting and asked for all the ministers to hand in letters of resignation, a common tactic when shuffling a cabinet. A confident Laval submitted his letter never guessing that his own job was the one in danger. Pétain then accepted only two of the letters, Laval's and that of the education minister, Laval's closest ally in the cabinet. Pétain then ordered Laval placed under house arrest.[87]

What happened next proved that even Vichy's nominal control over its own internal affairs was little more than a fiction. Otto Abetz, the German ambassador to France, took the removal of Laval as a personal insult. He had just invited Pétain to Paris for a ceremony to mark the return of the remains of Napoleon's son, the Duke of Reichstadt, to Les Invalides, where Napoleon himself is entombed.[88] Abetz saw the Laval dismissal as a deliberate slap in the face following this German gesture of friendship and reconciliation. He reacted to Laval's arrest with fury, sending an armed German detachment across the demarcation line to Laval's house to bring him to Paris. Abetz himself stormed into the main government building in Vichy waving a pistol, demanding Laval's release, and sending an unmistakable message about who really called the shots, even in the unoccupied zone.

Despite the chaos, Pétain seemed to have emerged the winner, although, with the full support of the Nazis, Laval could pose an even greater danger to the United States from Paris if he convinced the Germans to seize the French Empire or the fleet from his rivals Pétain and Darlan. During the brief period of his house arrest, he met with Robert Murphy for more than an hour. Laval showed Murphy a giant oil painting of Joan of Arc and praised her triumph over the British, speaking of the events of long ago "as though they happened yesterday." The British in the 1930s, Laval believed, had tricked the French once again into fighting a war more in Britain's interest than France's. This time, however, Laval promised that "the British, not the French, would pay for the war."[89] Notwithstanding France's massive defeat, Laval still saw opportunity for France at British expense.

Murphy described Vichy as "absurdly isolated" and "inbred." He compared the mood there to something more akin to Alice in Wonderland than the norms of international politics. Laval questioned Murphy about Donovan's trip, prompting Murphy to deny knowledge of it and say only that Donovan was "a well-known private American citizen whose judgment is respected in the United States." Laval once again blamed "the efforts of a number of discredited French émigrés now in the United States, plus the antagonism of certain American and foreign Jews" for obscuring what he called the "verities of the French situation." He expressed his confidence in an eventual German victory over the British and, "with a bland smile," reaffirmed to Murphy that he still had faith in his own ability to wring major concessions out of the Germans at the end of the war. Confident even in captivity, he gave no indication whatsoever that his dismissal meant the end of his political career.[90]

H. Freeman Matthews, who watched Abetz's arrival in Vichy backed by a "carload of guards with submachine guns," nevertheless thought the mood at the end of 1940 more positive than at any time since France's fall. Tumultuous though it was, the widely despised Laval's dismissal had created "something akin to self-respect" throughout France, suggesting that "the country and its Government have not sunk to the degradation of Nazi enslavement."[91] Pétain and Darlan seemed "delighted" at the appointment of Leahy, and Hull authorized Murphy to tell French leaders that "there has been no change whatsoever in the established traditional friendship of the United States for France, whose continued independence and position of leadership in the civilized world is a matter of deep concern not only to this Government but the people of this country."[92]

Pétain's willingness to dismiss Laval certainly marked a courageous and positive sign for that friendship, but Leahy did not think that the beloved Vichy leader matched up to the propaganda image of him in the American media. "Marshal Pétain is remarkably capable for a man of his age," Leahy reported, "but the burden of work which he has assumed is beyond his physical capacity." Leahy noted that Pétain frequently fell asleep at meetings and often gave "every appearance of a tired, discouraged old man," especially in the afternoons.[93] Could he become a reliable American ally or at least a partner, or would the more energetic Laval and Darlan find ways to outmaneuver him? On this question might hinge the war and the future security of the United States.

4

WE MUSTN'T UNDERESTIMATE
AMERICAN BLUNDERING

Britain's Imperial Insecurity

DURING A VISIT TO Washington in the fall of 1940 to discuss strategy, Robert Murphy, the senior American diplomat in North Africa, reacquainted himself with an American naval attaché he had known in France before the war. Roscoe Hillenkoetter was a midwesterner like Murphy, tall and thin, with an angular face and a distinct military bearing. He had a reputation for being discreet, hardworking, supremely competent, and always in the right place at the right time. For these reasons, rumor had it that he was a rising star in the rapidly developing world of American espionage. After Paris fell, he had gone to Morocco and Algeria when most other Americans headed for the safety of neutral Spain, Portugal, or Switzerland. What he saw in North Africa sparked in him a hope for the future rare indeed among American officials at that desperate time. North Africa, he told Murphy, was not like Vichy. In Morocco and Algeria, Frenchmen, too, had sworn allegiance to Pétain, but many also burned for a chance to fight against the Germans and restore France's lost honor. Murphy noted that Hillenkoetter's reports seemed not to have made any particular impression on the professional diplomats in the State Department, but they made quite an impression in the White House. Before Murphy left the United States in November, President Franklin Roosevelt, influenced by Hillenkoetter's ideas, told him that "North Africa was the most likely place where French troops might be brought back into the war against Nazi Germany."[1]

Being technically neutral but of interest to everyone, North Africa became a hot bed of espionage activity, seemingly confirming in Murphy's mind what Hillenkoetter had told him. Reports reached American officials that German agents had begun to flood into the region disguised as commercial attachés.[2] If true, those agents could only have one possible mission: to prepare for a German takeover of French assets in the region. Murphy thus decided to invite Hillenkoetter, destined to become the head of the Central Intelligence Agency just seven years later, to come with him to Algiers. Hillenkoetter had the ideal background to start a spy war against the Germans in Africa. He knew Ambassador William Leahy from their navy days, and he spoke German, French, and Spanish. He had also worked with Jean-François Darlan before the war and knew Henri-Philippe Pétain from their overlapping time in Spain.[3]

Washington needed the skills Hillenkoetter could provide because, as Murphy later wrote, "North Africa was almost another planet to military intelligence."[4] The United States government had no officials in the region qualified in Arabic and had not yet even decided which branch of the government should take the lead for covert operations there. The government hadn't run an intelligence operation as big or as daring as the one Murphy had in mind since the last world war. The nascent Office of Strategic Services (OSS) did not yet have the resources to take charge, and the State Department worried about the fallout if it took the lead and its diplomats were unmasked as spies. The Germans might imprison or even execute them, pressuring the United States to respond with military action.

Murphy and Hillenkoetter thought the risk worthwhile because they retained faith that Maxime Weygand, the French general exiled to Algeria with whom William Donovan had tried to meet, might still become an American ally. The president told Murphy that he found it impossible to believe that "this honorable old soldier would tolerate indefinitely French subservience to Germany." Working far from the intrigues of Vichy, Weygand had developed a reputation as the new regime's most consistently anti-German voice, although he remained as difficult to read as ever. A friendship or alliance with him might make all the difference to American national security. Roosevelt told Murphy to use any card he could to cultivate a relationship with Weygand. He turned to Murphy "with a wink" and said, "You might even go to church with Weygand!" Murphy wryly noted in his memoirs that the incident proved that "the President seemed to have exaggerated ideas of the bond existing between Catholics because of their religion."[5]

WEYGAND MAY HAVE HARBORED anti-German sentiments, but he continued to show his loyalty to Pétain. He gave a speech over Vichy radio in early 1941 heard by 500,000 people, including all of the soldiers under his command. Weygand told his listeners "not to leave the path of order and discipline" and to remain faithful to Marshal Pétain and his National Revolution. Although he did not mention Charles de Gaulle by name, his listeners understood the message: France's future lay with Pétain and the legitimate government seated at Vichy, not with the rebellious de Gaulle causing trouble from London.[6] What the speech meant for American relations with Weygand remained unclear, but it seemed increasingly likely that the United States would have to make a choice not just between Pétain and de Gaulle but also between Weygand and de Gaulle.

Murphy, who had taken an instant dislike to de Gaulle in any case, determined to press on with plans to try to turn Weygand, even if doing so might place even greater strain on Anglo-American relations. Murphy hoped that he had found something far more powerful than a shared Catholic faith with which to try to influence Weygand's behavior. He had the ability to solve one of North Africa's most important problems: a severe lack of food. The poor French harvest of 1940 led Vichy to pressure North Africa to send as much food as possible to the mainland. As a result, food stocks in major cities like Casablanca, Oran, and Algiers hovered at crisis levels and local officials openly worried about a famine or food-related riots, especially among the Arab and Berber populations. Murphy recognized that extending the American food aid policy for French North Africa would not only serve a humanitarian purpose, but it might also ensure that Weygand maintained his pro-American orientation. A lack of food, on the other hand, could produce a rebellion among what Murphy described as "the restive native populations" in Africa. If food aid produced results, it could eventually lead to programs to supply Weygand with fuel, weapons, and ammunition, all of which his rudimentary military forces sorely lacked. They would need those supplies if they hoped to play a future military role against the Germans.[7]

The British, still concerned that American supplies would end up in German hands, objected to any plan to send precious material to France. The United States, moreover, had legally committed to respect the British blockade of North Africa. Nevertheless, the benefits of a food aid package seemed so manifest that Murphy and Weygand agreed to a deal in mid-January 1941. The United States would increase aid on the conditions that the French would amass no stockpiles that Vichy might send to Germany and that the money to pay for food and transportation would come from the sale of French assets the United States had frozen in 1940. To ensure French adherence to these conditions American officials demanded the right to inspect the distribution of the aid throughout North Africa.[8] As long as these conditions remained in place, the British grudgingly agreed not to interdict the shipments through the Strait of Gibraltar in the interests of keeping the United States happy. Cordell Hull and Leahy both agreed to the deal, and wanted it to go much further "so that," in Hull's recollections, "the Germans might not use the widespread misery of the people as a lever to swing the Pétain Government to open collaboration."[9]

HULL UNDERPLAYED THE MASSIVE EVIDENCE of open collaboration already in place. The British did not and remained the key sticking point to the execution of the deal. The Americans won them over because of reports that the French fleet might force the Strait of Gibraltar open if the British did not agree to allow food to come into North Africa. The British still opposed the idea of supplies going to France, but they could not afford a battle for control of the most important choke point in the Mediterranean. They insisted that the United States take basic items such as clothing and fish oils off the updated aid lists, but they approved the shipment of perishable food and milk that Vichy would have trouble stockpiling or transporting to metropolitan France before they spoiled. By mid-March, all the necessary parties, including the reluctant British, had agreed to Murphy's plan to use aid to draw Vichy closer to the United States.

In Murphy's eyes, this complex scheme of sending American food aid to North Africa served a dual purpose: providing needed relief to people there and giving the United States a way to begin to court the regime away from collaboration with Germany. Exactly what Weygand and the French forces in North Africa might do, especially given his recent pledge to remain loyal to Pétain, remained unclear to Americans, but from the perspective of Washington, the fears of 1940 had not abated. William Langer recalled the first months of 1941 as "on the whole, one of the blackest [periods] of the entire conflict." Similarly, Hull called that time frame "a low and dangerous depth" for American security.[10] The outcome of both the Battle of the Atlantic and the British Commonwealth's war in North Africa remained in doubt, the Axis presence in the Balkans had grown, and Japan continued to expand in East Asia. The Allies, moreover, had already seen too many surprises in the last few months for anyone to rest easy. Weygand might even turn his military power not against the Germans but against the Free French or even the British. "The situation remained extremely uncertain and appeared fraught with danger," Langer wrote, in large part to justify the controversial policy of continued engagement with Vichy.[11]

Given the fears of France entering the war on the Axis side, keeping warm relations with Weygand seemed to Hull, Langer, and other supporters worth the small price of recognition and food, even if no one yet knew exactly what Weygand planned to do. Providing food to North Africa would improve the image of the United States in the region, which might pay off at some later, still undetermined, point in time. As long as the funds to pay for the aid came from frozen French accounts in the United States, the scheme would not cost the United States anything but some manageable diplomatic friction with the British. If it kept the French fleet out of Axis hands and prevented the Germans from using French assets against the British, then such deals seemed to Washington officials like Hull to make obvious sense.

Roosevelt may have had faith in Weygand's honor eventually causing him to flip to the American side, but not all officials shared his views. Thomas Wasson, the American vice-consul in Casablanca, believed that Weygand wanted American supplies to prepare for operations against the British colonies in Africa, especially as anti-British sentiment continued to rise among the Vichy elite.[12] Winston Churchill also tried to warn Roosevelt away from a pro-Vichy policy of any kind, writing to the president that dealing with any Vichy officials equated to "dealing with Germany."[13]

Under those circumstances, providing anything, including food and milk, to any part of Vichy France could backfire, especially because the blockade formed such a central part of British strategy. Policy toward Vichy offered few easy answers.

Although complex and difficult, North Africa remained a key concern for both the United States and Great Britain. Port cities in Morocco gave anyone who controlled them an opportunity to bypass Gibraltar and gain direct access to the Atlantic Ocean. In April, Hull told the recently arrived British ambassador to the United States, Lord Halifax, that if Vichy gave Germany control over Morocco, the United States would take "definitive action," perhaps in concert with the British, to seize control of the ports of Casablanca and Dakar. This statement came as close as Hull ever did to drawing what strategists might today call red lines for American entry into the European war.[14]

A week after Hull's meeting with Halifax, Secretary of the Navy Frank Knox gave a speech in which he said that German control of French Africa would "cut us off from all commerce with South America and make of the Monroe Doctrine a scrap of paper." Knox had chosen his words carefully; Germany's chancellor had dismissed his country's invasion of Belgium in 1914 by claiming that the British guarantee of Belgian neutrality merely amounted to a "scrap of paper." The chancellor had guessed wrong. Invading Belgium led to British intervention in the war. Clearly, in 1941, Knox wanted to warn the Germans in the strongest possible terms against treating neutral North Africa and Senegal as their predecessors had treated neutral Belgium.[15]

IN SUCH A COMPLEX ENVIRONMENT, Murphy and Hillenkoetter went to work. They cleverly insisted that the twelve American officials in charge of monitoring food distribution receive the titles of vice-consul with unfettered right of movement throughout North Africa. American intelligence officers began calling them the Twelve Apostles. None of them had any experience in espionage; one had recently left his job as Coca-Cola's Marseille branch manager and another had been selling jewelry for Cartier. Status as a vice-consul could help to protect these amateurs because it meant that by international law, all of their communications became classified as diplomatic traffic. The French, desperate for the food, could hardly refuse, even though they must have known that the Americans would want to monitor more than food shipments.[16]

As Murphy noted, these agreements "became the basis of one of the most effective intelligence operations of the war."[17] William Eddy, a Lebanon-born Marine Corps officer and spy who spoke fluent French and Arabic, came to Tangier, controlled by neutral Spain, to run a clandestine radio network and establish communications between agents in North Africa and Allied headquarters in Gibraltar.[18] American diplomats and spies could then discover which Vichy officials in Algeria they should approach in order to try to persuade or bribe them to cooperate with the Allies. Officers in the British Special Operations Executive and the OSS added their support. A naval intelligence officer named Ian Fleming played a role in the planning of the British end of the scheme. Fleming codenamed it GOLD-ENEYE in recognition of the surveillance and intelligence gathering aspects of the operation.[19]

The vice-consuls sent back mountains of critical intelligence on harbors, roads, rail lines, fortifications, and the political leanings of French officers based in North Africa. Murphy, Hillenkoetter, and Eddy expanded their network to a series of five radio transmitters, hidden in a winepress in Tangier, the attic of a nervous vice-consul's house in Casablanca, and the offices of vice-consuls in Algiers, Tunis, and Oran.[20] The network's information proved invaluable in 1941 and in the planning for the invasion of North Africa the following year. The primitive State Department codes, however, became a problem. Despite Murphy's naive confidence that they were both unbreakable and protected by international law and diplomatic courtesy, German intelligence had, in fact, cracked and read them. The cables showed American faith in Weygand as a potential anti-German collaborator. They also revealed how central he had become to American designs, although they did not suggest any interest on his part to cooperate with the United States. Nevertheless, both the Germans and senior leaders in Vichy grew suspicious of Weygand and began to look for ways to get him out of the picture.

NOTWITHSTANDING MURPHY'S FOOD AID SCHEME, Vichy grew dangerously closer to Germany after a period of relative inactivity at the end

of 1940. The immediate spark for the change in this global war of inter-
locking conflicts was an anti-British movement at the other end of the Arab
world in Iraq. The anti-British former prime minister Rashid Ali al-Gailani
sought to take advantage of the war to reduce British influence in his
country. His Golden Square movement led a coup in April 1941 that put
at risk both British oil supplies and the security of British India. Once back
in power, al-Gailani abrogated a treaty granting the British military basing
rights in Iraq and the right to move troops through Iraqi territory. An Iraqi
military force tried to isolate the international section of Baghdad while
another surrounded the main British airfield west of the city.[21] Freya Stark,
a British propagandist fluent in Arabic and a person not easily given to
panic, described the atmosphere in her diary as "frothing milk about to
boil." She had just come from the tension of wartime Cairo but found the
situation in Baghdad even more worrisome, although, with her characteristic sangfroid, she refused to cancel the teas she had planned with prominent pro-British Iraqis.[22]

The powerful grand mufti of Jerusalem, Amin al-Husseini, turned up
the heat on the frothing milk even more by issuing a fatwa against the
British and in support of the Iraqi coup. He belonged to the al-Muthanna
Club, a group of pro-fascist Arab leaders active since the mid-1930s. Stark
met him in Baghdad and described him as having the look of a "just-fallen
Lucifer about him" and "venom in his glance." Al-Husseini had links to
key leaders in Nazi Germany; later in the year he went to Berlin to build
connections between Nazism and his Palestinian nationalist movement.[23]
Al-Husseini commanded an enormous following not just in Palestine and
Iraq but across the Muslim world. His influence plus his links to Berlin
threatened to export the problems in Baghdad across the entire region.[24]

The coup in Iraq could undermine Britain's entire global strategy,
especially if al-Husseini helped to inspire similar coups in Egypt, Transjordan, and maybe even in India.[25] A furious Churchill ordered a swift
military response, initially in the form of a force of several thousand
soldiers who would march triumphantly from Palestine through Transjordan to Baghdad, reasserting British authority over the Middle East as it
went. The British also dispatched Royal Air Force fighter squadrons and a
division of Indian troops to Basra. In spring 1941, Iraq sat at the center of
global attention. "For two desperate months," recalled American journalist
Artour Derounian, the revolt "threatened to turn the entire Middle East
into a Nazi camp."[26]

For a time, the Germans thought they sensed an opportunity to tie the British down in Iraq just when German troops had encircled British Commonwealth forces near the Libyan port of Tobruk. Germany considered offering direct support to al-Gailani and his government in order to pressure the British on both sides of the Arab Middle East. Adolf Hitler also made a public pronouncement that "the Arab liberation movement is our natural ally."[27] Officials in London grew despondent, aware that the simultaneous losses of Tobruk and Iraq could mean the end of the British Empire in the region. British politician Harold Nicolson confided to his diary that "Libya is the main preoccupation and Libya is bad indeed. We cannot trust Egypt and Iraq is already gone."[28]

Amid all this confusion and danger, British officials in the region reported that an "exceedingly dangerous" femme fatale they knew as Mlle. Lachnor had mysteriously and suddenly arrived in the Middle East from Vichy. Austrian-born but living in France since the mid-1930s, British intelligence knew her as a master spy, mistress to several high-ranking officials in both the Vichy administration and the Gestapo, and a key liaison between senior German politicians and the leadership in Vichy. Her arrival in the region added an air of mystery and intrigue to a situation that the British already feared could undermine their entire empire.[29]

Vichy had more than a mysterious female spy in its corner. France also held the key to the military aspects of the Iraqi problem. If the Germans wanted their Middle East strategy to succeed, they needed the help of Vichy, whose bases in Syria and Tunisia could provide the necessary logistical support. Without that support, the Germans had no way to move men, weapons, and supplies to Iraq. Hitler therefore reached out to Darlan through German ambassador to France Otto Abetz, inviting the French military leader to meet at his mountain retreat at Berchtesgaden. It represented one of the few moments that Nazi Germany deigned to treat Vichy France as anything like an equal.

A CRAVEN DARLAN, FLATTERED AT THE INVITATION and sensing an opportunity to get for France what his rival Pierre Laval had not, offered to grant access to French naval bases in exchange for Germany loosening the tight controls on the demarcation line between Vichy and occupied France. He also wanted the occupation costs the Germans imposed on the

French reduced, and he asked for maximum publicity for any deal he negotiated in order to demonstrate the closeness of Franco-German relations.
Darlan wanted to show the world that Vichy's future lay with Germany. He
also wanted his fellow Frenchmen to see that he, and he alone, could negotiate
favorable terms for France.

Word of the Darlan-Hitler meeting terrified the Allies and ought to have
provided definitive proof of the failure of American policy. In a world of
constantly shifting crises, Ambassador Leahy worried that the attempted
coup in Iraq might trigger much deeper Vichy-German military agreements
worldwide that could prove detrimental to British and American interests.
He told President Roosevelt of his continued faith in Pétain as a person,
but he also warned that the marshal "has no power with which to oppose
German demands" such as the use of French airfields in Syria. The dark
picture Leahy painted of Vichy boded poorly for the American policy of
recognition and aid. "It is my conviction that any demands whatever that
may be made by the Germans will either be granted by the Vichy Government or permitted without active opposition. I find no indication whatever of a possibility that the Marshal might move his government to North
Africa or that he might direct General Weygand to join cause with the democracies." Pétain had given Leahy his word "that the fleet and the naval
bases will not be turned over to Germany, but that does not give assurance
that Germany will not take the ships and will not occupy the bases."[30]

Darlan's decision to grant base access in Syria and Tunisia showed
Vichy's true colors. The further agreements that Leahy feared, moreover, soon
followed. Given their relative powerlessness, the French tried to cut rea-
sonably favorable deals where they could, using the bases as their bargaining
chips. In May 1941, Darlan and Abetz initialed an agreement known as
the Paris Protocols. Germany agreed to reduce the occupation costs by
25 percent, release several thousand First World War veterans from German
prisoner of war camps, ease the restrictions on movement between the two
zones, and acknowledge the eventual right of the Vichy government to assume unfettered authority over domestic matters inside all of France. In
return, Darlan agreed to give the Germans the right to use French airfields,
trucks, and stockpiled military supplies in Syria to support al-Gailani, the
use of the Tunisian port city of Bizerte to support Erwin Rommel's war
against the British, and, at some undetermined point in the future, access
to the French naval base at Dakar, Senegal.[31] American intelligence also

knew that Germany had secretly agreed to allow the French to rearm six destroyers to help in a future attempt to break the British blockade or as part of operations to oust Gaullist forces from sub-Saharan Africa. In his meeting with Darlan at Berchtesgaden, Hitler held out the lure of France gaining Wallonia and the French-speaking parts of Switzerland as well as parts of the British Empire in exchange for further help. Darlan responded by agreeing in principle to join in the war against Britain and its African empire, telling Hitler that the British "must be disposed of."[32]

Shortly after his return from those negotiations, Darlan gave a bombshell interview to a Vichy journalist. In it, he said that "we now realize how completely enslaved we were by England for seventy years. The English made us hate the Germans as our implacable enemies. Now that we are free from these shackles, we want to see whether it will not be to our advantage to work with the Germans." Around the same time, Laval told *Paris-Soir* that he blamed "the cruel and bloody force" of the democratic powers for postponing "the hour when France can march toward the future." He said that he supported ceding to Germany Alsace and Lorraine in order to end what he described as an unnecessary historic dispute between the two countries but that he would resist with force any attempt by the United States to seize any part of the French Empire.[33]

Shaken by these comments and unsure of what else the two sides might have agreed to, American concern rose to near-panic levels. The Paris Protocols seemed to prove that Vichy had in fact opted for the "open collaboration" with the Nazis that Murphy and Leahy had feared.[34] William Langer called May 1941 "a period of prolonged crisis" over French policy because of these fears.[35] A formal Vichy alliance with Germany or a Vichy declaration of war against the British could force a premature American declaration of war that might prove unpopular at home. Pétain certainly provided little comfort. He gave a public radio address supporting the Paris Protocols and saying that "if, through our close discipline and our public spirit, we can conduct the negotiations [now] in progress, France will surmount her defeat and preserve in the world her rank as a European and colonial power." When Leahy challenged him to explain his comments, Pétain replied that he spoke only in general terms and claimed that he had no specific knowledge of the details of the agreements between Darlan and the Germans. Thanks to Murphy's spy network, Leahy seemed to know more about the details of the Paris Protocols than Pétain did. With so much

The supremely ambitious Vichy prime minister Pierre Laval, described by one American magazine as "a squatty, villainous faced old man." The British and the Americans both hated him for his avowedly pro-German policies.

of American policy riding on the personality of Pétain, that simple fact did not augur well for the future.[36]

BACK IN WASHINGTON, Roosevelt and Secretary of State Cordell Hull met twice to discuss the Paris Protocols and the appropriate American response to them. Roosevelt and Undersecretary of State Sumner Welles wanted to take a hard line. The president proposed sending a message to Congress asking for permission to claim Liberia and much of North Africa as an American security zone, although it is not clear what they thought such a status might mean or how they thought they might enforce it. Roosevelt also wanted to send a message warning Vichy about the risks of any further "acquiescence in the use of French territory by the Germans." He gave a radio address in which he said that "the people of the United States can hardly believe that the present Government of France could be brought to lend itself to a plan of voluntary alliance, implied or otherwise, which would apparently deliver up France and its colonial empire, including French African colonies and their Atlantic coasts with the menace which that involves to the peace and safety of the American people."[37]

Hull, however, counseled caution, warning the president against any "unwise" or drastic change in policy that might give Germany an incentive to seize North Africa outright. He argued instead for keeping the policy of engagement in place as a way to buy time for America to rearm. "As you and I have agreed in our discussions of our handling of the Vichy Government, our only way of keeping our relations with the Marshal stabilized as much as possible is to continue to keep in touch with him and to support him insofar as we can without interfering with British war measures."[38] He did, however, agree with Roosevelt's decision to seize French merchant ships detained in American ports in 1940 in order to prevent them sailing to Africa and potentially being turned over to the Germans or Italians. Any French assets that fell into German hands, Hull acknowledged to the president, represented "an attempt to slit the throat of the United States indirectly."[39]

Roosevelt deferred to his secretary of state, but the tensions in America's Vichy policy had begun to cause increasing problems both at the highest levels of the government and in American society more generally. Most importantly, the policy had made America less secure, not more. Even Hull admitted that the Vichy leadership had "gone straight into the arms of the German government," and "having done so, their first thoughts were to deliver France body and soul to Hitler." Despite America's blending of carrots and sticks, Darlan continued to negotiate directly with Abetz for even more concessions. Roosevelt, Hull, and other officials gave increasingly tough speeches. Roosevelt informed the American people at the end of May about Nazi interest in controlling Dakar, which would give German submarines a strategic place from which to interrupt the main trans-Atlantic shipping lanes. "The war is approaching the brink of the Western Hemisphere itself," he warned. "It is coming very close to home." Roosevelt also ordered a study to determine the feasibility of sending a 25,000-man expeditionary force to the Azores, although that idea never got past the initial planning stages.[40]

Still, Hull ordered no major changes to America's shaky Vichy policy, even though he acknowledged that the Paris Protocols "fulfilled our worst expectation." Hull also knew that American public opinion had begun to shift toward a pro–de Gaulle line, but he resisted all suggestions that the

United States should recognize the Free France movement as the legitimate government of France. He argued that recognition of a "desperately temperamental" de Gaulle would mean a "complete break with Vichy" and "a rupture of the fruitful contact we were maintaining with Weygand in North Africa."[41] Roosevelt himself said that given the fast-moving situation, America's French policy had to proceed "hour to hour and day to day."[42] For the moment, that meant that the United States would stick with Pétain despite the demonstrable lack of success in the policy. As Hull bragged, "The president and I never wavered in adopting and sticking to a consistent policy." He wanted to continue to resist the "emotional wave" from the American people "in favor of breaking with the legal Government at Vichy."[43]

Hull had deluded himself if he believed that American actions had any "fruitful" influence on Vichy's behavior. Vichy archives show their dismissive and condescending views of the United States. Cables sent to the Vichy cabinet from the French embassy in Washington described a United States unwilling and unable to go to war because of two decades of isolation and parsimony on defense. In the view of Washington-based Vichy officials, the small elements in the country that did want war mostly included the Jews, who controlled "the entire economic and financial power" of the country and held Roosevelt as a "slave." They alone advocated a "fight to the death against fascism and National Socialism." Others in the hypercapitalist United States, the embassy advised, would only support war if they could profit from it. Donovan, Wendell Willkie, and others represented this financial elite, who "know very well that we have only arrived at the *hors d'oeuvres* of an interminable menu" of international spoils for America's taking. Vichy officials assumed that the Americans had their eyes on Dakar and unfettered control of the Atlantic Ocean, but they also assumed that the victorious Axis could buy off the greedy Americans by promising them parts of the British Empire instead.[44] Clearly, Vichy had misread the United States just as badly as the United States had misread Vichy.

BY MID-JULY, the British and Free French had reasserted their authority and calmed the situation in the Middle East. After the surrender of Vichy forces in Syria and Lebanon, the senior ranking general to declare loyalty to de Gaulle, General Georges Catroux, assumed command of Free French forces in the Levant. The two men had formed a close friendship in a German prisoner of war camp during the First World War, but they soon clashed bitterly over policy for the Middle East. The British argued that the Free French would have to renegotiate the 1936 treaty that formed the legal basis of French presence in Syria or risk open rebellion from an angry population. Catroux, to de Gaulle's fury, agreed. He soon went even further, announcing his support for Syrian independence after the war. De Gaulle sensed a British plot to increase their influence in an area he insisted should remain a French sphere of influence; his relationship with Catroux, whom he suspected of being too easily swayed by the British, never recovered. The entire episode left behind a bitter legacy of recrimination between rival French groups as well as between de Gaulle and the British, whom he angrily accused of undermining his authority in Syria.[45]

They also led to a rise in anti-Semitism in both the Middle East and Vichy, as Jews in both places faced charges of aiding the Allies.[46] The anti-Semitism of the Vichy regime, frequently expressed in both its policies and its propaganda, undoubtedly conditioned its views of the United States as a predatory capitalist country far more interested in profit than ideals or even basic security. One report described Charlie Chaplin, "a Jewish clown," as the "supreme ideal of the United States."[47] No evidence exists, at least for 1940 and 1941, that American awareness of this anti-Semitism had any effect on policy. American officials did not make any meaningful protest against the anti-Semitic actions of the Vichy regime, such as the October 1940 exclusion of Jews from the army, press, civil service, and even many private sector jobs; the removal of French citizenship from naturalized Jews; or the authorization to local authorities to inter Jews in special camps.[48] Nor does any evidence from private papers suggest that anti-Semitism inside the Vichy state disinclined American officials to want to continue the policy of engagement.[49]

Washington officials could not, however, claim that they did not know about Vichy's increasing persecution of Jews. Leahy reported to the State Department on the increasingly anti-Semitic behavior he witnessed, including Vichy's requirement that Jews register with their local police. The French government also ordered Jews to leave Vichy's *département* of Allier. In June 1941, Leahy advised Washington that "the [Vichy] Government will take increasing steps to make the lots of persons of the Jewish race more difficult."[50] Still, the American ambassador sounded no major alarms, merely noting that the persecution of Jews seemed roughly consistent with German persecution of ethnic Frenchmen and Frenchwomen in Alsace and Lorraine. From Washington, American officials only asked Leahy to ensure that the new discriminatory laws did not apply to any American Jews who might live in North Africa.[51] Even when Vichy gave equivocal answers to his inquiries to that effect, Leahy raised no formal objections. In his defense, Leahy could not then have known that the Germans would decide on industrial genocide just a few months later.[52]

Vichy officials had already concluded that even if the Americans did object to their policies, they could do little about it. A cable sent from the French embassy in Washington in January 1941 estimated that America could not achieve its rearmament plan until 1950 at the earliest, by which time the war in Europe would surely have ended. Even if the United States did build planes and ships, it would still lack the pilots, crews, and technicians to translate its economic power into military power. American rearmament therefore represented a public relations stunt more than a serious military plan of action, "a verbal offensive" more than a strategic one.[53] The Germans, by contrast, could turn up the heat on France anytime they wished by making the occupation more onerous or by refusing to release any more of the hundreds of thousands of French prisoners of war. It therefore made far more sense for Vichy officials to worry about mollifying the nearby Germans than the faraway Americans or the hated British. As Darlan's behavior demonstrates, Vichy in 1941 looked for ways to offer the Germans more, even if what they had to offer (such as bases and the use of the French fleet) increased the chances of conflict with the United States.

By early summer 1941, the failure in America's Vichy had become clear for all to see, but Washington officials clung to it regardless. Władysław Sikorski, the influential leader of the Polish government in exile in London, passed to Roosevelt and Churchill a report that Weygand might soon grant the Germans "use of [France's] colonial as well as metropolitan ports and airfields as bases against the British." These reports contradicted Murphy's own assessment of Weygand's leanings. If true, they would not only prove Weygand's duplicity and unreliability, but they would also prove the basic worthlessness of American policy. Murphy went to confront Weygand on the matter, but Weygand sneaked out of Algiers on the excuse of inspecting units in the countryside, leaving the Americans even more confused about his intentions.[54] The war, however, was about to change in an instant and with it America's increasingly bizarre relationship with France.

ALTHOUGH HE HAD SUPPOSEDLY LEFT town on an inspection tour, Weygand called Murphy the next morning, June 22, 1941, urgently asking him to come to his residence. The news had just broken that the Germans had invaded the Soviet Union. Both Murphy and Weygand knew immediately that the Germans, now tied down in the east, could no longer afford to send more forces to Africa or try to take over the French Empire there. Weygand also shared with Murphy his conviction that Germany would now surely lose the war. Murphy reported the conversation to Roosevelt, who authorized Murphy to tell Weygand that the United States would send him American fighter planes in exchange for his help. When the Frenchman asked if America was ready to become a belligerent, Murphy replied, "In a sense we already were that," an answer that, unsurprisingly, failed to satisfy Weygand. Murphy did, however, begin to see that with the Germans preoccupied in the Soviet Union for months or years to come, North Africa might become the perfect place for the United States to begin its war as soon as it did join, hopefully with Weygand's help.[55] The time might soon come to put Hillenkoetter and Roosevelt's vision into action.

Most Vichy officials initially disagreed with Weygand's assessment and thought the Germans would win the war in the east. If they had beaten the modern, well-trained French army, they reasoned, then the decrepit Soviet one should prove no match. The British, moreover, stood in no position to help the Soviets and the Japanese might take advantage of the crisis by invading Siberia. Murphy even had a bet with a French admiral who thought that the Soviets would sue for peace within two months.

The invasion led American officials to stick with their failing policy rather than risk major change at such a crucial moment. Thus, despite mounting evidence that the United States had had no positive influence on Vichy leaders, the Roosevelt administration continued to rebuff de Gaulle and his Free French movement for fear of offending Vichy or risking a full German takeover of France. Prominent French exiles, including André Maurois, Antoine de Saint-Exupéry, Camille Chautemps, and Jean

Renoir all mistrusted de Gaulle and influenced American officials to keep him at arm's length. Roosevelt, Hull, and Welles continued to refuse to meet with René Pleven, de Gaulle's representative in the United States.[56]

On the other hand, the offer of airplanes to Weygand never went any further, as Roosevelt may have known all along; he told Murphy not to write anything down but to deliver the offer to Weygand orally. The number of players and the fast pace of events left American leaders confused and searching for someone they could trust. For the time being, the United States would stick with Vichy and keep its options open on both Pétain and Weygand, even as its diplomats began to report on the frustration of the French people toward Vichy's spinelessness and craven docility.[57]

Leahy still saw Pétain as "an old gentleman whom I hold in the highest regard as a patriot completely devoted to the welfare of his people." Nevertheless, he knew that many Frenchmen and Frenchwomen "would join a de Gaulle movement in France if it should ever appear to promise a prospect of success." Leahy had also received remarkable reports of French families telling American consuls that they would prefer their children go without American food aid if some of the aid ended up in German hands.[58] Roosevelt had repeatedly said that he did not want to choose France's form of government either during or after the war, but how much longer could the United States support a government whose legitimacy had begun to vanish in the eyes of its people?

The German invasion of the Soviet Union convinced Darlan, recently named Pétain's successor in the event that anything should befall the marshal, of the need for even greater Franco-German military cooperation. Darlan told Leahy that the invasion of the Soviet Union would last no longer than a few weeks, that the British blockade could not impede the German offensive, and that a Soviet victory would mean the unacceptable triumph of communism worldwide.[59] To him, the war no longer meant defeating the British but defeating the Soviets and their dangerous communist ideology. The conservative leadership in Vichy therefore initially welcomed this new war, which they expected the Germans to win in short order against a Soviet threat that it viewed as existential not just to France but to all of civilized Europe.

That the hated British and the evil Soviets had now become allies made the new geostrategic situation even clearer for Vichy. The war now seemed to Darlan and many others in the senior leadership to take on a sharper ideological meaning and in ways more favorable to the French. Now France could justify its support to the Germans not as vengeance for their anger against the British but as part of a wider war against the common enemy of bolshevism. That war might even draw some support from the French people, most of whom had shown little interest in a war against the British. France could thereafter more confidently present the Germans with a wide range of options for working together in exchange for further concessions and a leading role in the new anti-communist Europe to come. The postwar peace treaty would now not only crush the British but the Soviet Union as well. The Germans, most Vichy officials assumed, would need France as a reliable partner in this new world order. Even the capitalist Americans could hardly object to Vichy supporting Germany if it meant contributing to the defeat of communism.

Or so Darlan had reasoned. The reality was not quite so clean and neat. Within a month of the invasion, Leahy reported that many junior officers in the French military had begun to sense that the Germans might not achieve their aims in Russia after all. Whereas they had once thought that the decadent Russians could not last longer than the modern French had, now they began to see signs of Russian endurance. Rumors swirled around Vichy of one million German prisoners of war and mass casualties in gigantic battles the likes of which Europe had not seen since the last world war. Anti-German French officers speculated about an upcoming winter "such as that which ruined the Russian campaign of Napoleon." Young French officers hoped for a stalemate in the east that would break German power and liberate them from "permanent slavery under German masters." Others openly began to hope for American assistance to take advantage of Germany's distraction in Russia.[60]

IF THE GERMAN INVASION OF THE Soviet Union clarified strategic aims for senior French leaders, it had the opposite effect in Washington, at least for relations with France. "It is impossible to guess what will happen in France tomorrow or the next day," Leahy wrote to Roosevelt. "It is almost as difficult to point to any useful accomplishment that we have made here since my arrival six months ago." The fast-moving pace of events put pressure on a tired Pétain to cede more and more control of the government to

Pétain and the head of the Vichy armed forces, Admiral Jean-François Darlan (to Pétain's left) attend a ceremony for veterans at Vichy. Darlan remained loyal to Pétain but constantly sought ways to increase his own power inside the Vichy system.

Darlan, who no longer allowed Pétain and Leahy to meet without him. The American worried that in the near future, Darlan would seize all real power and reduce the aging Pétain, the bedrock of America's Vichy strategy, to making "speeches to school children and veterans." With not a little bit of flattery intended, Leahy told the president that the French people increasingly looked to him (Roosevelt) as "their one and only hope for release from Nazi rule."[61]

Soon, the challenges of Vichy gave the Americans more to worry about beyond Europe. In a late-July meeting, Darlan told Leahy that France had decided to accede to a Japanese ultimatum for the use of French bases in Indochina, including the deepwater port of Cam Ranh Bay and the airfield at Bien Hoa. The ability to deploy military forces in Indochina would give Japan a powerful presence to the west of the American colony in the Philippines. It therefore offered Japan a tremendous advantage in Southeast Asia just as tensions between the United States and Japan had begun to rise to a breaking point. The French decision reinforced the view in America of a spineless and weak Vichy willing to do whatever the Axis powers asked of it. When the news became public in the United States, Cordell Hull noted, "Popular opinion here to the [Japanese] occupation [of French Indochina] seemed more bitter against Vichy France for legalizing the move than against Japan for making it." Both the *New York Times* and the *New York Post* ran editorials arguing for breaking diplomatic relations with Vichy and seizing Martinique to prevent it similarly falling into Axis hands. William Langer recalled the tone of those editorials as, "First in Syria, now in Indochina, the Darlan regime, despite its protestations, was yielding without even a show of resistance."[62]

When he learned of the Franco-Japanese agreement over Indochina, Leahy wrote in his diary, "Here Endeth the French Colonies in Asia."[63] The remark could have referred to the Japanese takeover or the now nearly universal reluctance in Washington to allowing Indochina to return to French control after the war. Roosevelt and his team thereafter made much more forthright statements about Indochina entering into some kind of international trusteeship after the war. French officials across the spectrum, from Vichy to de Gaulle, vehemently opposed these ideas. They may have disagreed on virtually everything else, but all French officials insisted that Indochina, like the rest of the French Empire, should remain under full French control after the war.

America's own war in Indochina would come soon enough. More immediately, French actions there set in motion the final steps toward Pearl Harbor. American intelligence analysts noted the arrival of Japanese warships and troop transports in Indochina, suggesting Japanese intention to act against the Philippines, the Dutch East Indies, Hong Kong, or Singapore. President Roosevelt, recognizing the consequences of the new threat, took a more confrontational turn with Japan, freezing Japanese assets in the United States and ending oil exports. Because 80 percent of Japan's oil came from the United States, the embargo put the two nations on a collision course that they could not avoid. And some of the footprints went all the way back to Vichy.[64]

Vichy's powerlessness and subservience in the face of Axis demands continued to present existential crises for American strategists. Vichy looked more and more like an active Axis partner. Still, Cordell Hull continued stubbornly to argue that "nothing had occurred to change the basic points on which the President and I were resolved to maintain diplomatic ties with the Pétain Government."[65] For now, the American government chose to blame the Japanese, not the French, for the seizure of Indochina, even as public opinion showed more anger toward France for its cowardly habit of giving in to Japan's (and Germany's) demands.

The government's dealings with Vichy remained deeply unpopular with the American people and among leading voices in the media. A public opinion poll taken just before Pearl Harbor showed 75 percent of Americans agreeing with the statement that Vichy took its orders from Germany and 65 percent were convinced that Vichy would turn over its fleet if the Germans so demanded.[66] Dr. Seuss drew cartoons critical of Laval, Darlan (whom he called "the new Fuehrer"), the Vichy government they led, and America's policy toward it.[67] Samuel Grafton, a syndicated columnist for the *New York Post* who reached millions of readers every day, asked, "Why do we recognize fascism when it is called Hitler but not when it is called Pétain? Why does a simple change of name that would not fool a hotel clerk bewilder our State Department?"[68] No one in the United States government seemed to have a good answer.

IN AUGUST 1941, Murphy and the consul-general in Algiers warned of "disquieting reports that the tide at Vichy is running rapidly in the direction of concessions to the Germans in French Africa." He believed that Vichy might "go all out in support of the German program" if the war against the Soviet Union went well. The evidence, he reported, was "unmistakable" that Pétain's power had waned and that the Vichy elite "simply operates under German domination and controls." Murphy suggested reaching out to Weygand with a final offer of military assistance in exchange for his taking action against Germany. Weygand remained adamantly anti-German and had tolerated the spy network Murphy ran in French North Africa. These signs suggested a possibility of further interaction with him. Murphy believed that Weygand held the "African trump, which is the last France has," and that he might play it if he thought it could turn the tide.[69] Hull replied four days later, telling Murphy to reassure Weygand that "his needs are not being overlooked," hardly a clarion call for either to take action.[70]

Even Leahy, who still supported American relations with Vichy as long as Pétain remained in charge, began to reconsider his views. In the middle of August, Pétain invited him to a speech he gave in the Vichy Opera House. Rather than announce a change in foreign policy or indicate a stiffening of French resolve, he announced a suspension of public gatherings and a ban on the distribution of all political literature. He also announced a doubling of the Vichy police. "As I listened," Leahy recalled with evident sorrow, "I had a feeling that Hitler must have written the speech."[71] Still, the ambassador thought that Darlan and his minions must have misinformed Pétain of the true situation in the country. He continued to believe that Laval and Darlan, not Pétain, represented the true problem.

Just before Pearl Harbor, relations began to take yet another turn for the worse. Rumors once again spread that Vichy would soon give the Germans full use of the ports in Bizerte, Oran, Dakar, Toulon, and Marseille in order to support Erwin Rommel's campaign against the British in North Africa. With the Russian war not going well, the Germans needed to wrap up the Mediterranean one in order to focus on just one front. On December 1, Pétain, Darlan, and General Alphonse Juin met with Hermann Göring. Pétain told his host that Germany could win a war without France, but it could not win a peace. Pétain pledged further collaboration but only on terms of equality.[72] He wanted a promise from Göring to honor the commitment Hitler made to Darlan during the Paris Protocols discussion to "give France a place of honor in the new European federation," albeit one "guided by Germany."[73] Göring, however, exploded in anger, reminding Pétain of the French army's collapse the year before. "I want you to know who is the conqueror and who is the conquered," he screamed.[74]

Perhaps most importantly, in mid-November the Germans forced the resignation of Weygand who had strongly opposed the Paris Protocols and seemed to have grown too close to the Americans for comfort. The Germans may also have gotten wind of Weygand's discussions with Murphy. They handed Pétain a written demand for Weygand's dismissal on November 15. Leahy described it as a "brutal ultimatum" that threatened a full German occupation of France if Weygand remained in government.[75] The note warned that if France refused to dismiss Weygand, the Germans would occupy the entire country and "permit the native population to die of hunger." Pétain asked Weygand to come to Vichy for meetings, then dissolved his post of delegate-general.[76] In response for firing Weygand, the

Pétain tried but failed to convince the Germans that France could be an active partner in peacemaking and in the postwar period to follow. His meetings with Hitler and Hermann Göring (seen here with Pétain and Darlan in December 1941) convinced many Americans that working with Vichy was not only futile but immoral.

Germans rewarded Darlan by releasing 5,000 naval officers from prisoner of war camps.[77] A concerned Leahy wrote to Washington that Vichy officials displayed what he called "jellyfish reactions" to Nazi threats.[78]

Even with Weygand, the most pro-American Vichy official now out of office, Leahy and Hull continued to place their bets on Pétain, although the tone had clearly begun to change. In a letter to Roosevelt, Leahy called Pétain "a feeble, frightened old man surrounded by self-seeking conspirators."[79] Nevertheless, the United States did not give up on him. American officials allowed themselves to believe that the marshal could not have known the full details of what Darlan and Hitler had agreed to at Berchtesgaden or he would have stopped it. Still, such supine behavior, Leahy argued, "justifies the stoppage of all [American] assistance to [Vichy] France."[80] He suspended that aid after Darlan met with Göring, and the State Department announced that America's France policy would experience a complete review. That review, however, produced no substantive change, with Hull continuing to argue that only American support for Vichy prevented a full German takeover of France, its fleets, and its ports. He pressed for a resumption of American aid in return for a promise from Pétain to reaffirm his pledge to keep the French fleet out of German hands. He still argued that the price America had paid for all the benefits of his Vichy policy was "comparatively infinitesimal. . . . We had sacrificed no principles. We had made no political commitments." In Hull's view, the United States had received in exchange a sufficient guarantee that France would secure its fleet and an encouragement to anti-German officers inside Vichy.[81]

But without Weygand, American policy no longer made any sense. Darlan had moved Vichy closer and closer to the Germans, and despite Leahy's continued admiration of him, Pétain lacked the power to do anything but make more empty promises. The only saving grace seemed to be that Laval remained out of the government in Paris. He survived an August assassination attempt while at a ceremony at Versailles honoring the new collaborationist paramilitary force known as the Légion de volontaires français, and for a while afterward he kept a lower profile. For the time being, at any rate, Laval posed no great threat to American interests, but he remained menacingly on the sidelines, ready to do Germany's bidding or maybe even to replace Pétain.

Just days before Pearl Harbor and the subsequent German declaration of war against the United States, Darlan made it quite clear to the Americans that Vichy's future lay with Germany. He told H. Freeman Matthews that "you can never beat the Germans militarily and to think that they threaten your security is laughable." Having missed its chance to influence the war in 1940 and 1941, Darlan argued that the only role for America in 1942 was to help negotiate a peace, presumably at Britain's expense. "It is always the same story," he told Matthews. "America is too late."[82]

THE ATTACK ON PEARL HARBOR stunned American officials in North Africa but also brought some much-needed clarity. "I could feel relief that the chips were drawn at last," Murphy recalled, "and Americans no longer need pretend to be neutral."[83] Four days after the shocking attack, Leahy told Darlan that he had placed all American relations with France "in suspense."[84] He then bluntly warned Pétain that "any assistance which France might give to Germany, such as cession of bases, permitting the Germans to take possession of North Africa, or use of the fleet, would in fact amount to giving active military assistance to Germany against the United States." Pétain promised that he would keep Vichy neutral in the war between the United States and the Axis powers. Leahy believed in Pétain's intentions, but he warned Washington that he had "no reason to believe that under German pressure the Marshal will be able to carry out the policies" of neutrality as promised.[85] Darlan's decision in late December to give Germany use of the port of Bizerte in Tunisia seemed a clear sign that Leahy had reason to worry.

In the terrifying new environment of full American belligerency in the war, the United States needed to decide whether Vichy would become an American enemy, a possible ally, or as Pétain promised, remain indefinitely neutral. A series of top-secret assessments written in the chaotic week after Pearl Harbor by Donovan's new office of Coordinator of Information (COI), and undoubtedly based on intelligence from Murphy's network as well as Donovan's own impressions from his recent trip, painted a dark picture.[86] The reports predicted that Germany would pressure Vichy to break relations with the United States and send troops to bolster the defenses and submarine pens of Dakar. "The Nazi hammer may descend at any time upon the hapless Pétain," the report read, with the "willing and convinced collaborator" Darlan, "a hater alike of Britain and America," ready to take full control of Vichy's political and military power. Already, Vichy was preparing to ship 3,600 tons of gasoline and 1,100 trucks to the Germans to support operations in North Africa. More active French assistance to the Germans, they predicted, would follow, although the details remained ominously unclear. "A Nazi ultimatum will arrive shortly after the beginning of the new year," one report guessed. "There is no telling what will happen."[87]

One COI report in particular would have set alarm bells ringing all over official Washington. For months, rumors had circulated that the French had offered to give the Germans access to airbases in West Africa; Darlan and the Vichy ambassador in Washington had both hinted as much during tense meetings with American officials.[88] The COI report warned that France had built two airfields in Senegal (with three more under construction) that had runways longer than any plane in the Vichy air fleet could possibly need. The COI drew the conclusion that Vichy had designed the new airfields to accommodate long-range German bombers.[89] Although fully armed German bombers could not reach the United States from Senegal, the He 177 did have sufficient "ferry range" to fly from Senegal to Martinique or Brazil by carrying extra fuel tanks instead of bombs. More ominously, the reports might mean that the Germans had completed the long-feared four-engine Me 264. Menacingly nicknamed the Amerika Bomber, it had a range of 7,400 miles even at its full payload of 5 tons.[90] It would not have taken much imagination in those panicked days after Pearl Harbor to envision German planes flying from Senegal to the western hemisphere, then being armed and refueled somewhere in the Americas (perhaps even Martinique) from where they would certainly have the range to hit a variety of American cities and maybe even fulfill Göring's pledge to deploy bombers that could hit New York City.[91]

If the reports about the airfields reached Secretary of State Cordell Hull, they would help to explain his extreme reaction to a minor incident regarding the French islands of Saint-Pierre and Miquelon. Sitting just off the coast of Newfoundland, in theory, German submarines might seek to refuel there in order to extend their range and continue their campaign of sinking transport ships in the North Atlantic. The islands also hosted a valuable weather station and a radio transmitter that the pro-Vichy governor used to broadcast propaganda into Quebec. Still, Canadian officials told the Americans not to worry: the islands had just eleven policemen, no military assets, and no port facilities that could support military ships. Nor did they have airfields. Canada opposed any American attempt to seize the islands or occupy any part of them, including the radio transmitter, for fear of creating a crisis over an insignificant issue.

It wasn't the Americans or the Canadians, however, but de Gaulle who created a crisis over the islands. Rumors had been spreading for weeks that he might dispatch a naval force to claim the islands for Free France. Cordell Hull had responded on December 18 by promising Vichy that the United States would not recognize any transfer of French territory in the Americas. But de Gaulle went ahead anyway, bolstered by reports that the population despised the pro-Vichy governor and wanted to become part of Free France. Anxious to isolate the transmitter and respond to overwhelming pro-Gaullist sentiment among the 4,000 residents, de Gaulle sent a small fleet of three corvettes and one submarine to the islands to claim them for Free France on Christmas Eve, 1941. The residents welcomed the ships without violence, deposed the Vichy-appointed governor less than an hour later, and pushed forward a referendum first proposed in April on the islands' future. It voted nearly unanimously for de Gaulle the next day. There this tiny incident would have ended, except for the reaction in Washington.[92]

Cordell Hull quite unexpectedly exploded in fury at what he described as a Free French violation of the Monroe Doctrine. The United States had rejected an overture by de Gaulle's representatives to support an operation against the islands earlier in the month on the grounds that he had no legal standing to challenge Vichy's sovereignty. Hull derogatorily referred to the "so-called Free French" and demanded the islands' immediate return to Vichy control, although he proposed that the United States and Canada should take joint control of the radio transmitter to stop its pro-Axis broadcasts. De Gaulle's actions infuriated him so much that Hull canceled his Christmas vacation and returned to Washington to monitor the situation. He also lashed out at the Canadian and British governments for allegedly being involved in the scheme without telling the United States.[93] Winston Churchill had trouble understanding Hull's anger, especially in the heated and terrifying days after Pearl Harbor, remarking, "I was struck by the fact that, amid gigantic events, one small incident seemed to dominate his mind."[94] De Gaulle, too, was taken aback by the intensity of Hull's response.[95]

Hull's reaction was wildly out of proportion to the incident. The government of Canada continued to dismiss Hull's fears about any military potential for the islands, reporting that Saint-Pierre and Miquelon lacked the necessary facilities to support military operations and had a population almost entirely pro-Canadian and pro-American. Still, for Hull, de Gaulle's coup to grab the islands put the United States and its policy toward Vichy on the horns of a major dilemma. Supporting de Gaulle's claim had the advantage of standing up for a British ally and cutting off pro-Axis propaganda, including false claims that his forces had perpetrated a "blood bath" on the islands and murdered two priests in cold blood. On the other hand, to admit de Gaulle's claim to legitimacy in any part of France meant not only a shift in policy away from Vichy but also an acknowledgment that the policy itself had been wrong in the first place. A pro–de Gaulle line might even drive Vichy fully into a marriage with Germany, with use of the five West African airfields as part of the bride's dowry. Hull therefore insisted that Saint-Pierre and Miquelon return to full Vichy sovereignty, a strange approach to take given the results of the referendum and the support for de Gaulle from the British and Canadian governments as well as a large section of the American people.

Hull's decision to cause so much friction over so small an issue reveals the fundamental difficulties inherent in America's choices over Vichy. The problem of Saint-Pierre and Miquelon certainly did not stem from any potential military threat. The United States military had cared so little about the place that it had just one map of the islands, an old hydrographic chart in the navy map collection that did not even fully show the islands themselves. The United States Army had done a brief survey in September and found no threat to American interests. The population there, the army estimated, was 98 percent pro-American, a conclusion that the referendum reinforced.[96]

Canadian prime minister Mackenzie King hurried to Washington to calm Hull and to tell him that "while we had nothing to do with the matter, Canadian feeling was relieved and pleased with the de Gaulle accomplishment." Canada favored honoring the referendum and keeping the islands in de Gaulle's hands. "I told him that it would not do to have the Governor restored as he was pro-Axis, and his wife a German," King reported.[97] Hull nevertheless insisted, evidently quite forcefully, that Canada join the United States in backing Vichy's claim and helping to expel de Gaulle's men from the islands, with force if necessary. Canada's undersecretary of foreign affairs, the future prime minister Lester B. Pearson, dug in his heels, noting, "We made it clear that we were no banana republic to be pushed around by Washington."[98] Winston Churchill stirred Hull to further fury when he came to Canada and, before the Canadian Parliament, praised de Gaulle's expedition as an example of courageous democratic spirit in action. "Frenchmen there were," he told his audience in Ottawa, "who would not bow their knees and who under General de Gaulle have continued to fight on the side of the Allies."[99] Hull interpreted Churchill's speech as a direct attack on him and America's Vichy policy.[100]

The American people, however, agreed with Churchill and King. *Time* praised de Gaulle for turning two islands only ever useful to Americans as a "rumrunners' rendezvous in Prohibition days" into a symbol of freedom and democracy. By seizing the islands, de Gaulle had effectively told Vichy to "go to hell," a sentiment the American people cheered. The international score might still be "Jeanne d'Arc 1, Axis 10," but at long last, Free France was on the scoreboard.[101] During a depressing Christmas season when Hong Kong fell and the Axis seemed to be on the rise everywhere, Saint-Pierre and Miquelon represented to Americans a victory for the side of the Allies and one close to home at that.[102]

President Roosevelt's support for Churchill in the matter infuriated Hull enough that he drafted a letter of resignation over the matter, although he never gave it to the president. Hull knew that he was out of step with American opinion and bemoaned the fact that his department faced a barrage of "editorials, radio attacks, and representatives from various organizations" opposing his Vichy policy and his position on Saint-Pierre and Miquelon, which had become a symbol of the wider American shift away from Vichy. Hull thought that his opponents "did not comprehend [the] broader issues" involved.[103]

Clearly, Hull had misread the symbolic importance of the islands to American opinion. Hull further miscalculated by dismissing American public opinion, which universally favored de Gaulle in this case and subsequently gave Hull "every sort of abuse" from across the political spectrum.[104] Now engaged in a total war, public opinion mattered more by the end of 1941 than it had at the start of the year. Public sentiment forced Hull to back down and accept the transfer of the islands to de Gaulle's government, even if the United States had not yet recognized Free France. The issue for Hull was about much more than the technicalities over an insignificant set of nearly barren islands. The Saint-Pierre and Miquelon crisis publicly revealed the tenuous and contradictory nature of his own policy of talking tough to Vichy leaders in private but working with them in public. His plan to bring the British and Vichy together through Churchill's offer of six divisions for North Africa had already collapsed. Now the Saint-Pierre and Miquelon affair had forced him to acknowledge that the basis of American policy in relation to Vichy had failed in the eyes of the American people.[105]

Hull's policy had not only failed, but it also nearly blew up in his face. The great historian of Vichy Robert Paxton argues that the Vichy cabinet did seriously discuss declaring war on the United States in return for further German concessions to France. Pétain, Darlan, and others in the cabinet showed a willingness to enter the war if Germany agreed to "profound modifications" in its policy toward France. In the end, German success in North Africa disinclined the Germans to cut a deal with the French because they thought they could win the war there without French help. Darlan, too, seems to have gotten cold feet, promising only in January 1942 that Vichy would declare war on the Allies if they tried to invade part of the French Empire. Within a year, the war would test how far Darlan might go to keep that promise.[106]

Vichy's decision to back away from war with the United States may also have resulted from signs that German momentum in the east had slowed. By the end of 1941, more and more officials inside Vichy had ended their initial infatuation with Germany's invasion of the Soviet Union. As winter set in and the Germans failed to capture Moscow, the hopes of a quick German victory vanished. Pétain's prediction of a short war in the east because the Germans only wanted to set up vassal states in Poland and Ukraine proved terribly wrong. The Germans instead bogged down in a total war that even as early as December 1941 some Vichy officials believed they could never win.[107] Vichy might, therefore, have to find itself more amenable to working with the United States in 1942.

The fast-moving pace of events at the end of December threatened to overturn everything the United States had tried to build in regard to France. France's decision to cede its bases in Indochina to the Japanese now directly threatened American interests in the Pacific. Maybe more importantly, although Pétain had pledged to keep France neutral, the risks of Germany seizing French ports or French warships had now exponentially increased the danger to the United States. As 1941 became 1942, no one knew what to expect next. As William Langer wrote, "We were operating pretty much in the dark. All we knew was that Vichy was a Pandora's Box, and we must be ready for anything."[108]

5

THEY'RE ASLEEP IN NEW YORK

The Allies Look for Answers

IN APRIL 1942, IN A DAMP, gloomy castle near Dresden, a tall sixty-three-year-old man in excellent physical shape took a rope he had fashioned from bedsheets, copper wire, and strips torn from clothes his wife sent him. He tied one end of the rope around the bars of his cell in the castle's prison, known as the Saxon Bastille for its size and bulk. On his first try, or so he later claimed, he realized halfway down the forty-five-meter wall that the rope was not quite long enough, so he climbed back to his cell and went back to work. He bided his time by eavesdropping on his German captors to improve his German and memorizing a map of the area smuggled into the prison by agents of the British Special Operations Executive (SOE). The second time he tried, now with a longer rope, General Henri Honoré Giraud succeeded in rappelling down the prison's walls and disappearing into a nearby forest. He then located his SOE contacts who gave him money, civilian clothes, and a map showing him an escape route through Switzerland.[1]

Giraud dodged German agents all the way to Vichy where he met with Henri-Philippe Pétain. The daring escape and sudden appearance in the heart of the new French government by the man *Newsweek* called "this escapist extraordinary" made headlines worldwide. Giraud had already gained fame as commander of the French Seventh Army in 1940, keeping it intact and fighting until the end. One of his last messages before his capture brashly announced, "I am surrounded by 100 German tanks. I am destroying them one by one."[2]

In a country with few heroes from the recent months, Giraud became an important symbol of defiance. His escape from prison restored a modicum of pride to a French nation desperately in need of a man it could admire for his wartime courage. That he had embarrassed the Germans in the process only made the story more enthralling. The "daring old man on his flying trapeze," as *Time* described him to its American readers, had defied the enemy with a brilliant escape, just as he had as a junior officer in 1914, when he had received help from none other than the soon-to-be martyred British nurse Edith Cavell.[3] American officials also took notice. On hearing the news of the escape, Robert Murphy instantly remembered Giraud as the confident general he had met in 1939 in Paris's Gare du Nord. He seemed to have lost none of his self-assurance despite France's defeat.

The State Department's historian and apologist for America's flawed Vichy policy William Langer quickly dubbed Giraud the "new star" in French politics. He struck Murphy, Langer, and many others as the perfect man to offer a chance to reset America's policy toward France. He surely did seem tailor-made for the part, and his face soon graced the cover of American magazines.[4] With his bushy Gallic mustache and youthful looks, he gave every appearance of a brave French soldier with plenty of fight still left in him. He won more supporters by offering to return to captivity if the Germans would first release 500,000 French soldiers from their prisoner of war camps, but the Germans refused. Instead, they offered him parole if he first turned himself in; Giraud publicly responded that he would never again trust the word of a German.

Giraud appeared like a gift from the heavens to American policymakers looking for answers in the new strategic environment of 1942. The strategic geometry of America's Vichy problem grew more complex when Japan and Germany became American enemies. If, as most Americans assumed, Vichy France was actively assisting America's new foes in Tokyo and Berlin, then how could the administration justify its continued policy of engagement and even sending food and fuel? Even if Vichy had not signed on as a formal German and Japanese ally, and even if its leaders continued to pledge neutrality, a moment would come sooner or later when Vichy would have to choose sides. Given the pressure that Germany could put on France,

Franklin Roosevelt meeting with the "man of the future," French general Henri Giraud. The Americans desperately hoped that Giraud could help them find a way out of their failed Vichy policy. He proved to be a difficult ally.

few people doubted which side Vichy would choose. When they did, the United States would at long last have to recognize the failures of its own policies. There might even come a time when American forces cooperated with British forces in an invasion of France itself. They would need men like Giraud to have any hope of success.

Giraud found Vichy much more craven and pro-German than he had expected. He mistrusted the collaborationist officials he talked to at lower levels and he found their despondency deeply troubling. Disappointed by what he interpreted as Pétain's cowardice and timidity, Giraud sneaked out of Vichy and made his way to London via Lisbon. Giraud's second daring trip in as many months only increased his stature in American eyes. Meeting Giraud for the first time in his London headquarters, General Dwight Eisenhower, destined to deal with Giraud frequently throughout the next two years, described him as a "gallant if bedraggled figure" whose long imprisonment and tiring escape "had not daunted his fighting spirit." Giraud,

Eisenhower noted, "looked very much a soldier."[5] Could he be the man to provide a powerful counter to both Vichy and Charles de Gaulle?

LIKE MOST AMERICANS, the Pearl Harbor attack put William Leahy in a confrontational mood. He told Pétain in January 1942 that the United States would bring "everything we could bring to bear" to help France if it joined the Allies. If, however, France helped the Axis, the United States would have no choice but to conclude that the Vichy leadership was "playing the German game." An actively pro-Axis Vichy, he warned, "the United States could not accept without taking action." Pétain, fearing a German reprisal against any overtures he might make to the United States, replied by turning down further American assistance, renewing his promise of French neutrality, and insisting that France would defend North Africa against any nation that tried to take it away from French control. The meeting convinced Leahy that Pétain felt himself powerless to take definitive action.[6] Perhaps the time had come to look for other French leaders.

The time had also come to turn up the heat on Vichy, at least from the shadows. Elizabeth "Betty" Thorpe, an American socialite unhappily married to a British intelligence officer, played a leading role. She had conducted operations in Spain and Warsaw before the war, then became one of the most effective spies in Washington. In the months before Pearl Harbor, she wooed several Axis diplomats, gaining access to their secrets. She then turned her attention to Charles Brousse, the press secretary at the Vichy embassy in Washington. Together, they photographed the code books in the embassy safe, eavesdropped on sensitive meetings, and read secret documents from the ambassador's own files. Their handler, Canadian spy William Stephenson, drank his martinis with vodka, and always shaken, never stirred. He later became one of the models for his friend Ian Fleming's creation, James Bond.[7]

Even with the intelligence coming in from Washington and Algiers, the dizzying pace of change in the months after Pearl Harbor made it almost impossible for American officials to figure out what Vichy intended to do. Pétain showed occasional signs of "stiffening" and said that France "could expect nothing but grief" from Germany, but he gave no indications to suggest a forthcoming break with the Nazis or a decisive move toward helping the Allies.[8] British strategist J. R. M. Butler noted the confusion when he wrote later about the "many shades of grey between the black malevolence of Laval, the vacillation of the senile chief [Pétain], and the latent sympathies of Weygand."[9] Murphy recalled in his memoirs that the confusion and chaos in North Africa kept him awake with dreams of a new assignment in Sweden.[10]

However confusing and hard to read, Vichy became increasingly critical to the Allies in early 1942 as the war in North Africa continued to seesaw back and forth. In May, the Afrika Corps under Erwin Rommel launched a new offensive in Libya toward British positions near the key port city of Tobruk. In June, Tobruk finally fell, with 33,000 British and Commonwealth soldiers going into captivity. The British had suffered a complete humiliation and the road now seemed open for the Germans to drive on the Suez Canal and cut British lifelines to India.

Vichy, whose troops could have played a decisive role in support of the Allies had they chosen to, remained on the sidelines. Its continuing neutrality infuriated the British, but American officials stuck to their policy of recognition of Vichy and isolation of de Gaulle. The Americans may have wanted to buy time to see if Giraud could grow into the leadership role that they wanted to see him play. As a result, nothing changed in American policy toward Vichy despite the United States' formal entry into the war. Officials in Washington, in the view of the exasperated British ambassador Lord Halifax, "have got it so firmly fixed in their minds that they must do nothing which can possibly jeopardize their position in Vichy and in North Africa at the present moment that it seems unlikely that they will be prepared to have closer relations with [de Gaulle's] Free French."[11] The Americans and Vichy French seemed to have a tacit agreement in place: as long as Pétain did not openly cooperate militarily with the Germans, the United States would not do so with de Gaulle.

While Vichy's forces sat on the sidelines, Free French forces, although small and inexperienced, acquitted themselves quite well. As part of the Battle of Gazala outside Tobruk, Free French forces under the command of General Marie-Pierre Koenig drove back repeated German attacks on their positions near the Libyan oasis of Bir Hakeim. With only enough men to form a half brigade, they repulsed a force ten times their own size, even drawing the praise of Adolf Hitler who (in a thinly veiled swipe at the Italians) called the Free French the second-best troops in Africa. De Gaulle's "Fighting French" were killing and dying in common cause with the Allies while the Vichy French continued to assist the Axis. Yet the United States recognized the latter and snubbed the former. Even while fighting continued at Bir Hakeim, de Gaulle bitterly complained that American officials had invited Vichy's military attachés to attend Washington's Memorial Day parade, in his eyes a symbol of the evident failures of America's Vichy policy.[12]

OBSERVING THE SITUATION FROM VICHY, Leahy concluded well before Tobruk, Bir Hakeim, and Giraud's daring escape that his country had chosen the wrong side. In February 1942, he asked President Franklin Roosevelt to use the Saint-Pierre and Miquelon controversy as a pretext to recall him for consultations, but the president told him to stay. A month later, Leahy repeated the request to Undersecretary of State Sumner Welles, who had come to agree with him on the failure of American policy. Roosevelt once more asked Leahy to remain in Vichy, telling him that the United States still needed "to hold Vichy to its promises not to give away the French fleet or make French territory available as bases for military operations." Leahy therefore needed to stay in France and do what he could to "strengthen those elements which are locally resisting the extension of German influence." Leahy knew that at the senior level, such elements did not really exist. Welles, however, told him that the United States had begun quietly to look for ways to support the Free French as the dust had begun to settle after the conclusion of the Saint-Pierre and Miquelon affair. American policy thus remained in a state of deep confusion, supporting both French movements, one in public and one in the shadows. "The time may come at an early date when these two are no longer compatible," Welles recognized. Until then, however, Leahy must remain in Vichy and do his best.[13]

At about the same time Leahy heard, likely from Murphy's spy network, that Jean-François Darlan had agreed to ship 500 French trucks to Tunisia to help ease the strains on German logistics. Leahy challenged Darlan on the issue, who told him that the Germans had threatened to seize the Tunisian port of Bizerte outright if France did not oblige. Leahy, aware of how Darlan's decision could irreparably harm the British then fighting to hold

Egypt, snapped back that France should prefer to lose Bizerte in battle than to surrender it. Leahy also noted in his diary that Darlan arrogantly told him that he had expected to keep the trucks agreement secret, "a stupid expectation in view of our well-known sources of information in Africa as well as in Vichy," a compliment to the efficiency of the American intelligence network.[14]

The British decided to turn up the heat on France. Royal Air Force bombers struck French industry and transportation lines with regularity. On March 3, in the largest raid to date, the British dropped 2,000 bombs, including incendiary devices, on and around a large Renault factory in the western suburbs of Paris that made spare parts for tanks. The raid gave Vichy and German propagandists a badly needed weapon in the information war. Vichy officials described the raid as a "bloodbath" and exaggerated the number of dead from 391 to 2,000. Still, even 391 dead shocked a capital not accustomed to facing aerial bombardments. Darlan, in Paris for meetings with Otto Abetz, rushed to the bedside of some of the victims and made certain to bring a camera crew and reporters with him. The raid, Vichy claimed, proved that Great Britain and de Gaulle would see Paris destroyed if it helped the Soviet Union spread communism throughout Europe. De Gaulle's alliance with the British and the Americans, the propagandists alleged, only proved their subservience to the Jews and the Soviets. French fascist Jacques Doriot called for a declaration of war against Britain, and the collaborationist writer Jacques Benoist-Méchin proposed displaying the coffins of the dead on the place de la Concorde and marching the entire city of Paris past them in homage.[15] One propaganda poster produced shortly after the raid showed a bloody and demented Winston Churchill as the head of an octopus with tentacles reaching out to Somalia, Egypt, Dakar, Syria, Germany, Norway, and Mers-el-Kébir. The text read, "Confidence: His Amputations Are Proceeding Methodically."[16]

Roosevelt and Cordell Hull supported the air attacks, as did the American people whose faith in Vichy, the London *Times* reported, "is so completely gone that [Americans] have long urged a stiffening of American policy."[17] Still, Hull resisted pressures for any major change in his France policy. A memo from Hull to Roosevelt written in April noted that the United States might recognize de Gaulle as "the head of a military movement" but never as the head of a government. The arrogant Free French leader, Hull complained, "will permit no other expression than his own to be voiced" in the political future of France; therefore, the United States should take no action that seemed to validate his unwarranted claims to political power or it might look like the Americans wanted to install a puppet regime. If he wanted American help, Hull argued, then de Gaulle should "continue the fight for French freedom and leave politics alone until the day of victory when the people of France shall themselves be free to select a government of their own choosing."[18] Hull was naive if he believed that military actions during the war had no political purpose after it, especially in the minds of French leaders who would have to deal with the reconstruction of their country after the catastrophe of 1940.

POLITICS, OF COURSE, REMAINED FRONT and center at all times in this rapidly changing environment. In April, at about the same time that Hull wrote his memo, came the bombshell announcement that Pétain had caved to German pressure and reinstated Pierre Laval as prime minister. Laval had gained stature in German eyes by promising to help the Germans recruit French laborers for German industry. His return confirmed Vichy's complete subservience to the Nazis. Leahy still had faith that Pétain had France's best interests at heart, but he could also see Pétain's power and influence waning with each passing week. He had no interest in remaining in Vichy if staying meant dealing on a daily basis with a government run by Laval and his pro-Nazi sycophants.[19]

American intelligence concurred, reporting that Laval's return meant that "collaboration wins the day at Vichy" and that Germany aimed to "remove American influence and sympathy with the Allies from places of importance around Marshal Pétain." Laval would then have an unchallenged position to chart the "collaborationist course for France" that he has "long cherished." The Germans had scored "a diplomatic victory of far-reaching implications," reducing Pétain to a "political front for the Laval regime." American analysts expected Laval to remove government officials suspected of holding anti-German sentiments, assign loyal officers to key jobs in North Africa, and use Vichy's remaining military power to reconquer the parts of the empire that had declared allegiance to de Gaulle. Under Laval's rule, Vichy would become a willing and eager ally of Nazi Germany.[20]

"The bad days are over. Papa is making money in Germany." The poster attempts to promote a deeply unpopular labor scheme that Pierre Laval designed to send French workers to German factories. It provided further proof of Vichy's subservience to the Germans.

It is hard to overstate the hatred with which Americans in spring 1942 viewed Laval. *Time* depicted him in a cartoon as a rat returning to a sinking French ship commanded by Darlan. Another cartoon showed him as a goose-stepping, Nazi-saluting pig that could only say "Oui, oui, oui." The American media pulled no punches, describing him alternatively as "a fearfully hated Hitler stooge," "a creased, oily, white-tied lawyer," and "a squatty, villainous faced old man who made political capital of his own nation's dis-unity and pushed France into subservient collaboration with its 20th century invaders." Perhaps most imaginatively, one editorial wrote that "many Frenchmen who had stomached the idea of Marshal Pétain as a possible savior of France, vomited all hope for Vichy when Pierre Laval took over."[21]

Laval's return meant, in the words of one United Press report, adding "France's gears to the German war machine" that had now officially de-clared war against the United States.[22] At a press conference, Undersecre-tary of State Sumner Welles mentioned that Laval had gone to Paris to ne-gotiate the formation of new cabinet. A reporter asked whether he had met with Frenchmen or Germans. Welles just smiled, but news soon fil-tered back to Washington that Laval had in fact met almost exclusively with Germans and that Germans had even written his press releases.[23] One American news report concluded that "through two long years of bitter misery and intense danger the French people have rejected Hitler's advances only to have Hitler's creature forced on them in the end."[24]

Laval's return to power invalidated all American efforts and proved that the policy of recognition had completely failed. Leahy renewed his plea that he should abandon his failed mission in Vichy in order to distance the United States from any regime run by Laval. Leahy's wife had died sud-denly of an embolism, and the political situation had taken a negative turn for the United States from which it would never recover. This time, Wash-ington officials agreed and brought Leahy back to assume the post that would become chairman of the Joint Chiefs of Staff. Welles argued for breaking relations with Vichy. Hull and Roosevelt did not yet want to go that far, but they temporarily suspended food and oil shipments and rec-ognized de Gaulle's control of the parts of French Equatorial Africa that had declared its loyalty to him.

American newspapers denigrated the government's failed policy, with several using the explosive word *appeasement*.[25] The *Miami Herald* pub-lished a provocative front-page article warning that the Germans could use the numerous inlets of the French Caribbean island of Guadeloupe (which it called "as Vichy as Martinique") to hide or resupply U-boats. Al-luding to fifth columnists on the islands, the story argued that many French "cays and shoals [were] accessible to large ships with 'local knowledge'" standing by to guide German crews. The Germans could also lean on thousands of "non-descript native fishing and trading craft" to convey infor-mation and maybe weapons "far out to sea" with Vichy's acquiescence or active assistance.[26] Just over a month later, a front-page headline in the paper read simply, "Seize Martinique." "The United States should move in at once," read the accompanying article. "This is no time to fool with diplomatic niceties with an open enemy. National safety demands that we take over immediately every inch of territory held by France in this hemisphere."[27]

Despite the increasing sense of threat, Hull resisted calls for any drastic shift of approach. Starting symbolically on July 4, the United States began regular radio broadcasts into French North Africa, presenting the news in a pro-American light, countering Nazi propaganda, and most of all, using statements from American industrialists to promote the idea of increased trade after the war to help the French economy rebuild.[28] Hull did occasionally deliver tough-sounding speeches, like one he gave at the end of July warning that "nations who refuse to fight for their liberty and freedom cannot expect the same support from the United States as those who do." Hull did not mention any specific nation in the speech, although a spokesperson later confirmed that he had Vichy France and India's Congress Party in mind.[29]

Although only a small number of people knew it, France and North Africa had begun to move to the heart of Allied strategy. American planners had conceived an operation code named SLEDGEHAMMER to invade mainland France in late 1942 or early 1943. British generals objected to the concept, arguing that occupied France was too heavily defended and the Americans far too inexperienced for such a dangerous and complex operation. They urged instead an invasion of French North Africa. The Americans pleaded with Roosevelt to authorize the more direct approach called for in SLEDGEHAMMER, but he sided with the British. In July, the president decided that American and British forces would invade Morocco and Algeria, in hopes of trapping the Germans between the invading forces and British forces advancing west from Egypt. The plan, code named TORCH, made the response of the leaders of Vichy France critical to American success or failure. Hull therefore saw value in keeping the door to Vichy even the slightest bit ajar.[30]

WITH AN INVASION OF NORTH AFRICA now being planned, Robert Murphy arrived in Washington at the end of August to find senior officials from military planners to the president himself anxious to talk to him.

The Anglo-Canadian fiasco at the French port of Dieppe that same month meant that executing a major cross-Channel attack in 1942, or in all likelihood, 1943 had become highly unlikely.[31] Clever minds, even those that did not know about Roosevelt's decision for TORCH, shifted their map gazing toward North Africa as a possible place to get Americans fighting before the end of the year. But American officials knew so little about the place or the Vichy officials who governed it that Murphy found his expertise in high demand. Secretary of War Henry Stimson and Army Chief of Staff General George Marshall opposed an invasion of North Africa, in no small part because of their intense mistrust of Vichy officials. Leahy, however, found in the North Africa scheme a way to justify his time spent in France. He greeted Murphy in Washington by exclaiming, "Well, maybe you and I didn't waste our time cultivating those people in Vichy!"[32]

As to those people in Vichy, Murphy reported that he had gotten nowhere with two of the regime's most important military figures. Neither General Charles Noguès, commander in chief of ground forces in Morocco, nor Admiral François Michelier, Casablanca's naval commander, responded positively to any of Murphy's discreet overtures. Both men remained firm Darlan loyalists.[33] Some French officials at lower levels had hinted that they might support a full-scale Allied landing in North Africa but not a hit-and-run raid on the model of Dieppe. Darlan himself continued to be opaque, promising nothing and meeting with Murphy as infrequently as he could. "Never before," Murphy recalled, "had Americans been confronted with a situation like this and we had to play it by ear," even as military planners tried to eliminate as much ambiguity as possible.[34]

In early September, Leahy flew with Murphy to Hyde Park to brief President Roosevelt and his close adviser Harry Hopkins. Leahy, now the president's senior military adviser, wanted Murphy to help him convince Roosevelt of the likelihood of the Allies conducting successful operations in North Africa. As they sat down for an informal discussion in the president's hot, airless study, however, Murphy found a man who needed no convincing. The president seemed enchanted by the adventure and exotic mystery of North Africa. Roosevelt also foresaw a key role for the navy, always the service nearest and dearest to his heart. Murphy came away believing that the British had not talked a naive Roosevelt into the invasion of North Africa, as American generals had warned him. The invasion had, Murphy thought, been Roosevelt's idea all along.

Nevertheless, the president saw the problems of getting involved in so complex a place. The United States could not ask in advance for Pétain's permission to move Allied forces through North Africa for fear of that information finding its way to the Germans or leading Vichy to sever diplomatic relations. But an Anglo-American landing in North Africa without that permission meant violating the neutrality of Vichy and thereby increasing the chances of Vichy forces resisting the landings, especially if British forces played a prominent role. Roosevelt told Murphy not to share details of their conversation with anyone, not even with Secretary of State Cordell Hull. For operational security reasons, neither the Free French nor the Department of State could know about the details of TORCH. Roosevelt believed that a sufficiently large American force, combined with what he called "diplomatic maneuvering" behind the scenes by Murphy, would suffice to bring French officials in North Africa to the Allied side.[35] Murphy would have been forgiven if he had dreamed of Sweden again that night.

While Murphy wrapped up his trip in Washington, Vichy showed still more signs of lining up with the Germans, complicating Roosevelt's already shaky schemes. In August, Pétain sent an unseemly congratulatory telegram to Hitler after the Allied fiasco at Dieppe. In a symbolic gesture of gratitude, the Germans released all French prisoners of war born there.[36] American agents also reported that Vichy would soon create a German-equipped French armored division backed by one hundred modern tanks built in French factories like the one that the Royal Air Force had bombed in March. If successfully raised, trained, equipped, and deployed to North Africa, a modern French armored division could make an Anglo-American operation there, such as the one then under planning, prohibitively risky.[37] The same Office of Strategic Services (OSS) agents thought that some Vichy officials had guessed (correctly) that the Allies would invade North Africa before they tried to liberate metropolitan France and that such an invasion could happen as early as the end of the year.[38]

The spy ring that Murphy and Donovan created now became central to American planning. If Vichy resisted the landings, Anglo-American forces might suffer huge, perhaps unsustainable, casualties; if, on the other hand, Vichy leaders like Noguès and Michelier cooperated, then the landings would go smoothly and change the entire course of the war in the Allies' favor. The Americans would have to play the leading role because Vichy officials deeply mistrusted the British after the Mers-el-Kébir attack. As one

Vichy senior officer said to an American agent, "If the British come, I will pick up a rifle and shoot until I am killed. If the Americans come, I will welcome them with open arms."[39]

American informants reported that most Vichy officers in North Africa tended to have both anti-British and anti-German sentiments. By the summer of 1942, they knew that Germany's gains in the east had come at a high material and human cost. They began to see that Germany might not have the ability to sustain those losses long enough to win a war against the Soviet Union, especially with another winter approaching. Still, such beliefs did not necessarily mean that the Americans could expect cooperation from Vichy officials. American analysts believed that the French military would have no choice but to obey orders to resist any Allied landing in Africa, if for no other reason than to avoid a loss of prestige in the eyes of their Muslim subjects.[40]

Continued French control of the region and the empire more generally after the war remained a central strategic aim of Vichy officials. Except for Murphy and a few other professionals on the scene, Americans never did understand the importance of North Africa to Frenchmen of all political stripes. Morocco and Algeria provided three-quarters of prewar food imports to the metropole and one-fifth of the total economic output of France.[41] French North Africa, moreover, had become home to one million Europeans who lived among a much larger population of Arabs, Berbers, and Jews. The Europeans, from the desperately poor *pieds noirs* to the wealthy landowners known as *colons* had all the rights of Frenchmen living in the metropole.[42] As one popular saying went, the Mediterranean ran through France just as surely as the Seine ran through Paris.[43]

In the eyes of Vichy's leaders, Algiers and Casablanca were every bit as French as Marseille and Nice. Algiers had in fact been under French control three decades longer than Nice. The new French government had thus repeatedly pledged to defend Morocco and Algeria against all invaders, be they German, British, Italian, Free French, or American.[44]

From 1940 to 1942, Vichy officials worried that any appearance of weakness in the empire on their part might diminish France's ability to prevent a further rise in Arab nationalism that would undermine French control. Subsequent events proved that French officials had reason to worry about their long-term ability to retain control of North Africa in the face of Arab nationalism and American anti-colonialism, factors that Murphy recognized early on.[45] For all of their disagreements with Vichy officials, on North African affairs, de Gaulle and Giraud, too, were imperialists who wanted to do nothing that might undermine French control in Algeria and Morocco.[46]

Militarily, senior Vichy officials, including Darlan and Laval, still believed that Germany would find a way to win the war or at least negotiate a peace agreement from a position of relative strength. They continued to despise the British and mistrust the Americans. For their part, the Allies had not yet set unconditional surrender as their strategic goal, leading Vichy officials to expect the war to end by a negotiated settlement. By allowing Germany to build matériel in French factories, granting Germany access to French air bases in Syria, and giving the Germans the use of French fuel and vehicles in Tunisia, they thought that they had positioned France for favorable postwar treatment from Germany in those negotiations. Placing their bets on Germany, they believed, gave them their best chance to keep control over North Africa after the war. Although most Vichy leaders wanted to remain neutral, some wanted to bring France into the war on Germany's side in exchange for promises of further territorial gains in Africa at Britain's expense. French fascist politicians Jacques Doriot and Marcel Déat proposed that Germany should hold the line against the Soviets in the east, while France took on the responsibility of defending the Axis southern flank in North Africa from British, Gaullist, and American aggression.[47]

DESPITE ITS OCCASIONAL HIGH-MINDED anti-imperial rhetoric, in 1942 Americans did not care about North Africa's political status as much as French leaders feared. They wanted an anti-Vichy general who could govern the region and keep it calm as Allied forces moved east into Tunisia. Enter Henri Giraud, the French general who had escaped from his German captors in May. Giraud had an anti-German orientation, a great personal story, and a seemingly endless reservoir of courage. By having spent 1940–1942 in a German prison, he had no connection to the collaboration of Pétain and Laval, and he had made no pledge to follow the orders of the Vichy government. At the same time, he had no links to the Free French whom the Americans still mistrusted. "Clearly he was the man of the future,"

Langer wrote with unwarranted optimism.[48] Giraud, however, remained in the dark about American plans because he did not see the war in the same way that they did. He wanted to liberate mainland France first, then turn to North Africa. Giraud thus began to dream up joint Franco-American operations that he would command to liberate France in 1943, the same kinds of operations that the British rejected as too risky.

Americans who did not know him well, such as Hull and Langer, believed that Giraud could become the ideal person to lead a French unity government. Even at this relatively early stage of the war, American, British, and French officials all feared the possibility of a civil war in France as soon as the Germans finally left.[49] President Roosevelt had stated repeatedly that the United States would not determine the form of the postwar French government, but France would still need a provisional government, if only to keep mutually antagonistic French groups from settling old scores.[50] Leahy and a few others seem to have thought that Pétain could still serve this role, at least as a figurehead, but at his age and with his evidently declining power and prestige, he seemed ill-suited for such a massive job. Whoever emerged as this leader, he would have to come from the military, as all prominent French politicians had connections either to Vichy or to the discredited Third Republic. Giraud had solid credentials as an anti-communist and his conservative politics might help him attract the farmers, industrialists, and Catholics who had initially supported Vichy but had grown disenchanted with it.[51]

The British, however, did not share the United States' high opinion of Giraud and had already committed to de Gaulle instead. Sir Alexander Cadogan, the British permanent undersecretary of state for foreign affairs, disliked de Gaulle as a person but nevertheless acknowledged that "when France was prostrate, de Gaulle was the only Frenchman of any note who remained staunch. . . . With all his faults, we believe him to be a sincere patriot untainted by collaboration."[52]

Senior American officials, on the other hand, had no faith in de Gaulle, whom they saw as unreliable, untested, and arrogant. Hull remained angry with him for his handling of the Saint-Pierre and Miquelon affair. De Gaulle had an anti-communist orientation, but in the interest of building a unified French resistance under his control, he had reached out to many communist and socialist leaders. William Bullitt, a former ambassador to both the Soviet Union and France, warned Roosevelt that Joseph Stalin would take advantage of de Gaulle's promises of a widely inclusive provisional government. Communists could join that government, then "crush the democratic elements" therein and seize power in postwar France.[53] Undersecretary of State Sumner Welles also opposed de Gaulle, telling Lord Halifax that the Free French movement had nothing to commend it and "no outstanding men with qualities of leadership," an obvious insult aimed at de Gaulle.[54]

British officials practically begged the United States to change their minds and join them in recognizing de Gaulle. They argued that America's continuing policy of supporting Vichy increased the likelihood of Frenchmen looking to the Soviet Union after the war instead of the United States and Britain. "If the Vichy rulers have retained any authority over the French people," noted one British report in a clear swipe at the United States, "it is largely due to the support given to Vichy by some foreign governments." The sooner the United States dropped its recognition of Vichy in favor of de Gaulle, the British contended, the greater the likelihood of France emerging from the war strong, whole, and pro-Western.[55]

De Gaulle proved a difficult man to deal with; he had a knack for angering the same people whose support he most needed. Duff Cooper, who became Britain's first postwar ambassador to France, thought de Gaulle played up his anti-British attitudes intentionally in order to avoid the charge that he was nothing more than a "paid puppet of the British. . . . There was no criticism that he resented more bitterly." Churchill described him to Cooper as "a man [who is] Fascist-minded, opportunist, unscrupulous, ambitious to the last degree." Cooper tended to agree, later arguing that de Gaulle "possesses none of the grace usually associated with the French character."[56] And this from the British, de Gaulle's primary backers.

Still, even Cooper and Churchill could see that de Gaulle remained the only obvious alternative to Vichy especially as momentum for him built both inside and outside France. De Gaulle, the British claimed, would have had even greater support in France and in the United States "were it not for the attitude of the State Department, which acts as a deterrent, particularly on those Frenchmen who . . . are reluctant to support a movement which does not appear to be viewed with favour by the United States Administration."[57] British officials alleged that the State Department had purposefully underplayed the success of de Gaulle's movement because to admit his growing influence in France would "constitute an implied criticism of the State Department's own policy towards Vichy. How could the State Department continue to maintain its relations with Vichy and give so little encouragement to the Fighting French, if it was publicly to state how strong and effective these movements were proving to be?"[58]

De Gaulle had begun to gain adherents to his cause among the American people, if not its government. Often denigrated as a secret royalist or a would-be dictator, in July 1942, de Gaulle vastly improved his image with a speech promising a five-point plan for postwar France: free elections, a complete dismemberment of the Vichy system, a restoration of dignity to France, a resumption of liberty, equality, and fraternity for all Frenchmen, and French support for a world organization to maintain peace. The French people, he promised, would decide the form of the postwar French government and the shape of a new constitution through free elections. France would have neither a dictatorship nor a return to the discredited Third Republic. The speech convinced American media outlets like *Time* that the United States should recognize de Gaulle as the head of the French government and "the custodian of French democratic ambitions."[59] The United States government, however, remained unconvinced.

THE POSTWAR PROBLEM of who would govern France, while serious, would have to wait. First the Allies had to win the war, and American officials held to the position that Giraud, not de Gaulle, gave them the best option. But as with most of America's recent policy choices in regard to France, this one came with its own limitations. Three problems quickly emerged with the American decision to back Giraud. First, de Gaulle and Giraud thoroughly detested each other and had since 1937, when Giraud had been de Gaulle's commanding officer. They showed absolutely no desire to share power five years later.[60] Second, neither man had done anything to demonstrate that he had the support of the French people. Roosevelt therefore hesitated to put America's imprimatur on either one as anything more than a commander of the Free French military. Third, and most important, neither Giraud nor de Gaulle had any influence over Vichy forces in North Africa. Vichy had in fact labeled both as traitors for working with the Allies.

The man who did control Vichy's armed forces, Admiral Darlan, did not enjoy the confidence of anyone in London or Washington. Darlan still loathed the British for their attack on his fleet at Mers-el-Kébir, and he showed little affection for the Americans because of their alliance with the British. British officials warned the Americans that they saw Darlan as "synonymous to the British people with [Norwegian collaborator Vidkun] Quisling, if not with little Dr. Goebbels and Adolph himself."[61] Most senior American officials hated him as well, and some had openly fantasized about putting Darlan in jail at the first opportunity, but only Darlan, the commander in chief of the Vichy military, had the power to order French forces in North Africa to lay down their arms. Arresting him might satisfy a cathartic desire for justice, but it would not advance American or British interests. Darlan had also handpicked the most senior commanders in North Africa, ensuring their loyalty to him. Getting him out of the picture would not be easy, nor did there seem any way to convince him to switch sides.

With the invasion of North Africa approaching, Murphy, Donovan, and the OSS came up with a new plan to help Giraud's chances that the British initially dismissed as "crazy."[62] Murphy would use his network to arrange a secret meeting between General Charles Mast, a high-ranking Giraud ally based in Algeria, and American major general Mark Clark, who would use one of Britain's new submarines to land on the Algerian coast. Clark, Eisenhower's deputy for planning, would have the authority to negotiate a deal "on a hypothetical basis" and would come to Algeria with gold coins to help fund French resistance operations against key Vichy-controlled targets like the power, telegraph, and road networks.[63] If the meetings seemed to go well, the Americans could also offer to provide men and weapons in exchange for Mast's promises to prevent Vichy troops from moving against Gibraltar or the Anglo-American landing zones. Eisenhower authorized Clark to give Mast information about GOLDENEYE's network of radio transmitters in hopes that it might provide a way for American and French officials to communicate during and after the landings.[64] He could not, however, tell Mast about the timing of the invasion, the exact landing points, or the American decision to exclude Giraud from the command structure of the operation.

Clark, two high-ranking deputies, and three British commandos went in the highest of secrecy on October 20 to a villa near the town of Cherchell, located 90 kilometers west of Algiers. Clark knew, but Mast did not, that the landings would begin in less than two weeks.[65] Clark and the deputies came ashore in collapsible canoes and met with Murphy, Mast, and a handful of other senior French officials for what Murphy called "one of the oddest conferences of the war."[66] Mast told Clark that French officers in North Africa had begun to doubt Germany's ability to win the war because of reports of colossal German losses on the Russian front. They would, he assured Clark, work with the Americans, but probably not the British, in exchange for Giraud being given authority over French domestic matters and a senior role in the planning of the invasion itself. He also told Clark that Giraud wanted time to plan a simultaneous landing in southern France and that Giraud expected to be commander in chief of any operation that took place on French soil. The conferees had no ideas for neutralizing or co-opting Darlan, but Mast hoped that Giraud could swing the French army to the Allied side with or without Darlan's help. Mast also gave Clark "detailed and voluminous reports of information on strength, location of troops and naval units, supplies, and details of airports, also where resistance would be the heaviest."[67] This information took courage for Mast to share. It undoubtedly saved American lives but cost French ones.

The Clark mission almost ended in complete disaster. Servants at the house took Clark and his deputies for smugglers and called the police hoping to pick up reward money.[68] The Americans hid in a cramped wine cellar or outside in the bushes with pistols drawn ready to shoot their way back to the submarine if necessary. A quick-thinking Murphy convinced the police that he had been hosting a party after curfew with women of ill repute. He bribed the police to keep the embarrassing incident a secret given his diplomatic standing. The ruse worked, allowing Clark and his team to swim through the rough surf back to the submarine, although the vain Clark lost his pants and the gold sewn into his belt in the process. Fortunately, senior Vichy officials became none the wiser about the true purpose of the meeting.

Despite the disruption, the men had had enough time to sketch out the rough outlines of a deal. Mast agreed to help the Americans in exchange for Giraud being given control over French North Africa with no American interference in internal French political matters once the invasion was over. In effect, Giraud would become an American-backed viceroy in exchange for Mast's help in limiting the bloodshed on the shorelines of North Africa. Giraud put his name to propaganda leaflets the Allies dropped on the day of the landings that ended with the words "Remember 1914–1918:

Save Your Bullets for the Boche!"[69] He also recorded a radio appeal to be broadcast during the landings to French forces that proclaimed, "One passion, France. One aim, Victory!"[70]

Given the hatred Vichy felt for the British and the inexperience of the Americans, Eisenhower and Clark thought they needed to make a deal with Giraud, even as they started to have second thoughts about his abilities to deliver on his end of the bargain. In addition to knowing almost nothing about French North Africa or the people who lived there, the Americans had no interest in governing the region. They therefore cut a deal with a French leader to solve a temporary problem. They would do so again before the year had ended.

Eisenhower called the Clark-Mast meeting "extremely encouraging" by providing some hope that French officers might help, especially in large cities like Oran and Algiers. He did not, however, change his plans based on such preliminary discussions.[71] Troops were already en route from North America or assembled in Scotland and Northern Ireland, weather reports had confirmed the dates Eisenhower had chosen, and no one wanted to take the risk that the Germans would detect the movement of so many ships toward Africa. The operation would go forward with or without solid agreements with the French.

BY THE TIME THAT THE OPERATION BEGAN, a real crisis in American relations with Vichy France had developed on both the international and domestic sides. On the international level, American intelligence continued to report on the evolving military closeness between Vichy and Germany. German submarines had begun to use the French Mediterranean base at Toulon and the French had discussed turning over ten of their own submarines to the Germans. Other reports warned of Laval giving the Germans 70,000 tons of merchant shipping, initiating a joint Franco-German defense of Dakar, and breaking relations with the United States to please the Germans. One intelligence summary argued that "nothing favorable to the United Nations can be expected from Pétain whose influence is less every day."[72] Occupying French North Africa might be the only way to keep it out of German hands for much longer. Once the Germans took over its defense, the Americans and British would face a much tougher military problem.[73]

At home, what William Langer called America's Vichy gamble had become intolerably unpopular for Roosevelt and his still-unproven wartime leadership. One British report warned that Roosevelt worried about "waning public confidence over the war" and that much of that lack of faith traced back to his government's failed Vichy policy.[74] Just as the midterm elections of 1942 entered their final phase, former Republican presidential candidate Wendell Willkie, recently back from a world tour, cited America's support for "the vicious and subversive" Vichy regime as evidence that the Roosevelt administration was "losing its grip" on foreign affairs and grand strategy. America's "lack of courageous leadership" on the Vichy problem, he alleged, "is becoming more and more obvious."[75] Willkie's support had been crucial to Roosevelt's depiction of his strategy as bipartisan. He could not afford to lose that support, especially over Vichy where his administration's policy was particularly vulnerable. Prominent journalists like Walter Lippmann had also come out in opposition to Vichy, which he argued "is seeking by every means in its power to aid Hitler."[76]

The Vichy state had by then developed a terrible reputation in the United States. The Humphrey Bogart / Ingrid Bergman blockbuster *Casablanca*, made during 1942, reveals an intimate American awareness of the craven nature of the Vichy system. In one scene, Bogart's character asks a nervous French police prefect terrified of visiting German officers if he is pro-Vichy or Free French. The prefect, played by Claude Rains, refuses to answer. At the end of the movie, however, he symbolically tosses a bottle of Vichy water into the trash just before agreeing to join Bogart's quest to find a Free French unit across the Sahara Desert in Brazzaville.[77]

Frank Capra's *Divide and Conquer,* part of the popular *Why We Fight* series, also criticized Vichy. It described Pétain as a tired old man "egged on by men like Laval, who saw in a German victory his chance for personal power." Together, they had willingly delivered France into the slavery and subjugation of the Nazis. Vichy, the film told its American viewers, represented the antithesis of the great French democracy they had once known. Symbolically, at the end of the film, French battle flags are loaded onto ships bound for North Africa to keep them out of Nazi hands.[78] American policy may have served short-term interests, but it produced tension in both the United States and Britain, where it called into question America's commitment to its own stated principles.

Town hall meetings across the country debated the war and revealed a sharp anti-Vichy tone. One such meeting in Ohio, broadcast nationally via radio, featured as a speaker Williams College professor Frederick Schuman, who blasted America's support for the "Nazimen of Vichy" and argued that "our whole attitude . . . is one of cold shouldering the Free French while we continue to give Hitler's dupes at Vichy the enormous political and psychological advantage of diplomatic recognition as the lawful government of France." Pétain, Laval, and Darlan, he charged, were "the three men who, more than any others, helped Germany and Japan to prepare their attacks on the United States." Schuman's debating opponent, Pulitzer Prize winner Felix Morley, did not make a pro-Vichy argument in his reply. Instead, he argued that the French people were also victims of Laval and that maintaining diplomatic relations remained the only way to protect them from their venality of their own government.[79]

Pressure built for the United States not just to break with Vichy but to also take active steps to destroy it. In late October, just before Mark Clark sailed in his submarine to Algeria, *PM* magazine featured a cartoon showing the widely loathed Laval as a marionette controlled by strings attached to a swastika. The accompanying article was titled "Africa Is a Good Place for a Second Front."[80] *PM* became a leading anti-Vichy voice, as did the *Chicago Sun,* which began to syndicate articles by Camille Chautemps, a three-time prime minister of France who defected from Pétain's cabinet while on an official mission to the United States. Chautemps blasted Laval's return to the government as "a mortal coup to the existing confidence between the French and American governments." Pétain would have stopped Laval's return, Chautemps argued, if he still had the energy and power to resist. That he did not only proved France's complete subservience to Germany.[81] Dr. Seuss drew a cartoon showing Hitler, as a cat, dragging a stinking, ratlike Laval back to Pétain's front door. A few weeks later, he drew another one with Hitler as a violinist and a grinning Laval as the violin. The text above it reads, "Not a bad tone, pal, but what I want is more volume!"[82]

At the same time, sympathy for de Gaulle continued to rise among Americans. Edward R. Murrow became a vocal supporter of Free France, as did other prominent journalists. Lippmann compared de Gaulle to

George Washington while calling Laval "Hitler's second."[83] A giant Croix de Lorraine, the symbol of Charles de Gaulle and Free France, appeared to great fanfare in Rockefeller Center in New York City while a large crowd with dozens of VIPs in attendance roared their approval.[84] The mood in America had become pro–Free French, but American policy had not kept pace.

American newspapers wanted more than recognition of de Gaulle. They called for military action against Vichy. The *Philadelphia Record* argued for a lightning strike to seize 300,000 tons of French merchant ships in order to prevent Laval from handing them over to Germany, and the *New York Times* called for an invasion of North Africa because the Vichy leadership "carries out the instructions of Hitler. They are the underlings of underlings, the puppets of puppets, the tools of tools."[85] A letter signed by 900 ministers titled "The Conscience of Humanity Has Kept Silent for Too Long" also demanded a second front in North Africa.[86] Roosevelt worried about the political pressure so much that he tried unsuccessfully to press General George Marshall to start the landings no later than October 30 in order to guarantee that they would have a positive impact on the 1942 midterm elections on November 3.[87]

VICHY ITSELF SEEMED TO SIT at a tipping point. In September, Laval introduced a deeply unpopular labor scheme called Relève that would release one French prisoner of war from 1940 still languishing in German camps for every three Frenchmen who went to work in German factories. His support of the scheme had partly led the Germans to insist that he return to government. Laval had hoped to raise 150,000 skilled workers and 450,000 laborers through the plan, thus releasing 200,000 French prisoners, but only 22,000 Frenchmen, most of them unskilled and unemployed, volunteered.[88]

The plan proved deeply unpopular in France and helped lead to the creation of numerous French resistance cells. Laval began a series of more coercive moves to find his workers, such as closing nonmilitarily essential factories in order to force French workers to go to Germany or face unemployment. One intelligence report described the French people as seeing Laval's actions as "blackmail."[89] Cordell Hull warned Laval that he saw the scheme as "aid to an enemy of the United States and inconsistent with the obligations of France under international law."[90] Robert Paxton cites the introduction of Relève as the moment when Vichy "irrevocably lost its mass base of acceptance," and several high-ranking Vichy officials began to reconsider their support of the regime.[91] Five members of the French embassy staff in Washington reacted by resigning their posts and declaring their loyalty to de Gaulle.[92] One of them said he would no longer work for a government run by "a German agent" like Laval.[93] At least two of them went to work for the OSS.

Allied intelligence agents managed to obtain copies of Vichy postal censorship reports from the first half of 1942. They painted a picture of confusion and division. "The atmosphere in the drawing rooms is like that at the time of the Dreyfus Affair," with families divided and everyone convinced that someone else in France had it better.[94] Food had become so scarce that, in the words of one letter writer, "cats have almost disappeared, though one finds the skins lying about. I know people who prefer them to rabbits." Other letters suggested a society of the verge of civil war. "Hatred exists everywhere and increases by the day with the famine, the excessive requisitions, the shootings, and the arbitrary imprisonments," read one letter from the occupied zone to the unoccupied zone. Another, speaking of the collaborationists and war profiteers, read "Hate is growing, and I hope we shall know how to retain this hate and not forget as we did in 1918. There is no forgiveness for these mad dogs."

The report revealed that French faith in Pétain remained "unshaken" but that Laval was "bitterly hated," with not a single letter surveyed praising him. Significantly, neither de Gaulle's nor Giraud's name appeared at all. The Allied intelligence officers analyzing the reports concluded that "nobody is pro-German" any longer but that the Vichy government still held some minimal call to French loyalty because it represented the only government France had. "The miners must work and the workmen must eat. So they collaborate." The French-based American journalist Janet Flanner reported that food conditions in France had gotten so bad that stillborn babies far outnumbered live births and four-fifths of French children were underweight. Pétain, the French hoped, would see them through somehow. The report summarized French opinion as "the Marshal knows what [French interests] are better than any of us, so let us stay united in his support."[95]

Vichy's repression of Jews greatly increased under Laval, forcing senior American officials to make their first public acknowledgment of the mass murder of Europe's Jews. In August 1942, the State Department received a telegram from Zionist Gerhardt Riegner in Switzerland warning that the Germans had decided that "3 1/2 to 4 millions [of Jews] should, after deportation and concentration in the East, be at one blow exterminated."[96] Some still-unidentified State Department official, quite possibly Cordell Hull himself, sent back the now-infamous Cable 354, ordering American officials not to send any more evidence of atrocities from Europe.[97] The State Department's callous reaction infuriated Undersecretary of State Sumner Welles and Treasury Secretary Henry Morgenthau. Morgenthau appealed directly to Roosevelt as part of an unsuccessful effort to find out who had sent the cable and why.

American officials remained reluctant to speak out against the still-unclear reports of forced labor and mass murder of Jews. Yet America's complex relationship with Vichy finally forced Hull to admit what he knew about the fate of Europe's Jews. On September 16, barely a month after he may have personally ordered inaction in the face of the Riegner telegram, Hull harshly criticized the "revolting and fiendish" Vichy policy of sending Jewish refugees back to their native Axis countries or to camps in the east. In denouncing Vichy, he noted that the Germans "have announced—and in a considerable degree executed—their intention to enslave, maltreat, and eventually exterminate [Jews] under conditions of most extreme cruelty."[98] It likely represents the first public admission by any senior American official that the United States government knew that the Nazis aimed not to relocate Jews but to commit genocide.[99]

Vichy's central role in the mass murder of Europe's Jews soon made headlines in a way that gave Hull no room for plausible deniability of American knowledge of genocide. Lord Halifax, in Washington as the British ambassador, noted reports that the Germans were killing 100,000 Jews per month. "They are supposed to make various things they want out of the boiled down corpses," he wrote. Three weeks later, on September 23, he wrote that American rabbi Stephen Wise "gave a terrible picture of what the Germans were doing with Jews—deporting them from the west in truckloads literally to kill." No one, not even Hull, could any longer deny Vichy's active complicity. "How vile it is of Laval to hand any more poor wretches over," Halifax wrote.[100]

Hull certainly knew more about the condition of Europe's Jews than Halifax did. The first OSS reports on the increasingly harsh treatment of French Jews had arrived in Washington in July 1942. They indicated that Vichy police had rounded up 15,000 Jews and sent them to labor camps. The documents concluded that Vichy's leaders, even those not naturally inclined toward anti-Semitism, would continue to persecute Jews in order to remain in the good graces of the Germans. Further evidence then began to arrive from the OSS that Vichy had supported German plans to isolate Jewish children from their parents and destroy the identity papers of naturalized French Jews so that they could not prove their citizenship.[101]

The OSS informed the United States government of the Vel d'Hiv *rafles* (roundups) in which Vichy police arrested 13,000 Jews, including 4,000 children, then held them in an indoor bicycle racecourse in Paris known as the Velodrome d'Hiver. Neither American officials nor the American media knew for certain that the Nazis would soon murder these Jews, and thousands of other French Jews, in death camps like Auschwitz. The *New York Times* reported that French Jews would become "serfs, destined to hard labor and the scantiest food and shelter after they have been deported to eastern Europe."[102]

By August, American media reports had begun at long last to report on Vichy's complicity. From Switzerland, the *Washington Evening Star*'s Frank Brutto wrote about the increasing evidence of the mass murder of Polish and Russian Jews. He also told his readers that Laval had personally directed the deportation of Jewish children to suspected death camps in "war-devastated, Nazi-occupied Russia." Reports had reached Brutto of Jewish women in Paris jumping to their deaths with their children in their arms rather than face deportation to the east.[103] When asked for a response, Laval merely said that if the Americans did not like France's policy toward its Jews, he would gladly send them all to the United States.[104]

WITH THE INVASION DATE APPROACHING and tensions building, Hull's increasingly sharp critiques of Vichy helped pro-German French propagandists to cast the United States as an enemy of France. Paris newspapers, acting under orders from their German masters, stoked the tensions between the United States and Vichy. Recognizing the likelihood of an attack on France or parts of its empire, the Paris press depicted the United States as agents of world Jewry and communism and also alleged that the United States had begun to concentrate military forces in England and Brazil for an attack on France. More Allied bombing raids over France provided additional grist for the propaganda mill. The Vichy media concluded that the French government would have no choice but to ask for German help in defending Morocco and the rest of its empire against Anglo-American aggression.[105]

Vichy newspapers also highlighted the close links between the United States and Britain, the latter still widely vilified for its attacks on Mers-el-Kébir and Dieppe, as well as the bombing raids over Paris. "There is a bellicose atmosphere in Paris these days," reported British newspapers. "America is the chief target of this campaign, which aims at forcing Vichy to break completely with Washington."[106] This propaganda effort had only one purpose: to lay the groundwork for a German takeover of the French Empire and fleet. From a military perspective, replacing the Vichy forces that American intelligence judged as mediocre with higher-quality German units would make a successful landing in North Africa all that much harder to achieve.

Moving quickly against North Africa might preempt that problem.[107] American intelligence officers reported that on October 17, the German consul-general in Casablanca had proposed to Berlin that the Germans occupy Morocco as quickly as possible with as many as four armored divisions. Another report warned that the Germans would manufacture an Arab revolt as a "necessary pretext to intervene and occupy Tunisian ports." Eisenhower's headquarters even prepared a draft message for Roosevelt to read after the TORCH landings had begun that read that "the Axis powers are planning to occupy French North Africa and to use the territory as a base for their military operations. The United Nations have therefore been compelled to forestall the Axis plans."[108]

German interference on this level only further underscored the image of Vichy weakness. George Marshall told Eisenhower on October 16 that Vichy's collapse "may be expected in as little as ten days."[109] American newspapers judged that, in the words of one editorial, the Vichy regime was "tottering" and that a "showdown" between Vichy leaders had become inevitable.[110] That showdown could result in a collapse of the Vichy state, a full German occupation of France, or the appointment of even more

German puppets to key positions. The leading candidate for one of those jobs, Jacques Doriot, had spent the war cultivating his links with Germans in Paris. Unlike the opportunistic Laval, he had long-standing credentials as a fascist. Pétain had successfully kept him out of Vichy to this point, but the Germans could insist on Doriot occupying a dominant place in a new Vichy government. A US Army intelligence report noted that Doriot and his fascist Parti populaire français were "preparing the ground for action when the time is ripe," including forming their own military units to fight as part of the Wehrmacht. Doriot himself had joined, had had himself photographed in a German uniform, and received the Iron Cross from the Nazis.[111]

Time reported that the upcoming showdown would prove that Pétain was "indisputably through" as a French leader. One of its historically minded journalists compared his time in Vichy to the Directory, the largely ineffective group of five men who took power in France in 1795 after the chaos of Robespierre and the Terror then ruled until 1799 when Napoleon's coup swept them from office and cleared the way for his dictatorship. Similarly, the instability of the Third Republic had led to Pétain, who had, like the Directory, now outlived his utility. The crisis in Vichy in fall 1942 might clear the way for a coup by a Doriot and his Parti populaire français, allowing him to emerge as a "dictator-Gauleiter" in full control of France and its empire with German backing.[112]

Laval's deep unpopularity might lead to an anti-Vichy uprising by the French people, but as Hull's American critics noted, the United States government's recognition of Vichy sent an ambiguous signal to the French people. Hull called on them to reject Vichy, but as the *Philadelphia Record* argued, he had effectively asked that they rise against a government the United States recognized in support of a Free French movement that it did not. The paper demanded that the United States break with Vichy, recognize de Gaulle as head of a French government in exile, seize Martinique, and invade North Africa. "Only then will we have the right to ask the French people to revolt."[113]

Nor was the *Philadelphia Record* alone. Virtually all armchair strategists seem to have come up with a plan to defeat Vichy in 1942. Scripps-Howard's military affairs correspondent William P. Simms thought the United States could defeat "Hitler, Mussolini, Laval, and other Axisites" by occupying Dakar, then flying troops and supplies over the Sahara Desert to attack

Vichy along its lightly defended southern frontiers. His counterpart at the *Washington Post* argued for staging American forces in Liberia, from where they could attack either Dakar or Morocco.[114] Even the Congress of Industrial Organizations, a labor union representing 500,000 war workers, passed a resolution in September demanding an end of American aid to "Hitler's friends" in Vichy and the opening of a second front.[115]

AT LEAST A PART OF THESE PLANS had already begun. The United States Army's War Plans Division, using intelligence gathered by Murphy and Donovan, did not need any media pressure to begin studying the possibilities of invading French North Africa. Vichy, it guessed, controlled eight divisions in the region, amounting to approximately 120,000 soldiers backed by powerful, modern French warships and land-based airplanes in Moroccan and Algerian airfields. Although Vichy ground forces had an inefficient command structure, outdated equipment, and uncertain morale, the officers in the War Plans Division estimated that if they decided to resist an Allied landing, Vichy forces could delay American movement toward Tunisia by three months.[116]

The problems involved in such an operation continued to multiply. Murphy described North Africa to Eisenhower as a place of "bewildering complexities." Eisenhower listened to Murphy with "horrified fascination" as the diplomat explained all the ways that the invasion could still go wrong.[117] Eisenhower faced a military problem unprecedented in American history. Logistically, TORCH involved three task forces leaving the United States and Great Britain timed to arrive precisely on schedule without being discovered en route. Politically, no one knew how Vichy forces or the Arabs would react to the Americans, let alone to the British. French phrase books handed to American soldiers contained translations for both the phrase "I am your friend" and "I will shoot you if you resist."[118]

Roosevelt tried to deal with the complications with characteristic American optimism. He told Churchill that "an American expedition led . . . by American officers will meet little resistance from the French Army in Africa." British politicians thought Roosevelt savored the opportunity to determine France's future; British generals read his statement as an attempt to give full control of TORCH to the Americans. The president, however, seems genuinely to have believed that the mere idea of America held an attraction to French officers, even ones who had sworn allegiance to Vichy. Roosevelt, observed de Gaulle, "felt a genuine affection for France, or at least for the notion of it he had once been able to conceive." De Gaulle did not share the president's optimism, given his own negative views of the Vichy leadership in North Africa and mistrust of Giraud.[119]

For his part, Eisenhower had lost his faith in Giraud. The Frenchman proved himself a difficult ally once he learned that he would not command anything until it became clear that the landings had succeeded and Allied forces had moved on to Tunisia. Without a guarantee of support from anyone inside Vichy, American and British forces would have to assume a hostile response from the French.

As the day of the operation grew near, American intelligence officers grew increasingly worried about the probable response of Vichy forces in North Africa. American naval intelligence knew that in August, the French cabinet in Vichy had discussed rumors of a pending Anglo-American attack on Dakar and / or Casablanca and that subsequent troop movements in mid-October seemed to suggest that they put some faith in those rumors.[120] The key question, therefore, remained the same as it had been all summer: how would Vichy forces respond to British and American forces when they showed up off the coast of Morocco and Algeria? Naval intelligence remained pessimistic. Based on interrogations of recently captured French naval officers, they judged French forces in North Africa "100% anti-German," but hoping for a stalemate more than an Allied victory because a stalemate could give France the best chance at "preservation of as much independence and power as possible." Vichy forces would therefore resist any attempt by any nation, including the United States, to interfere with their control over their empire. As to de Gaulle, Vichy officers saw him as a "renegade" more interested in fighting Vichy and creating "irreparable divisions in French national unity" than in fighting Germans. The French officers made no mention at all of Giraud.[121]

Murphy, who surely knew the situation and the people involved better than anyone, refused to hazard a guess about Vichy's response, although he hoped he had convinced many French officers to support the Allies once the invasion began. The final preinvasion reports from the army's G-2 (Intelligence) Bureau believed the French would fight but not out of ideology. Because Vichy had purposely assigned officers to North Africa without allowing their families to accompany them, "the Germans can lay their hands on the families of many of the French officers." The French would therefore have to fight to protect their own families back in the occupied zone. Many Vichy officers, moreover, still hated the British and would assume that any British or American ships coming to North Africa had hostile intent. Many of the most pro-Allied officer, moreover, had already defected, leaving die-hard pro-Vichy officers in their place. On the question, "Will the French resist?" the report ominously concluded, "They will."[122]

6

A BEAUTIFUL FRIENDSHIP?

The Invasion of French North Africa

IN EARLY NOVEMBER 1942, as American and British forces began to move toward North Africa for the start of Operation TORCH, a Royal Navy submarine arrived off the French Mediterranean coast near Toulon. It marked the second dangerous clandestine mission in almost as many months for the sub, which had earlier brought Mark Clark and his team to the coast of Algeria for their meeting with Charles Mast. The brand-new, state-of-the-art submarine, HMS *Seraph,* was British but commanded by one of the United States Navy's most talented officers, Captain Jerauld Wright. It represented the first time in history that an American had commanded a British ship. But Jerauld Wright was no ordinary officer—and this was no ordinary mission.

Wright, a former naval aide to two American presidents, had served on the Clark mission to Cherchell and he had all the markings of a man destined for high rank and great responsibilities.[1] However, he had little recent experience with submarines, let alone those of a foreign navy. He was so nervous that a British officer on the ship decided to play a joke on him to ease the tension. With a grave face, he handed Wright a rolled-up document and told him that it contained a set of rules and regulations that all captains must memorize and obey before putting to sea in a Royal Navy vessel. Wright opened the document to find a pin-up girl poster from an issue of *La vie parisienne* that Special Operations Executive (SOE) officers had smuggled out of France.[2]

Wright had plenty of reasons to feel nervous. He had not commanded a submarine in many years, and a clandestine operation in enemy-infested waters on a foreign ship hardly seemed the right time to try to knock the rust off an old skill. His delicate mission, moreover, could easily go wrong. Wright had to find and embark Henri Giraud, who had sneaked himself into southern France to try to organize allies for an Anglo-American-French operation under his command to liberate southern France from Vichy control. If the Vichy police found out about his plans, they would surely look to arrest or even kill him.

Giraud had also refused to cooperate with the British and there was no American submarine nearby, thus the subterfuge of temporarily placing the *Seraph* under an American commander. Wright had to get Giraud embarked on the submarine at a prearranged spot in the dark of night, then find another prearranged spot out at sea for transfer to a seaplane to fly him to Gibraltar. No one wanted Giraud to refuse to board the *Seraph* because he heard British accents. Wright, moreover, knew what Giraud did not: that the Allies would invade North Africa instead of southern France, and that a talented but untested American, Dwight Eisenhower, would command the operation.

The rendezvous ran into a few problems owing to weather and bad signals, but the submarine's crew managed to get Giraud safely on board and then to the seaplane that flew him to Gibraltar. The mission had succeeded, but somehow, Wright's signal to Gibraltar of "task done" had arrived as "task gone," sending headquarters into confusion and panic. Had Giraud chosen not to show up? Had he been assassinated? Had he discovered that the ship was British and refused to embark? The *Seraph* itself reached the Rock on November 7, just hours before the first of 73,000 American and British soldiers landed on the shores of Morocco and Algeria.[3] Wright then rushed to Eisenhower's headquarters sporting a growth of beard and a dirty uniform, profusely apologizing for his radio transmission having somehow arrived incorrectly.[4]

THE MEETING BETWEEN EISENHOWER and Giraud did not mark a smooth start to the liberation of French North Africa. Giraud spoke in

rapid-fire formal French, not slowing down for the translators, and referring to himself in the third person, none of which endeared him to the
Americans. He came with his own set of plans for invading southern France
that he expected the Allies to adopt in lieu of Eisenhower's own painstakingly developed ones for North Africa. Once informed that the British and
the Americans had already begun moving toward North Africa, not southern
France, Giraud demanded a three-week delay so he could prepare his own
alternative plans. The Americans told him that any changes at this late
stage were absolutely out of the question, sending Giraud into a fit of anger.
After the meeting, a frustrated Eisenhower turned to Mark Clark and jok-
ingly (or so one hopes) asked about the possibility of arranging for a plane
crash for Giraud. Eisenhower later wrote in his diary, "Giraud is difficult to
deal with—wants much in power, equipment, etc., but seems little disposed
to do his part to stop [French forces from] fighting."[5] Eisenhower also complained to his chief of staff, Lt. General Walter Bedell Smith, "It isn't this
operation that's wearing me down—it's the petty intrigue and the necessity
of dealing with selfish, conceited worms that call themselves men."[6]

Despite his stubborn unwillingness to conform to American plans,
Giraud remained central to American strategy, especially as estimates of
French will to resist began to rise in the last few weeks before TORCH.
Giraud's ally in Algiers, General Charles Mast, had developed a network
of volunteers willing to support the Allies, especially in Algiers and Oran.
They included civilians such as the leaders of a youth organization known
as the Chantiers de la Jeunesse. Although they had few weapons, little coordination with anyone in Gibraltar, and no training for such dangerous
work, they planned to surround key sites such as police stations, telephone
exchanges, and the Villa des Oliviers, the official residence of the commander of Vichy ground forces in Algeria, General Alphonse Juin. They
also had a list of pro-Vichy officials they planned to place in "protective
custody" until the Allies had safely landed and Giraud had taken control
of the government.[7]

Mast also made contact with a group of key figures in North Africa
known simply as the Five, who showed a willingness to work with the
Americans as long as French officials retained political control in North
Africa. Henri d'Astier de la Vigerie, one of the attendees at the Cherchell
conference with Mark Clark weeks earlier, led the group. One of his friends

described d'Astier as completely loyal to France and a "brilliant, persuasive charmer fascinated with intrigue, and at heart a royalist."[8] After Maxime Weygand refused to participate in their planning, d'Astier reached out to the Comte de Paris, a direct descendant of the last French king, Louis-Philippe. The Comte then lived as a gentleman farmer in Morocco while trying to influence events from behind the scenes.

The Five and many of their followers belonged to a cryptic, royalist (and sometimes fascist) society called the Cagoule, who wore Ku Klux Klan–style hoods at their meetings. They had committed acts of violence over the years, notably as part of a failed coup they attempted against the Third Republic in 1937.[9] Their followers had an anti-Vichy and anti-German ideology, but they wanted no fundamental change to the structure of French control over North Africa. They flatly refused to work with de Gaulle, whom they all mistrusted, but their feelings toward Americans remained hard to discern.[10] They wanted American help in getting rid of collaborationist Vichy officials, but at the same time, they wanted to ensure that the Americans did not try to change the structure of French governance in North Africa. The Five used their links to Mast to communicate with Giraud, who had himself probably joined the Cagoule at one point. To American eyes, all of the strange nodes in the anti-Vichy resistance did not form a single, effective network. Politically, they ran the gamut from moderate republicans to conservative royalists. In many cases, the members maintained healthy suspicions of one another, or they looked to avenge real and perceived slights from the political chaos of the 1930s and the terrible days of 1940.

Odd though it certainly seemed, the Five and their network of local agents might prove critical to Allied success. A final intelligence report from the American planning staff for TORCH predicted "stiff resistance" from the French navy and army "in the initial stages" of the landings. In theory, Vichy could deploy as many as 120,000 soldiers against the first few waves. Some Allied intelligence officers also worried that they might have lost the element of surprise because of indications that Vichy had either learned or guessed about the invasion. Detection at sea remained a risk, as hundreds of Allied ships had to come from the United States and Britain, then through the Strait of Gibraltar and past both enemy submarines and coastal spies undetected. Vichy radio transmissions in North Africa had gone silent, suggesting that the French might be disguising their countermeasures. Intelligence reports further indicated that Vichy had transferred another 118,000 gross tons of Vichy shipping to the Germans, perhaps to help the Germans assume the defense of key ports and facilities in Dakar or Casablanca, the two most obvious places for Anglo-American operations to begin because they did not require moving ships through the narrow Strait of Gibraltar.

Nervous Allied intelligence officers did find some encouraging signs, however. The French had not canceled regular leave for their soldiers in North Africa, and American intelligence knew that Pierre Laval's most recent defense meetings with German officials had focused on Dakar, more than 1,500 miles away from the southernmost landing beach for TORCH.[11] Finally, although the terrain in North Africa lent itself to irregular warfare, the French had so little faith in the loyalty of indigenous troops that they had made no preparations for Arab or Berber guerrillas to support regular Vichy forces. As a result, the Allies would likely win or lose the campaign on the shores and in the ports in the first few hours.[12] The help Mast and his resistance cells could provide in those first few hours might therefore make the difference between victory and defeat.

The British remained far more pessimistic. They worried that the Americans had deluded themselves, despite manifest evidence to the contrary, into relying on a Franco-American "Lafayette tradition." Because of a mythic shared history (much of it anti-British) and a presumed shared revolutionary past, the Americans falsely believed that when push came to shove, the French would never fire on them.[13] Both the British and Charles de Gaulle blamed this optimism on Robert Murphy, whom they suspected of trying to leverage anti-British attitudes in North Africa in order to bolster the position of the United States. De Gaulle deeply mistrusted Murphy, snidely, but not wholly inaccurately, remarking that in the American's mind, "France consisted of the people he dined with in town."[14]

The odds seemed to favor the Allies, although as everyone around Eisenhower's headquarters knew, the plan could still go badly wrong, especially if Vichy mounted a stiff resistance on the beaches. Thanks to Murphy and William Donovan's spy network, the United States had a good picture of the French order of battle as well as a full account of the number and conditions of French planes, fortifications, and airfields in Morocco. They also had links to resistance groups ready to join the fight.[15] The wild card remained Vichy

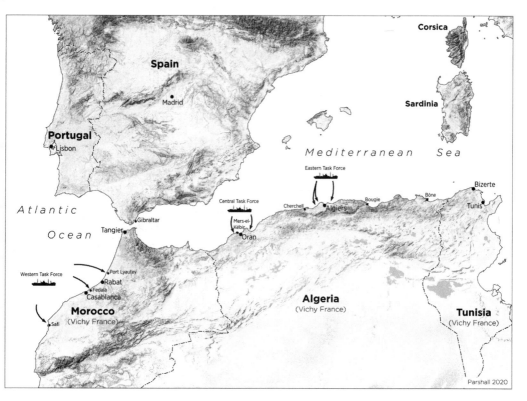

The French Empire in North Africa and Allied landing sites for Operation TORCH.

and how, "Lafayette tradition" or not, French officials on the ground in Morocco and Algeria would respond once the shooting began.

OUTWARDLY AT LEAST, AMERICAN OFFICIALS, including Murphy, continued to have faith in Giraud, hoping that he would, in the end, become the man they needed. Once in North Africa, he might still offer an anti-Vichy and pro-Allied voice with enough authority to compel French officers to obey him. One of Giraud's senior advisers said that with his photogenic looks, military bearing, and heroic personal story, he appeared to the Americans as a "typical Hollywood" character, thus they "could not help but accept him."[16] American planners promised to arm French units in Dakar and North Africa if they accepted Giraud's leadership.

The United States also abandoned its stated principles, pledging support for the restoration of the French Empire on its 1939 borders. Washington officials authorized Murphy to tell Mast that the full restoration of France, "in all her independence, in all her grandeur, and in all the areas which she possessed before the war, in Europe as well as overseas, is one of the war aims of the United Nations."[17] The Atlantic Charter and Franklin Roosevelt's high-minded anti-imperialism would have to wait. The United States had decided instead to use the restoration of the French Empire as a lure to unite the fissiparous groups in North Africa around their one major point of agreement: the continuance of the French Empire.

The American planners gambling on TORCH saw few viable alternatives because the confusing and ever-shifting political realities of Vichy France and North Africa offered no easy answers. The French people remained, in the abnormally playful description of the War Department, "Vichy Vashy," or content to wait and see what happened next. De Gaulle, the department believed, had too little support among the French armed forces to become an effective ally, Weygand had snubbed American requests for help, and Giraud was too stubborn and demanding.[18] Murphy later complained bitterly that "the ideal Frenchman, which our critics see from the heights of their ivory towers, we did not find. . . . Our critics are interested primarily in an ideological return to the France which they see in their memory and not in the military operation."[19] So much for the Lafayette tradition.

Their tepid support for Giraud notwithstanding, the Americans knew that they still had to find a way to deal with or isolate Admiral Jean-François Darlan. He had, in one Office of Strategic Services (OSS) assessment, become one of the most powerful people in Europe. "Never in French history," it concluded, "had a man who was not actually chief of state [had] so much power."[20] He had unlimited control over the French navy, had solidified his links to the Germans through his negotiations over the Paris Protocols, and had close allies in command of garrisons throughout North Africa, having replaced "those whose loyalty or sentiments are considered doubtful."[21] A single word from him could change the course of the war.

But no one in Washington or London trusted Darlan in the least. The British saw him as a collaborator through and through who genuinely wanted a German victory in the war, in large part to reduce the power of the British Empire he so despised. The OSS saw him as guided solely by "his ambition and his desire to be first everywhere." They wanted him arrested, not wooed over to the Allied side.[22] He rated only behind Laval in the amount of disgust Americans and Britons felt toward him. One American officer colorfully described him as "a short, bald-headed, pink-faced, needle-nosed, sharp-chinned little weasel," hardly an endorsement for seeing him as a potential American ally.[23] OSS spy and Arabic speaker William Eddy hated the idea of reaching out to Darlan, a notion that he compared to the extremely distasteful American alliance with Joseph Stalin. Roosevelt, Eddy thought, could sometimes be too quick to look for friends and too hesitant about dealing harshly with America's enemies. Eddy wrote to a fellow spy based in Gibraltar that he himself "would never have been realistic enough . . . to do it this way, so I am glad I do not act on the higher levels."[24]

The time the Americans had spent building relationships with Henri-Philippe Pétain and Weygand had been wasted, as neither now sat in a position to do much to help the Allies, even if they had been so inclined. Pétain, back in Vichy, remained committed to neutrality and the defense of the French Empire against all parties. He also had to worry about possible German responses if Vichy officials in North Africa aided the Allies. Weygand, now out of power, could do nothing at all. The alternatives seemed little better. The Americans had yet to come around to the British position that de Gaulle should be their main French ally. An OSS report noted that he had more "dignity" than the other French leaders, but it also argued that he was "not fitted for the part."[25]

American officials continued to deny de Gaulle any claim to political leadership in postwar France, even though Winston Churchill had begun to refer to him as "the head of a friendly state."[26] Officially, the Americans held to the position that de Gaulle could claim no such title; to them, he was nothing more than a recently promoted brigadier general whose assertions of political authority seemed more akin to delusions of grandeur than anything backed up by a legal title to the French government in exile. The Americans also worried about the links de Gaulle had established with the French socialist and communist groups that held the real levers of power in the Resistance inside occupied France, especially in the cities. He had developed an especially close working relationship with key figures on the left like Jean Moulin, a socialist destined to become one of the French Resistance's great heroes and martyrs.

The American military remained committed to Roosevelt's often-repeated sentiment that, as the OSS wrote, "no government created out-side of France without the consent of the French people can claim to be the successor to the Third Republic."[27] Some American analysts argued that because Vichy had had no right to end the Third Republic, it, not Vichy or de Gaulle, remained the legitimate government of France. Senior American officials thus hoped to limit their interactions with de Gaulle or Giraud to their role as military commanders only and sort out the complexities of the politics later. As the American official history of the campaign noted, "the Allies had no political course in mind other than to win campaigns in the field while allowing the French to work out their own internal prob-lems, unhampered and unaided."[28] This view was both politically naive and strategically misguided. For many French, the political problems of gov-erning North Africa and its relationship to the rest of France were as fun-damental as driving the Axis forces out of Tunisia. Their political divisions reflected more than personality issues; they represented differing views of how the French political system should emerge from the war. Eisenhower even counted on that division inside North Africa, writing that the French "might be so badly divided by internal dissension and by Allied political maneuvering that effective resistance will be negligible."[29]

Nor did the Allies yet have a complete understanding of those political divisions, despite the work of Murphy, the OSS, and the SOE, which Eisen-hower praised but still described as "exploratory."[30] In fairness, American agents could count airplanes much more easily than they could assess the inner workings of French politics or predict how individual French leaders might respond when the shooting actually began. Some optimistic anal-yses done by American intelligence concluded that Vichy attitudes toward the Allies in late 1942 were "much more favorable than a year before" and that the French air force and coastal artillery gunners had largely pro-American sentiments, although at the same time they remained mostly anti-British. They might therefore refuse to fire on a large American landing force, and they might support a plan to arrest key pro-German and pro-Vichy officers if given sufficient encouragement and resources. As to the Moroccans and Algerians, American and British intelligence officers argued before the landings that they were "extremely uninterested" in the outcome and would therefore most likely support whoever appeared to have the upper hand.[31] Eisenhower continued to hope that the French would see the value of working with him; his deputy Mark Clark became increasingly infuriated at all of the French officers.

Final orders from the chiefs of staff to their field commanders offered some cause for optimism, directing that Allied forces should not fire on Vichy positions unless the French "take definite hostile action against us." But if shooting began, Allied military assaults on French positions "should be opened with maximum intensity and continue with utmost vigor until active resistance has ceased." That resistance, they hoped, would not last long, both because of ammunition shortages on the Vichy side and the expectation that some French political leader would emerge who could arrange a ceasefire. The orders directed Allied commanders to try to spare facilities like ports, oil storage tanks, and transportation infrastructure so that Allied forces could themselves use them to support future operations. Any plane or ship heading toward the landing areas, Allied ships, or Gibraltar, however, should be treated as hostile.[32] Two coded phrases went out to every American unit. "Batter up" meant the French were resisting; "Play ball" meant that American units had authorization to shoot back.[33]

JUST TWO HOURS BEFORE THE LANDINGS, the BBC broadcast four not terribly creative code words, "Allô, Robert. Franklin arrive." As soon as "Robert" Murphy heard the words, he sent out instructions to the Five for resistance leaders to seize police headquarters, arrest key Vichy leaders (thus leaving Mast as the senior French official on the scene until Giraud arrived), hold key transportation nodes, and capture power plants and telephone exchanges. But the group had had too little time to plan and far too little advanced notice to do any proper organization.[34] Moreover, Murphy only reached out to Mast and his pro-Giraud network. Treating de Gaulle and his network "with ill-disguised contempt" meant that his network, including about 300 dedicated Algerian Jews, played no role.[35] As a result, the sabotage portion of the plan did not live up to expectations.[36]

For their part, Vichy military units had remained complacent because their leaders had guessed wrong about American intentions and capabilities. Just weeks before the landings, French intelligence had assessed that whereas in 1917–1918 the United States had used 480 ships to move one million men across the Atlantic, in 1942 the Americans would need 1,130

ships to repeat the feat because of the large number of vehicles and supplies their forces now required. In the last war, the United States had focused on shipping manpower almost exclusively because the French had
agreed to outfit American units with most of the vehicles, heavy weapons,
and other supplies that a modern army needed. This time, of course, the
Americans could rely on no such generosity from France. Moreover, given
the French assumption that at least half of American ships would go to
the Pacific, the United States would need a minimum of 2,260 ships plus
whatever it decided to retain in the western hemisphere for training and
home defense. No one in Vichy thought the Americans could muster even
a fraction of that number.[37] French and German officers also likely put too
much faith in the wildly overinflated reports coming out of Berlin on the
number of Allied ships sunk by U-boats in the Battle of the Atlantic.[38]
Little wonder, then, that French commanders like Charles Noguès in Casablanca had dismissed the possibility of the Allies building a force anywhere
near as large as the one then coming at them in waves.[39]

Vichy officials further convinced themselves that Admiral William
Leahy, "the president's military brain," understood from his time in Vichy
the futility of opening a premature second front in Europe or North Africa. Better, he and other Americans would surely argue, to let the Germans and Russians wear each other down while America bought itself time
to arm. Besides, like all American naval officers, Leahy would share the
common view that Japan posed the greater threat to the United States and
that therefore the vast majority of American assets must go to the Pacific.
"The watchword [mot d'ordre] of all American officers has not changed: we
must destroy the Japanese," the Vichy embassy in Washington reported just
two weeks before TORCH began. Leahy, the French therefore assumed,
would have the wisdom and the authority to halt any British plans for operations against France. Instead, he would urge reinforcing recent American successes in the Solomon Islands, halfway around the world from
North Africa. Under Leahy, they assumed, the Americans would wrest control of Allied grand strategy from amateurs like Churchill and keep the
focus in the Pacific where the American people screamed for revenge, not
in the Atlantic theater, which did not pose an immediate harm to core
American interests.[40]

Clearly, they had guessed wrong, not just about the potential size of an
invasion force but also on the importance of North Africa and Vichy to

American grand strategy. The Americans and British needed North Africa in order to "complete [the] annihilation of Axis forces opposing the British forces in the Western Desert," with or without French help.[41] They did not see North Africa as a sideshow or diversion but the start of a new theater that the Allies expected would produce decisive effects on the war. If the French wanted to help defeat the Germans, the Americans would arm them and leave them in full control of domestic policy. If, by contrast, the French decided to resist, they would have to take their chances not only on the battlefield but also in the peace conference to come after the war.

THREE ANGLO-AMERICAN TASK FORCES LANDED amid great confusion on the North African coast on November 8, 1942. Despite the intelligence that Donovan, Murphy, and Clark provided, Eisenhower noted in his report on the campaign that "the actual state of French sentiment in North Africa did not even remotely agree with some of our prior calculations." The French officer corps, still enthralled with "the magic name" of Pétain, had no idea how to respond to the extremely unusual circumstance of an unexpected and at least temporarily hostile landing by potential liberators. Having never lived directly under the Nazi yoke, Eisenhower thought that the Europeans living in North Africa had experienced no "spur to hatred of the Boches." Instead, they had lived for two years under Vichy's anti-American and anti-British propaganda. Thus, many of them did not immediately see the Anglo-American forces as friendly.[42]

Hoping for the best, the Allies had prepared neither an air bombardment nor offshore naval gunfire before the landings, although both airplanes and warships stood ready if commanders called for them. Instead, the Americans wanted to reach out quickly to French leaders and convince them to order French forces not to open fire. Murphy's agents knew that French forces had only gone on alert in Oran, so if the Allies could get to the right people in time, then all might go well without bloodshed.[43]

Once the shooting started, however, chaos reigned on the beaches of Morocco and Algeria, now turned into a major battlefield. Vichy commanders, confused and obligated to defend themselves and their men, initially ordered their forces to resist the landings. The commander of the garrison at the southernmost end of the operation, the normally quiet port of Safi on Morocco's Atlantic side, at first identified the ships off his coast as fishing boats coming back from sea. Once definitively identified as warships, he could not figure out whose navy they could possibly belong to or what they were doing near Safi of all places. Not until he heard the accents of the soldiers several hours later did he know that he faced Americans. By 10:15 a.m. on the first day, those Americans already had control of the port and effective control of the rest of the town, making his decision to cooperate with them easy.[44] In Casablanca, Noguès read the operation at first as nothing more than a small-scale raid. He assumed that German control of the Atlantic Ocean would have prevented the Americans from doing anything larger.[45] Unlike the commander at Safi, Noguès, confident in his ability to resist a raid, ordered his men to open fire. Soon, the coded call "Play ball" went out to American units, authorizing them to treat the French around Casablanca as hostile. There seemed no end to the confusion. Famed war correspondent Ernie Pyle arrived in Oran with American forces to find one French unit "firing with a machine gun at wounded Americans, while other Frenchmen in rowboats were facing the bullets trying to rescue the Americans."[46] It was, in many ways, the strangest battlefield the Americans fought on in the entire war.

Nor did America's French allies do much to clear up the confusion. To Eisenhower's fury, de Gaulle and Giraud refused to cooperate with each other or with him. Each had built up his own network of spies and political allies, Giraud's mostly among conservatives and royalists and de Gaulle's all over the political map. The Americans, to de Gaulle's frustration, had put all their bets on Giraud. De Gaulle noted that "the Americans grabbed Giraud with the idea that the announcement of his name would bring down the walls of Jericho."[47] They had, just as de Gaulle had predicted, badly overestimated both Giraud's influence and his political acumen. De Gaulle did not expect Giraud to last for long under such circumstances. Once the Americans abandoned him, France would need a stronger and more capable leader to pick up the pieces from the debacle of Vichy. De Gaulle had convinced himself that only he could perform that role.

For his part, Giraud, not entirely without reason, was furious that the Americans had misled him as to both the target and the start date of the operation. He had wanted more time to plan simultaneous operations inside France itself that the Americans and British thought premature and

An American tank moves through Casablanca after the TORCH landings. American planners had no desire to occupy or govern French North Africa. They wanted a reliable French ally to do the job for them.

far too risky. He also hated the idea of serving under Eisenhower, especially on French soil. He had expected the more junior Eisenhower to limit himself to "control of base and administrative functions near the ports and tak[ing] care of the arrival of Allied reinforcements." He had also expected to shift the direction of attack after the liberation of Morocco and Algeria to Corsica, then to mainland France. Instead, the Americans and British had set their eyes on Tunisia where the Anglo-American advances from the west would pin the Axis against the British drive out of Egypt following the massive victory at El Alamein occurring at roughly the same time as the TORCH landings. "Where is a better place to kill Germans?" Churchill asked Eisenhower in reference to Tunisia.[48]

For the drive on Tunisia to succeed, the Allies needed a Frenchman who could secure Morocco and Algeria after they had moved east. The Americans and British had begun to lose faith in America's erstwhile "man of the future." Giraud had proven not to be the grateful, willing ally they had envisioned. As William Langer noted, Giraud "flatly refused to participate in the operation in any other capacity than that of Supreme Allied Commander," a role the Americans could never give him.[49] In the end, he refused even to go to Algeria to rally the French forces there in person or to broadcast a radio message of support because of his anger with the planning process and the diminution of his role in an operation taking place on French soil. A livid Charles Mast told Clark that if the Americans had given him four days' notice (instead of two hours) and kept the British out of the operation, he could have assured the Allies that there would have been no resistance. Instead, men on both sides were dying on the beaches of Morocco and Algeria to no purpose.[50] The mutual finger-pointing did not make it any easier to find a solution.

De Gaulle, still in London, learned of the landings not through proper channels but from a sympathetic member of the British cabinet. He first reacted with an ungracious "Very well. I hope that the Vichyites throw them back into the sea." When he learned of the comment, Chief of the Imperial General Staff General Sir Alan Brooke sternly reproached de Gaulle by telling him, "I understand your bitterness; now overcome it." De Gaulle, to his credit, did overcome it, giving a stirring radio address calling on Frenchmen everywhere to "rise up. Help the Allies. Join them without reserve. Fighting France demands it of you. Do not worry about names or formulas."[51]

IF AMERICA'S CLOSEST FRENCH ALLIES would offer little help, perhaps one of Vichy's leaders might fill the void. Once he realized that neither de Gaulle nor Giraud would come to North Africa, Robert Murphy went to find Alphonse Juin, a hero of the last war and now the French ground forces commander in Algeria. Murphy had already identified him as one of the Vichy senior officers most likely to welcome the Americans. Juin would in fact soon declare his allegiance to de Gaulle and lead Free French forces with distinction for the remainder of the war, but in 1942, he was motivated mostly by the fear that the Arabs and Berbers might take advantage of the chaos to attempt an uprising as had happened in Iraq against the British the year before. He vehemently opposed any diminution of French power in North Africa.[52] Juin therefore calculated that France might need

American help to ensure that the transition of power did not adversely affect long-term national interests in North Africa. Murphy found a "startled and shocked" Juin a virtual prisoner at his headquarters in the Villa des Oliviers; the young men of the Chantiers de la Jeunesse had the villa surrounded and had cut the telephone lines.[53]

Meanwhile, the fighting on the beaches had begun to tilt in favor of the Allies. Their matériel superiority overwhelmed the ill-equipped and confused French forces. No one wanted the fighting to continue, but only Juin had the power to stop it. Murphy tried to impress upon him the seriousness of the situation and the need for decisive action from French leaders. He wildly exaggerated the size of the attacking force, boasting that the final contingents of a 500,000-man American and British force would soon land in North Africa and that the French could not possibly hope to stop a force that large.[54] The French, Murphy insisted, should order a cease-fire and work with the Americans rather than risk destruction at their hands in a war no one wanted.

Much as he might have wanted to work out a deal, however, Juin told Murphy that he could do nothing because he was no longer the senior ranking French officer in Algeria. By sheer coincidence, Admiral Darlan had arrived in Algiers to visit his son, Alain, suffering from polio in a local hospital. Although his initial itinerary had him returning to Vichy before the landings, Darlan decided to stay on at a friend's house in Algiers to spend more time with his son. Juin therefore saw no point in issuing orders that Darlan could quickly countermand.

The Americans found themselves in the totally unexpected situation of having Darlan in Algeria but neither Giraud nor de Gaulle. Murphy decided to take a chance and ask Juin to call Darlan, notwithstanding the disgust that most American and British officials felt toward him. Negotiating with a man as widely despised as Darlan might well cost Murphy his career, but it might also save the lives of thousands of Americans, Britons, and Frenchmen. Awakened by the call and not yet sure of the situation on the beaches, Darlan agreed to come to Juin's villa.

At first, a furious Darlan seemed to justify all the disgust and disdain American and British officials felt toward him. His face "purple" with anger, Darlan yelled at Murphy, "I have known for a long time that the British are stupid, but I have always believed Americans were more intelligent. Apparently, you have the same genius as the British for making massive blunders."[55] In another outburst, he yelled, "It is another one of these filthy tricks you Anglo-Saxons have abused us with for two years. I have orders from the Marshal! I will execute them! Since you want to pick a fight, we will fight."[56] In Darlan's eyes, the Allies had provocatively attacked a neutral country and had begun needlessly killing French military personnel on French soil. Under such circumstances, Darlan believed that the French had every right to defend themselves.

In an attempt to change Darlan's mind and get two French leaders to share power, Murphy told him of the arrangements with Giraud, who, Murphy said, would soon arrive in North Africa with full American backing. Darlan dismissed the whole basis of American strategy for North Africa, saying, "Giraud is not your man. Politically he is a child. He is just a good divisional commander. Nothing more."[57] Darlan warned Murphy that Vichy officers saw both Giraud and de Gaulle not as heroes but as traitors. "The Americans," he said, "must understand that they can have Giraud without the army or the army without Giraud."[58] Darlan's politics and loyalties might have conflicted with those of the United States, but as Murphy quickly recognized, he understood the situation better than anyone. He was, moreover, the only man who could stop the killing.

Juin recognized that with the landings succeeding, Vichy's time in North Africa would soon come to an end. In his eyes, the Americans represented not an invading force but France's best chance to maintain imperial control after the war. He tried to calm Darlan down, telling him of the scale of the Anglo-American landings, warning him of France's limited stocks of ammunition, and assuring him that the Americans did not intend to interfere with postwar French governance of Morocco and Algeria. He also informed his boss that French forces on the beaches had little interest in fighting the Americans, whom they tended to see as liberators. Juin issued creative orders for "an elastic but not aggressive" posture. This ambiguous guidance, he hoped, would allow local commanders to protect the lives of the men under their command without unduly antagonizing the Americans and British and thereby risk more pointless killing.[59] However, those orders could not protect French soldiers for long. Darlan would have to make a final political decision as the battle raged.

Despite his fury, Darlan could see how radically and fundamentally the situation was changing in the Allies' favor with each passing hour. The size of the landing force, if well below the 500,000 men that Murphy claimed, still made it clear that the Allies had something exponentially larger in mind than a raid on the model of Dieppe. He must also have understood that if he did not cooperate with the Americans and the British, they would find someone else, like Giraud, who would. Murphy managed to sneak a message to the Allied command begging them to get troops and a senior military commander into Algiers as quickly as possible. More Allied troops in and around the city might force Darlan to cooperate. "Situation well in hand," the note read, "but unwise to let this endure too long."[60]

In Darlan's mind, everything hinged on the Germans. If they responded to TORCH by crossing the demarcation line between occupied and unoccupied France, then they would carry the legal burden of violating the armistice, thus absolving France of the need to abide by its terms. French leaders could then act as they wished, although the consequences for both occupied and unoccupied France would undoubtedly be severe. Darlan sent a message to Pétain asking for guidance and any definitive evidence of German intentions before deciding on his next moves. Police soon arrived at the villa, pushing aside the adolescent Chantiers de la Jeunesse and temporarily detaining Murphy in the process. Elsewhere in Algiers, forces loyal to Darlan released from jail the officers that Mast's resistance groups had arrested. The tension mounted as the shooting continued and as tired men made life-or-death decisions. To American vice-consul Kenneth Pendar, the whole scene had an opéra bouffe quality to it, with various men arriving in an odd assortment of military uniforms and civilian clothes, all waving guns around and everyone threatening to arrest everyone else.[61]

WHILE THE STRANGE OPERA PLAYED ITSELF OUT, everything remained chaotic on the landing beaches. Vichy newspapers had spread anti-American propaganda, and news of British landings in the Algiers area would surely increase the determination of the defenders to fight. Major General George Patton, spoiling for a fight as commander of the Western Task Force, threatened to destroy the city of Casablanca with American naval guns. Some French commanders ordered armed resistance against the Americans whereas others hesitated, looking for ways to honor the letter of their orders to defend French soil while at the same time minimizing casualties on both sides. Still others actively assisted the Americans. Off the coast of

The modern French battleship *Jean Bart* after its destruction by American planes. Several days of combat between the Allies and Vichy forces cost both sides unneeded casualties and led to a search for a quick political solution.

Casablanca, the powerful French battleship *Jean Bart* offered stiff resistance until severely damaged by American warships, repaired with unexpected speed by French crews, then finally destroyed by American airplanes. At the major air base at Marrakech, by contrast, French commanders delayed implementing their orders as long as possible, thereby helping the Americans by denying Vichy forces on the coast reinforcements and air cover.[62] Similarly, Charles Mast showed up at the key fort of Sidi Ferruch near Algiers and ordered its commanders to hand it over to the Americans without violence.[63]

Throughout North Africa, French commanders began to choose sides. In Morocco, General Émile Béthouart, convinced that the Allies and Giraud offered the best chance of France retaining power in North Africa, supported the Allies. His superior officer in Casablanca, the anti-democratic and widely loathed General Charles Noguès, did not. He directed counteroffensives and ordered a crackdown on suspected anti-Vichy officers and resistance agents.[64] Laval's ally, the pro-German Admiral François Félix "Fritz" Michelier, furious at the "senseless and distressing bloodshed" among his men, refused all offers to talk to the Americans.[65] Orders flew back and forth from seemingly every direction. One French commander based in Tunisia wrote in his diary, "November 9 we fight the Germans. November 10, we fight nobody. November 10 (noon), we fight the Germans. November 11 (night), we fight nobody."[66] The confusion made it seem all the more imperative that the Americans cut a deal with someone who could put an end to the killing before it spiraled further out of control, even if that man was the detestable Darlan.

As American and British forces continued to make good progress and as men continued to die for no obvious purpose, Juin advised Darlan to open formal cease-fire negotiations with the Americans, now represented by Major General Charles Ryder, commander of the Eastern Task Force that landed near Algiers. Darlan, however, hesitated. He had orders from Laval to fight on and the Germans had not yet crossed the demarcation line. He did, however, cancel orders for a counterattack on Allied positions in the Algiers suburbs.[67] Pétain did not issue any orders to Darlan, but he did broadcast an angry message to Roosevelt that also aimed to stiffen Darlan's spine. It read: "You knew that we would defend the empire against any aggressor. . . . You knew that I would keep my word. We have been attacked, and we shall defend ourselves."[68] Laval responded by granting the Germans full use of Vichy airfields in Tunisia and ordered Darlan not to negotiate with the Americans, with whom Vichy would soon break diplomatic relations. Laval seemed ready to risk war rather than appear weak in the eyes of the Germans.

Darlan, growing increasingly aware of his impossible position, ignored Laval, a man whom, in any case, he despised. He began a series of tense meetings with Mark Clark on November 10. Murphy attended as well, partly to translate and partly to keep Clark calm. An angry and bombastic Clark, his men being shot at on the beaches, arrived in no mood for negotiations. He wanted nothing less than an end to the fighting in Morocco and Algeria so the Americans and British could push on to Tunisia as quickly as possible. For his part, Darlan still had an incomplete picture of the situation and still awaited word from Pétain. He also made it clear to Clark that he wanted no part of any arrangement that forced him to acknowledge the authority of Giraud, Mast, or de Gaulle.

According to the American official history's reconstruction of the conversation, Clark spoke in a "forthright and compelling" tone, although one imagines other, more colorful adjectives that would better describe the mood in the Villa des Oliviers. Clark told Darlan that he would not accept any further delay from the French. If Darlan did not agree to an immediate cease-fire without conditions, Clark warned, he would have Darlan arrested and order American forces to push their way through what remained of French defenses.[69] When Darlan mentioned the need to await instructions from Pétain, Clark shouted at him, "Pétain is nothing in our young lives. He has today broken relations with the United States and declared this landing as an act hostile to France. He has ordered resistance. As far as we are concerned, we don't recognize any authority of Pétain in North Africa." Clark wanted Darlan to take decisive action, but Darlan still wanted to wait until he knew for sure either that Pétain agreed or that the Germans had broken the terms of the armistice. Back in Washington, George Marshall complained to Eisenhower in an uncharacteristically blunt cable, "If these stupid French would only realize what side their bread is buttered on, what a chance they now have to execute a master stroke. They seem completely inept. . . . [They] have been too browbeaten and become too fearful to make quick and far-reaching decisions."[70]

Darlan knew that he could not resist Clark's demands for long or Clark would indeed arrest him and put Giraud in his place. Most of the fighting in Algeria had ended with American and British forces in control almost everywhere they went. Only in isolated pockets of Morocco did French units still offer effective resistance.[71] Darlan therefore ordered a cease-fire on the evening of November 10 that took effect the next morning (symbolically on November 11, the date of the 1918 armistice) at 7:00 a.m. He also ordered the French fleet in Toulon to sail to North Africa. Laval quickly learned of both orders, demanded that Darlan rescind them, and threatened to replace him with Noguès if he did not. When Clark found out, he repeated his own threat to arrest Darlan. Giraud, meanwhile, had finally agreed to leave Gibraltar but continued to refuse to meet face-to-face with American officials. Little wonder, then, that one of Eisenhower's close aides bemoaned what he called "that almost morbid sense of honor which had led the French initially to resist their deliverers, while leaving the back door open to their enemies."[72] A frustrated Eisenhower publicly praised Darlan for stopping the bloodshed in Morocco. In private, however, he was more direct, complaining that "all of these Frogs have a single thought—'ME.'"[73]

NEWS THAT THE GERMANS HAD in fact crossed the demarcation line clarified matters, at least as seen from Algeria. Darlan could now justify working with the Allies by arguing that Pétain had become a German prisoner whose orders he need not obey. The Vichy state itself, he could further contend, no longer existed in its 1940 form. Therefore, he felt himself released from all obligations to follow its orders. The military situation had also become hopeless for French forces. Patton's threats to level Casablanca with naval gunfire cowed even the hardline Noguès into ordering the city's surrender.

Clark noted "how miserable Darlan looked that day" as everything began to come apart around him.[74] Darlan knew that he had run out of options and would have to work out a deal or face imprisonment and a North Africa governed by Giraud or run directly by the anti-imperial Americans. Clark and Murphy knew that they needed an end to the chaos, and they had lost faith in Giraud as a partner. They therefore thought they needed Darlan. As Murphy later wrote, "The Good Lord knows we needed a military success in 1942," and Darlan could help deliver it.[75] In return for a cease-fire order, Darlan, not Giraud, would become the political leader of French North Africa; Giraud would command military forces only. The Americans promised to supply the new French forces with 30,000 machine guns, 5,000 tanks, 51 million rounds of ammunition, and 1,400 airplanes, enough to outfit eight new divisions. Darlan also reissued orders to the French fleet in Toulon to sail to Algeria, but its defiant commander responded with just one word: *merde*.[76]

Still, the admiral's anti-Darlan sentiment did not mean that he was pro-Vichy or willing to risk letting the ships fall into German or Italian hands. The French fleet scuttled itself rather than risk capture by the Germans. That act was brave and consistent with the pledge the French made in 1940 not to let a foreign power gain control of the French fleet, but it deprived France of more than 230,000 tons of warships including one battleship, two battle cruisers, seven cruisers, and twenty-nine destroyers.[77]

The fighting on the beaches gradually stopped, much to everyone's relief. Even Giraud grudgingly accepted that Darlan's intervention had saved lives and ended the killing faster than anyone else could have, including himself.[78] The North Africa landings succeeded but at a cost of more than 500 American, 570 British, and 1,300 French dead. The ramifications on France were severe. The Germans and Italians occupied the remainder of France, ending what limited autonomy the Vichy state had enjoyed. German forces flooded into Tunisia to fight the Allies, and Laval offered to bring France into the war on the Axis side in exchange for Germany recognizing

France in its 1914 borders (thus sacrificing Alsace and Lorraine) and with an empire "equivalent" to the one France had had in 1939. In practice, this equivalence would mean compensating France for any losses to Italy and Germany with large parts of British imperial territory. The Germans showed little interest in Laval's plan, in large part because a weakened Vichy France had so little to give Germany in return.[79]

French officers in North Africa did not yet respect de Gaulle or Giraud enough to obey their orders, so Darlan's presence in Algiers seemed to appear, in William Langer's words, like "nothing less than a miracle" because only he could offer something beyond a temporary cease-fire. Darlan gave the Americans the opportunity to end the fighting, calm the political situation, and enable Anglo-American forces to move east.[80] Eisenhower would have preferred not to deal with Darlan at all, but he felt that Giraud's refusal to serve in any role but supreme commander had given him little choice. Even while the fighting continued, Giraud complained on arrival in Algeria that no appropriate military honor guard greeted him. Thus, Darlan took on the role variously envisioned for Weygand, Giraud, and de Gaulle. On first hearing the details of Clark's deal with Darlan, a stunned Eisenhower reacted with a spontaneous "Je-e-e-e-e-suss Ch-e-rist! What I need around here is a good assassin."[81]

FEW AMERICANS IN NORTH AFRICA showed much interest in trying to sort out its bewildering social and political structures. Americans in general saw Vichy as "nothing more than a puppet of the Germans," but they also had little sympathy for the Arabs, whom many believed hated the French so much that they harbored pro-German tendencies. The region sat in dire poverty, with desperate shortages of food, fuel, and medical supplies. The French had it bad but not nearly as bad as the Arabs who walked around "in rags because of the poor economy" and were "on very bad terms with the French." The United States, no less than Darlan and Noguès, had no desire to see those Arabs rise up and rebel.[82]

Arab nationalism had grown immensely in the months before the Allied landings, in part as a result of the decline of French prestige. The use of martial law in Morocco and Tunisia since 1939 led to the emergence of nationalist leaders willing to challenge the French. In Tunisia, Sidi Mohamed el Moncref Bey (ruling as Muhammad VII from June 1942) openly questioned the authority of the French minister-resident, the Vichy loyalist Jean-Pierre Estéva. In August, Moncref Bey called for a sixteen-point plan of "Tunisification" that included free elections and the creation of a Tunisian Consultative Council. The situation resembled that in Morocco, where Mohammed ben Youssef (the future Sultan Mohammed V) gave increasing encouragement to a new generation of Moroccan nationalists.[83]

In Algeria, young nationalists like Hocine Aït Ahmed and Ferhat Abbas experienced French humiliation and the triumphant Allied landings as a political "earthquake." America brought with it the ideals of the Atlantic Charter and a generally anti-imperial ideology.[84] As Woodrow Wilson had a generation earlier, the rhetoric of Franklin Roosevelt motivated them to look to the United States as a model of democracy and freedom. Just as under Wilson, however, the huge chasm that separated America's words from its actions would leave them disillusioned and disappointed. The OSS recognized the dilemma. By leaving North Africa in French hands, the Arab intelligentsia felt "let down now that they realize that we are not going to change their status."[85] The problems of Arab nationalism would have to wait. As long as the war continued, Arab desires for political change appeared to American officials as a potentially disruptive force to resist, not a shared anti-imperial ideology to embrace.[86]

Murphy also pushed back against the State Department's call for a much more thorough purging of Vichy officials because "great care was necessary if we were to prevent racial uprisings which would be detrimental to the Allied military campaign." He even objected to restoring the Crémieux law of 1870 that gave Algerian Jews French citizenship; Vichy had abrogated it, taking away French citizenship from tens of thousands of Jews at a stroke.[87] "To infuriate nearly seven million [Muslim] inhabitants in order to favor some 140,000 [Jewish] inhabitants was simply more than Allied Force Headquarters felt capable of tackling while the war against the Nazis was being waged," Murphy reasoned.[88] Justice for Algeria's Jews and Muslims would have to wait while the Americans yielded to Darlan's desires for French control.

American officials shared with Darlan an interest in ensuring that the French could keep the Arab population from disrupting Allied plans. Darlan wanted to maintain French prestige across the empire, and the United States needed secure lines of communication as its forces moved east. The Americans also wanted to avoid having to dedicate an estimated 60,000 soldiers to occupy Morocco and countless thousands more to occupy Algeria.[89] This overlap of interests, plus the clear demonstration of Darlan's influence, led the United States to turn to the man they saw as better able to "control" the Arabs than de Gaulle or Giraud. French historian Christine Lévisse-Touzé argued that the shared desire for a continuation of the French imperial model led to Darlan and his cronies running a repressive imperial government under American aegis, or in her acerbic words, "vichyisme sous protectorat américain."[90]

This shared Franco-American desire to contain Arab nationalism played a much greater role in setting American policy than the more famous disputes with the prickly personalities of de Gaulle and Giraud. However much Roosevelt and other Americans may have spoken of independence and the end of colonialism, they did not want to begin serious discussions about the issue until after the war, if they believed in it at all. Murphy, clearly, did not. Darlan, a staunch conservative with like-minded political allies across French North Africa, offered Americans a much better chance of keeping the region subjugated than either de Gaulle or Giraud.

Clark arranged for Darlan, Giraud, Mast, and Noguès to meet in hopes of working out a comprehensive power-sharing deal. He wanted to solidify the agreement that made Darlan the political leader of French North Africa, with a subdued Giraud as the military commander in chief and Juin as his deputy. Noguès, whose instincts for self-preservation soon turned him reliably pro-American, would remain as commander in Morocco. The meeting, however, did not go well as old animosities and current power struggles emerged. At one point, Darlan shouted at Giraud, "You are nothing here, nothing but a rebel in the train of a foreign army!" Clark considered arresting all of the "yellow bellied sons of bitches" and starting from scratch, but no one knew who could possibly fill in the resulting political void. Clark certainly had no desire for the United States Army to do so.[91]

EISENHOWER ASKED FOR MINIMAL PUBLICITY on the resulting deal out of fear of the response from the British, but he also pledged to Darlan that "the North African Empire will remain French."[92] Darlan would receive the title of high commissioner but with the understanding that the United

States would not recognize him as anything more than the head of a civil administration pending future decisions on the shape of the French government. The title did not matter to Darlan. He had what he wanted and what he thought France needed—namely, himself at the head of a French administration in North Africa. Besides, he knew that the Americans had no long-term plan to stay and neither Giraud nor de Gaulle had their backing as he now did. Eisenhower decided to keep de Gaulle out of North Africa for the time being, in part because of how much he, Giraud, and Darlan all hated one another. As Eisenhower wrote to Sumner Welles, "Sometimes the best way to keep peace in the family is to keep the members of the family apart for a while." Darlan knew that he did not need to keep the family apart for long; once the Americans moved on to Tunisia, he could consolidate his power even further and isolate both de Gaulle and Giraud.[93]

One other Frenchman might have played a role in this unusual drama. After the landings, Pétain sent for Weygand, but instead of offering him the command of forces in North Africa that Weygand had hoped for, he offered the mostly symbolic command of the weak military forces inside unoccupied France. This offer suggests that Pétain knew that Darlan had no intention of returning to Vichy or that Pétain saw the need to keep the pro-American Weygand close at hand. In any case, Weygand had no interest in Pétain's offer of a what amounted at best to a powerless sinecure. On November 12, on his way out of Vichy, SS officers stopped his car and arrested him to prevent his return to Africa. He spent the rest of the war in German jails.[94]

As a result, the Americans found themselves with Darlan as their closest ally in North Africa despite an outcry in the United States when the details of the deals with him became known. Giving power to Darlan proved a step too far even for the hardhearted Henry Stimson, who saw the logic of it but nevertheless called it "one of the most violently controversial decisions of the war."[95] George Marshall hated the idea of working with Darlan, as did Wendell Willkie and Treasury Secretary Henry Morgenthau. The arrangement, they feared, made the United States an active accomplice to Vichy's own fascist behavior. Dorothy Thompson, Walter Lippmann, and other influential journalists criticized the arrangement as setting a terrible precedent for the rest of the war. Edward R. Murrow asked, "Are we at some future time going to occupy Norway and turn it over to [Norwegian collaborator Vidkun] Quisling?"[96] At another point, Murrow wrote, "Are we fighting the Nazis or sleeping with them?"[97]

It seemed to American critics of the Darlan deal that the United States had not so much liberated French North Africa from its Vichy overlords as legitimized and even reinforced a repulsive imperial regime. The *New Yorker*'s A. J. Liebling found in Algeria a European population fearful of a Muslim uprising and grateful for the authoritarianism and racism of Vichy. Of the powerful landowners known as *colons* he wrote, "They had not really collaborated with the Nazis; the Nazis had come along belatedly and collaborated with them" in passing anti-Semitic laws and strengthening the power of conservative Frenchmen like Darlan.[98] Even the American official history noted that the decision to back Darlan "produced an abrupt change in the prevailing optimism" after the success of TORCH.[99] William Bullitt said that dealing with Darlan was "as though Jesus had called upon Judas and said, 'On this rock I found my church.'"[100] Watching it all happen on the ground in Oran, Ernie Pyle could not believe that the Americans allowed fascist societies to continue to meet and pro-Axis functionaries to stay in their jobs. "Our enemies saw it, laughed, and called us soft. Both sides were puzzled by a country at war which still let enemies run loose against it."[101]

Cutting a deal with Vichy officials stunned Americans like Pyle and Liebling, but the basic idea had its roots in preinvasion planning. In mid-October, Army Civil Affairs, with Eisenhower's approval, had decided to "retain the civil governments and their officials and employees in their present positions." The sticking point, apparently, was Darlan at the head. In other words, the Americans had no problem with leaving Vichy officials in charge or with dropping their own high-minded anti-imperial ideals. They had just hoped that Giraud or Weygand would end up in charge, not Darlan.[102]

Americans like George Marshall hoped at least to get Darlan to remove some of Vichy's more reprehensible policies, such as the one that banned Jews from "professions that influence people."[103] According to the deal, however, such issues fell under the category of internal French political matters. They remained in place for months, as did many of the most odious Vichy leaders, including Morocco's reactionary governor-general Charles Noguès, who formed an odd and unseemly friendship with George Patton that helped him consolidate power. Even more than American support,

Darlan believed he needed to ensure the compliance and quiescence of North Africa's Arabs. Keeping the hardline Noguès in his job and anti-Semitic legislation in place seemed to advance those goals. As Darlan predicted, the Americans might not like it, but they would do little to stop him.

Nor did the Darlan deal do America any favors with its allies and potential allies. De Gaulle complained bitterly to an American admiral that "the United States rewards the acts of traitors if it appears profitable, but she will not pay with the honor of France." The war, he argued, was one of ideas as much as weapons. Supporting Vichy leaders like Darlan, he worried, would only make the ideas of the communists more appealing as an alternative in the postwar world.[104] Alexandre Tixier, one of de Gaulle's senior representatives in Washington, said that "Darlan's appearance on the air, speaking from American headquarters, as the government of North Africa, caused the greatest confusion in Free French circles in France. These were men risking their lives to help the Allies; and to find Darlan, who had been killing them wherever possible, suddenly appearing on the air, naturally gave rise to confusion."[105] For the time being, at any rate, de Gaulle had the gist of American policy right: military necessity would justify almost anything, even an alliance with Darlan to reinforce the power of empire.

Churchill, too, was appalled at American willingness to work with someone as loathsome as Darlan because dealing with him and Noguès would make it much harder for the British and Americans to claim the moral high ground in any future political dealings. He gave a closed-door speech to a skeptical House of Commons in December promising that British officials had had nothing to do with any deal with Darlan.[106] A senior official in the British Foreign Office said that "we are fighting for international decency and Darlan is the antithesis of this."[107] British officials told their angry Soviet counterparts that Britain "accepts no responsibility" for the Darlan deal.[108]

The British saw the Darlan deal as a symbol of all that had gone wrong in America's Vichy policy. Alexander Cadogan wrote in his diary that American diplomatic dealings in North Africa "generally take the form of the Vichy French telling the Americans what they want, and the Americans giving it to them with both hands regardless of our interests or feelings."[109] Churchill called Darlan's presence in Algiers at the moment of the Allied landings "an odd and formidable coincidence." Cadogan, who did not believe in coincidences as odd and formidable as this one, suspected an OSS plot with Murphy's fingerprints all over it. "I wouldn't put it past them," he remarked, promising a "God-Almighty showdown" with the Americans if it were true.[110]

NO EVIDENCE EXISTS TO PROVE an American plot to have Darlan in Algiers at just the right moment. A cable to Leahy just before the landings warned that Darlan had unexpectedly arrived in the city and that his presence might prove "embarrassing," but it also noted that Darlan would return to Vichy before the Allied landings began.[111] At that moment, the Americans did not care much more for him than the British did. A photograph taken after the meeting in Algiers on November 13 shows the tensions. Eisenhower and Mark Clark appear in crisp, pressed dress uniforms practically glaring at the photographer and daring him to take the picture. Standing between them is a small and serious-looking Darlan, notably dressed not in his uniform like the other military men but in a three-piece suit and a fedora. His clothes symbolize the end of his long military career and the start of his purely political one as an American-backed high commissioner for North Africa, or as Clark derisively called him, a mere "politico." He seems to shrink from the scene as if looking for a place to hide. The only other figure in the picture is Robert Murphy, standing off to the right and grinning widely with his eyes on Darlan like a proud impresario contemplating his new protégé. The Murphy in the photograph fits the description of Harry Butcher, Eisenhower's naval aide, as being "more like an American businessman canvassing the ins and outs of a prospective merger than either a diplomat or a soldier."[112] Murphy's original plan to merge Mast and Giraud with the American war effort may have failed, but he thought that he had found another way to gain a return on his investment, even if it meant making a deal with Darlan, one of the most despised men in the world. Notably, no British officials appear in the picture.[113]

President Roosevelt tried to hedge his bets by using the word *temporary* five times in his 450-word public statement on the Darlan deal.[114] He also insisted that American officials use words like *announcement* or *statement* rather than *protocol* or *agreement*.[115] The emergence of Darlan as a key ally struck most Americans, even someone as supportive of the government's Vichy policy as William Langer, as "certainly an uninspiring prelude to the

Admiral Darlan in his new role as a "politico," standing with Dwight Eisenhower, Mark Clark, and a grinning Robert Murphy. British leaders were appalled at American dealings with Darlan. One senior British official wanted to "push [Darlan] down a well" rather than work with him.

great crusade of freedom." The American-backed regime in North Africa seemed like the same malodorous Vichy water, sold in the same uninspiring bottles. Darlan even claimed to rule by the authority of Vichy, whose legitimacy he still did not doubt. De Gaulle, Giraud, and the British could hardly believe their eyes as the Americans helped Darlan build his new regime on Vichy's morally bankrupt foundation. He jailed Vichy opponents and allowed pro-Vichy paramilitaries to continue their intimidation of their domestic opponents, which included French Resistance cells in Algeria. He even spoke of his role as maintaining the mantle of Pétain's leadership until the marshal could resume full power in his own name. "If Admiral Darlan had to shoot Marshal Pétain," Winston Churchill wryly observed, "he would no doubt do it in Marshal Pétain's name."[116]

The OSS noted that "except for a small pro-Vichy element" in the navy, America's retention of notorious collaborators like Darlan and Noguès had damaged the reputation of the United States in metropolitan France as well. The OSS called the Darlan deal "withering" to the morale of the French

Resistance with which it had begun to work ever more closely. The Soviets also complained, calling American policy part of a "consistent effort to reach an understanding with reactionary clerical groups in Western Europe." World opinion on the matter, the OSS noted, created "an impression harmful to American prestige and difficult to correct." It noted that "the moral principles of the United Nations cannot find expression in immoral actions."[117]

THE AMERICANS' OWN SELF-IMAGE REQUIRED a vision of themselves as liberators, not occupiers or colonizers or even enablers of colonizers. They knew nothing at all about the people they were liberating, however. One OSS report spoke of the native Arabs and Berbers as noble savages, comparing them to "Indians on reservations." On the one hand, they were kind and simple, easily mollified with smiles and gifts from GIs such as "cigarettes, candy, chewing gum, and clothes." Most army units, the report paternalistically noted, "have adopted Arab [boys as] mascots" and won the hearts of the locals by giving away their extra rations. If given a voice, most Americans assumed, the locals would much prefer to live under American rule.[118] On the other hand, if not handled correctly, the Muslims in French North Africa might rebel and spark a "Holy War with the Islamic tribes" that no one wanted.[119]

For their part, the French wanted to keep American officials as far from the internal affairs of North Africa as possible. They pleaded with the Americans to leave North Africa in their hands, and the Americans largely agreed despite their assumption that the locals would live better lives under temporary American rule. "We have neither the personnel nor the local knowledge to police Morocco," read the most important OSS study of the problem. A report from Murphy to Eisenhower argued that "abrupt and radical changes . . . would bring about consequences that would be serious." The United States, he wrote, would "find it utterly impossible to cope with the Arab situation" should something go wrong. Better to leave North Africa in French hands.[120]

Although this news should have brought him joy, a despondent Darlan described himself to Clark as a lemon. Once the Americans had squeezed the juices dry, they would throw the lemon away and find another more to their liking.[121] Consequently, in exchange for the Americans leaving North African affairs almost exclusively in his hands, he proved as pliable for the Americans as he had for the Germans. His almost obsequious behavior disgusted some and pleased others. As the British minister-resident in Algeria, the future prime minister Harold Macmillan, said with thinly veiled revulsion, "Once bought, he stayed bought."[122] In maybe the worst baseball metaphor in all of military history, Mark Clark said, "Once we got him into the box for our side, he pitched big-league ball."[123]

American officials worried about how to balance the military help they got from Darlan with what one of them characterized as "a sordid nullification of the principles for which the United Nations were supposed to be fighting."[124] Still, given the problems they had with Giraud and de Gaulle, they held their noses and let Darlan become an American-backed dictator. H. Freeman Matthews thought Darlan belonged in jail, but he also thought that without him, the United States would have lost thousands of lives securing Dakar, Morocco, and Algeria because only Darlan could have spoken with any legitimate claim to Pétain's authority.

Clark and Eisenhower initially spoke of the Darlan deal as an emergency measure only. As Eisenhower explained it, "Giraud quickly gave up on trying to help us and it was only through Darlan's help that we are fighting the Boche in Tunisia instead of somewhere in the vicinity of Bône [today's Annaba, Algeria] or even west of that." The Americans saw no reason for the Darlan deal to require them to jettison Giraud as long as the former allowed the latter to have an important place in the new government. In a clear swipe at de Gaulle, "the thorn in our flesh," Matthews wrote that Giraud had "more real character and integrity than any other Frenchman either in North Africa or *London, repeat, London.*"[125]

To the British, however, the Darlan deal looked like another American mistake or maybe evidence of a plot to shut them out of a voice in determining the shape of postwar France and its empire. Churchill proved sensitive on this topic, as the future of the French Empire undoubtedly mattered more to British interests than American ones. He reflected the view of many British officials that the Americans had wanted Darlan all along once they finally grew disenchanted with the "most sweeping demands for plenary authority" that Giraud tried to force on the Allies. Churchill guessed that Roosevelt's promise of treating Darlan as a "temporary expedient justifiable solely by the stress of battle" would prove tough to keep.

Noting that events had moved "at a gallop" in North Africa, Churchill said, "There is no doubt that if you ask for a man's help and he gives it in a manner that is most valuable to you, on the faith of an agreement entered into amid dangers which are thereby relieved, you have contracted a certain obligation towards him."[126]

By the end of November, Darlan's "most cooperative attitude" did not change British minds, but it did silence some of his American critics, mostly those in Algeria itself.[127] Darlan ordered French officers in Dakar to cooperate fully with the Americans, arranged for the Allies to purchase North African raw materials, and loaned the Allies French merchant shipping. Eisenhower told George Marshall of his satisfaction with the arrangement and that he did not want anything to "lead Darlan and his colleagues to relax their efforts at this very critical stage."[128] Lord Halifax and Anthony Eden complained that the Americans in North Africa had gone far beyond the "temporary and local" deal with Darlan that Roosevelt had sold them, but they knew they had little power to interfere.[129]

Some American officials, mostly those back in Washington, did at least dream of finding ways to get rid of Darlan. Roosevelt told Eisenhower that he need not keep him in power "any longer than is absolutely necessary" and later told him that one is "permitted in time of great danger to walk with the devil until you have crossed the bridge."[130] The OSS thought that Darlan might accept a bribe to step down. Others proposed sending the entire Darlan family to Warm Springs, Georgia, where Alain Darlan could receive the same level of care for polio that Roosevelt himself received.[131] Darlan, however, refused to consider any plan that might leave de Gaulle in charge of French North Africa. The last few meetings between the Americans and Darlan in December had been cordial and productive. Darlan had not given any indication that he planned to leave office. Instead, he seemed more entrenched in his "temporary" job than ever. Little did anyone know, however, that the assassin Eisenhower had once so desperately wanted had his own ideas.

7

ROUND UP THE USUAL SUSPECTS

Assassination in Algiers

CHRISTMAS EVE, 1942, at roughly 3:30 p.m. High Commissioner Jean-François Darlan strolled confidently into his new headquarters in the elegant Moorish-style Summer Palace located in the hills south of Algiers. The Anglo-American liberation of French North Africa, the German takeover of the remainder of metropolitan France, and the start of a new Allied front in Tunisia had radically upset the existing order, but life in the Algerian capital had begun to settle down after the chaos of the previous six weeks. In this new environment, Darlan, now the unquestioned ruler of Morocco and Algeria, had an opportunity to secure the mainte- nance of French power in the region well into the foreseeable future. By making a deal with the Americans, he had preserved French sovereignty and, perhaps more importantly for Darlan, allowed him to shut out his hated rivals, Generals Henri Giraud and Charles de Gaulle, from a share of political power.

Fortuitously for Darlan, the Americans and the British quickly shifted their focus toward Tunisia. They had begun a "Run to Tunis," a lightning strike intended to capture the city and the nearby port of Bizerte before the Germans could reinforce it or use it to bring more Axis troops into the African theater. In a major operation supported by Free French soldiers commanded by Giraud, the Allies tried to drive a wedge between the Axis defenders, hopefully forcing one enemy column toward Tunis along the southern road and the other to Bizerte along the northern road. If they could complete that achievement, then the Allies could trap 15,500 Germans and 9,000 Italians, thus producing a quick and successful end to operations in North Africa.[1] The first attempt in late November, however, failed as Axis forces held their ground. By Christmas Eve, with the weather deteriorating and supplies running low, the Allies found themselves stuck; the Run to Tunis had failed and the Allies would have to plan for a North African campaign in 1943.[2] For Darlan, the stalemate in Tunisia meant that the Americans and British would likely remain preoccupied for many months to come. For the foreseeable future, he would have a free hand to solidify French control over Morocco and Algeria and ensure the continuance of the empire independent of British or American interference.

He never got the chance. Waiting for him upstairs in the Summer Palace was a twenty-two-year-old French royalist named Fernand Bonnier de la Chapelle who had used a set of forged identity papers given to him by a local priest to gain admission to the palace. Another resistance member had arranged for an office near Darlan's to be unlocked and empty for the day. Bonnier had in his pocket a pistol belonging to an Algerian-born Jew from a prominent local family named Mario Faivre, who had helped to arrange the clandestine beach house meeting for Mark Clark, Robert Murphy, and Charles Mast at Cherchell two long months earlier.[3] Bonnier waited until he heard Darlan ascend the stairs, then stepped out of the empty office and shot him twice, once in the chest and once in the face. He died immediately.

Bonnier belonged to a monarchist resistance cell closely tied to the Five that hated Vichy and Charles de Gaulle in equal measure. When the Americans put Darlan in power instead of in jail, the members of the cell grew disillusioned about the future of North Africa under American control and decided to take matters into their own hands. Veterans of several clandestine operations, they planned this one, their most daring by far, to the last detail. They expected that a massive public outcry of support for killing a man as reviled as Darlan would render it impossible for the French government to put them on trial; they would become such great heroes to the people of France that the state would not dare risk imprisoning them or turning them into martyrs.

Darlan's death would clear the way for Henri, the Comte de Paris, the pretender to the throne and great-great-grandson of the last king of France,

On hearing of Darlan's assassination, British foreign
secretary Anthony Eden wrote in his diary, "I have not felt
so relieved by any event for years." No one shed a tear for
Darlan, but his death left French North Africa with a
destabilizing power vacuum.

to come to Algiers and rule as King Henri VI.[4] His nonpartisan national
unity government would offer an anti-Vichy, anti-Gaullist, and anti-
communist vision for postwar France. Sailors and soldiers of the Vichy
armed forces would in theory rally to the comte, as would members of the
various cells of the nascent French resistance from across the political spectrum. Bonnier, one of four young men willing to give their lives for this
cause, had literally drawn the short straw and thereby became the man the
comte endorsed to carry out the assassination. If the scheme succeeded, of
course the comte would see to it that the plotters never faced a trial.[5]

Bonnier, Faivre, and the comte knew that the deal with Darlan had become extremely unpopular, both in French North Africa as well as among American officials and in the American media. In their youth and idealism, they expected that the Americans would welcome their act of bravery by vesting political power in the comte at least for the duration of the war and possibly well beyond it. Relatively unknown and living in semi-exile on a hog farm in Spanish Morocco, the thirty-four-year-old comte hardly seemed like the kind of charismatic figure that France needed. Few people, moreover, cared for the royalist symbolism that attached to him. The Third Republic may have failed in 1940, but only a minority of Frenchmen wanted to turn back the clock to 1848, when his ancestor King Louis-Philippe had abdicated in the face of revolution. Both the French and British governments had refused him permission to join their armed forces in 1939, although he did temporarily join the French Foreign Legion. Still, the comte's obscurity could, in theory, act as a strength. Precisely because so few people knew anything about him, he might stand above the bitter legacies of the partisan politics of the 1930s. He also had no connection in people's minds to the Third Republic, the collapse of 1940, or the collaboration of Vichy.

Notwithstanding Bonnier's courage, the plan never had a chance of succeeding. American agents, and likely Murphy himself, had already warned the comte that the United States would not recognize him as a head of a French government under any circumstances, certainly not if he gained power as the result of an assassination or coup. Allied officials also knew that he had previously reached out to both the Germans and to Vichy to offer his services; accordingly, they mistrusted him.[6] The comte and his followers, moreover, wanted to protect French sovereignty from the Americans and the British almost as much as from Darlan. They did not trust Washington for having dealt with Darlan (and for having betrayed Office of Strategic Services [OSS] promises to give them weapons) and they did not trust the British after their attack on the French fleet at Mers-el-Kébir.

Almost no one in Algeria, France, the United States, Germany, or Britain shed any tears on Darlan's behalf.[7] Clark described the assassination both as an "act of Providence" and, more imaginatively, as "the lancing of a troublesome boil."[8] An American correspondent observed that he had "never seen happier faces" than those on the streets of Algiers once news of the assassination broke.[9] As one British official noted, the end of Darlan's life was like a stone hitting a pond: "The ripples were only brief. It was as if

Darlan had never been."[10] Clark laconically dismissed him by saying, "He had served his purpose, and his death solved what could have been the very difficult problem of what to do with him in the future."[11] British foreign secretary Anthony Eden wrote in his diary that night, "I have not felt so relieved by any event for years."[12] Sir Alexander Cadogan, who described the Darlan assassination in his private diary as a "blessing," believed that with Darlan gone, the Americans had an opportunity to reset their misguided France policy, which had unnecessarily driven a wedge between the two allies. The Americans now had a chance to realize that they "had backed the wrong horse."[13] Maybe Darlan's assassination could close a difficult chapter in the story of the special relationship that both sides were trying to write.

DESPITE A GREAT DEAL OF CONJECTURE, no evidence exists that any American or British agent had anything to do with the assassination. Neither does any evidence exist that de Gaulle or his agents had any direct connection to the assassination, although there were circumstantial links and plenty of speculation. At a dinner with him in London on December 8, Cadogan noted that the Free French leader constantly came back to the same single "remedy" for France's problems: "Get rid of Darlan."[14] Free French circles in London ran wild with rumors of assassination plots against Darlan and anger at the United States for having cut such a favorable deal with him. American journalist Virginia Cowles recalled a dinner she attended in London where Free French officers criticized the United States for their support of Darlan. Cowles shot back, "Why do you go on about the Americans? Darlan is a Frenchman and it seems to me that the French ought to be able to deal with him themselves." Two days before the assassination, she got a telephone call from a man with a French accent who said he had heard about her remark and told her to keep an eye on the newspapers.[15]

There were ties between de Gaulle and some of the Algiers plotters as well. Henri d'Astier de la Vigerie supported the comte, but his two brothers had declared for de Gaulle. All three brothers had known key members of de Gaulle's inner circle for years. These links alone led US naval intelligence to deduce that a "Royalist–de Gaullist murder ring" had carried out the assassination.[16] One of the brothers, moreover, had gone to Algiers on a diplomatic mission on de Gaulle's behalf just days before the assassination, fueling speculation that he may have gone to deliver the order to kill Darlan. The priest who gave Bonnier the forged identity card that got him into the palace was also a Gaullist. Still, no compelling evidence links de Gaulle to the assassination.[17] Although all the elements for a good conspiracy certainly exist, d'Astier and Faivre likely acted on their own authority and that of the Comte de Paris with no direct help from de Gaulle, the Americans, or the British.

No one really wanted a full investigation into Darlan's death for fear of whose name might get tied to the murder, fairly or not. It seemed best to bury the hated admiral as quickly as possible and move forward.[18] Even if, as appears likely, Giraud had nothing to do with the assassination, an investigation might well reveal some unseemly connections between the Five, the fascist underground organization known as the Cagoule, and himself that even the Americans might find objectionable. As de Gaulle's most recent biographer has written, an investigation might have uncovered links or credible rumors to the many people who had a motive to want Darlan dead: "The Americans to be rid of an embarrassment; the Gaullists to be rid of an obstacle; Giraud to be rid of a rival."[19] Murphy thought that Darlan's own staff hurried the trial in order to conceal their own inexcusably lax security arrangements for their chief.[20]

Whatever the reason, a rushed military tribunal found Bonnier guilty, refused him an appeal, and executed him within hours. The tribunal ordered his casket prepared before the verdict had even been decided. Neither de Gaulle nor Giraud nor Murphy lifted a finger to try to save Bonnier or to insist on a fair trial. To the end, Bonnier thought himself a great hero and assumed that the members of the firing squad would spare his life by replacing their live rounds with blanks.[21]

WITH DARLAN NOW DEAD AND mourned by no one, the British and the Americans had to come up with a new plan to rule French North Africa. With the battle for Tunisia unsettled, they surely did not want to do the job themselves. Giraud officially inherited the title of high commissioner, but the title did not guarantee him the loyalty of French officials. He did not have Darlan's network of allies nor did he have the political savvy to build one of his own. If Giraud failed, the Allies would have to go back to square one. Dwight Eisenhower hoped that Giraud would remain in control, but he did not want to express a public preference for fear of unduly influencing French politics or making the unsettled situation in Algeria even more tense. No one could rule out further acts of political violence or even a civil war among rival French factions in North Africa.

The Allies had dealt with Darlan in large part to avoid having to get involved in what Harold Macmillan described as the incomprehensibly "odd *mise en scène* on which the . . . renaissance of France was being played."[22] British diplomat Roger Makins, also based in the region, described the situation as "two competing and irritated groups of Frenchmen . . . bitterly planning revenge." In a letter to a friend at the British treasury, Makins wrote, "I often have doubts, after a long day's contact with the French here, whether France has the capacity to revive."[23] Pessimism notwithstanding, France had to revive somehow, someway for Europe to rebuild. Yet de Gaulle remained unacceptable to the Americans, Giraud had proven unsuited for the task of governing, and after the heated controversy over the Darlan deal, Eisenhower understandably hesitated to reach out to former Vichy officials like Charles Noguès.

This situation was not completely unexpected. Darlan had so many enemies that rumors of plots against him had swirled constantly from London to Algiers.[24] Cadogan drew some perverse pleasure from watching the Americans struggle to control Darlan as he grew more powerful, but Cadogan knew, as he confided to his diary, that "we shall do no good until we have killed Darlan." To Foreign Minister Anthony Eden, he said that the Allies should "push [Darlan] down a well" as soon as they had control of Tunisia. Eden agreed.[25]

Darlan had had a sense that his life might come to a premature end and he worried about who might replace him. The day before the assassination, he told Murphy that he knew of at least four plots to kill him. "Suppose one of these plots is successful," he said. "What would you Americans do then?" Murphy had no response, so Darlan showed him a list of potential successors that the United States might approach instead of de Gaulle or Giraud. It included veteran civilian politicians, including former prime ministers from across the political spectrum. Darlan had evidently thought through what should happen after his death, a circumstance that Murphy observed Darlan spoke of dispassionately, "as though he were talking about the death of someone else."[26]

Whoever rose out of the mess to succeed Darlan would lead more than French North Africa; he would, in all likelihood, have the inside track to lead postwar France. He would therefore give "color and shape" to France in the war's final years and in the period following it. For that reason, Harold Macmillan and the British wanted the new French administration "stuffed by men of liberal ideas" who would "proceed in its acts upon liberal lines." Only with new men not tainted by Vichy's authoritarianism and fascist tendencies, he believed, could France move forward. The British did not think that such a transformation could ever happen under the leadership of the reactionary Giraud. De Gaulle, however, could, in the British view, build a new France around "people representing various shades of opinion with clean records as regards collaboration."[27]

The stumbling block remained the Americans, who had no such faith in de Gaulle. They accused him of all sorts of crimes and misdemeanors, including displaying ingratitude at the sacrifices made on France's behalf by the Allies, running an "active anti–United States propaganda campaign," and targeting exactly those Frenchmen who had "helped us to land in Africa." Later, Roosevelt all but accused him of organizing an assassination attempt on Giraud. Most of all, however, the Americans resented the arrogance of the unelected and unappointed de Gaulle assuming on his own authority the role of head of the French state. As one American report noted, "the tone of his communications . . . [is] reminiscent of exchanges between crown heads of the seventeenth century, the divine right of kings, and other ideologies for which this war is *not* being fought."[28]

For their part, both de Gaulle and Giraud bristled at the idea of the British and Americans having any voice at all in the future government of France. Neither wanted to meet with the other in the presence of American or British officials. Although no one in London or Washington wanted to force a showdown between rival anti-Vichy groups led by de Gaulle and Giraud, they had not yet come to an agreement on who should lead France.

The stakes could not have been higher. The future of France depended on the decisions made in the next few weeks. The Darlan deal at least had the advantage of postponing a confrontation between de Gaulle and Giraud as well as one between the British and Americans, but now the Allies and the French themselves would have to figure out a way forward among leaders who despised each other and showed little desire to work together, even with the future of France hanging in the balance. As Winston

Churchill warned Eisenhower, the situation could get out of hand; the British and the Americans, he warned, "cannot each have a pet Frenchman."[29]

THE ANGLO-AMERICAN SUMMIT AT CASABLANCA in mid-January 1943 forced the Allies to deal with the problem of Darlan's succession at the highest level.[30] The British and Americans already had a host of strategic issues to debate at the summit. The future of France would now appear on that list as one of the few political items on the agenda. Out of respect for the Soviet leadership who did not attend because of the ongoing battle at Stalingrad, the Americans and British limited the conference to military matters only. As a result, few diplomats attended. The Allies had had no intention of inviting Darlan, but now they would have to discuss the difficult and divisive question of his succession.

The coming clash between Giraud, backed by the Americans, and de Gaulle, backed by the British, soured the mood at Casablanca despite the recent military success of TORCH. In a bizarre and unnecessarily confrontational move, Secretary of State Cordell Hull turned up the temperature even further. He sent an angry letter to the British Foreign Office accusing the British government of encouraging London newspapers to criticize American support for both Darlan and Giraud as a part of a scheme to undermine American policy. Lord Halifax, the British ambassador in Washington, reported that Hull had warned him that "the emotional views of little men on political matters . . . should not be allowed to divert the attention of the two governments." An exasperated Halifax could only wonder why and how France always became such a divisive wedge between the two allies.[31]

The incident shows Hull at his worst, thin-skinned, stubborn, and sensitive to perceived slights from his British counterparts. As with the Saint-Pierre and Miquelon affair a year earlier, issues related to his France policy seemed to bring out disproportionate anger and frustration. Hull may have overreacted because he felt a compulsion to defend his own failed and deeply unpopular policies of first recognizing Vichy in 1940 and then supporting a deal with the odious Darlan in 1942. The head of the Czechoslovak government in exile, Eduard Beneš, who met frequently with American officials, told Eden that Hull and the Americans were frustrated that they "had backed Pétain and he had proved a broken reed. . . . They had burnt their fingers and were correspondingly sensitive" to criticism at home and especially abroad.[32] Macmillan agreed, laconically observing that "Americans hate backing a loser."[33]

Hull's tempest in a teapot reached all the way to Churchill, who wrote to Eden with advice on how to handle the American secretary of state. Churchill would not "involve H[is] M[ajesty's] G[overnment] in a direct attack on the freedom of Parliament and Press. There is surely a deep loathing in this country . . . against what are thought to be intrigues with Darlan and Vichy which are held to be contrary to the broad simple loyalties which unite the masses throughout the world against the common foe. . . . You should warn Hull that there is almost a passion on this subject."[34] In other words, Churchill wanted to make it clear that while the British did indeed disagree with American policy on the matter, they had taken no steps to influence newspaper editors who had come to despise American policy all by themselves. In a carefully worded jab, the Foreign Office added that British officials did not need to encourage criticism in the British media because Hull and his State Department "appeared to be subject to plenty of criticism in their own country."[35]

As Hull's second explosion in two years demonstrates, policy on France came to symbolize American missteps as much as it reflected an inability to force the British to hew to American desires. It may also have reminded Hull of American inexperience on the world stage. The British rarely missed an opportunity to remind their cousins of this fact, especially as the Casablanca conference neared. The Foreign Office noted that if a British general had commanded TORCH instead of an American, "the Darlan situation in Africa would not . . . have been allowed to arise." Now with Darlan dead, the political situation had deteriorated and "a brilliant *military* episode has been tarnished and tainted."[36]

American backing of Giraud, moreover, led to accusations in the Vichy and German media that the Americans had not liberated French North Africa but merely occupied it for their own purposes through a willing French puppet. Macmillan agreed, noting that the Allies had failed to demonstrate to the world "that the principles of freedom and justice which were the declared policy of the Allies would be put into practice in North Africa." The region would serve as a critical test in "this first experiment in Anglo-American cooperation since it would inevitably serve as a pattern of similar combined operations in the future of Europe." He argued that the Allies had to eliminate all traces of the "Nazi" system in North Africa to prove "the sincerity of the Allies in their declared fight for the 'rights of man.'"[37]

Macmillan, who had upset his American counterparts with his outspoken criticism of the Darlan deal, questioned American commitment to these values. In backing Giraud, the United States supported a man who shared not only many of the political aims of Vichy but depended on the backing of former Vichy officials in North Africa. As to the situation under his leadership in Algeria, "in spite of repeated promises, the political prisoners remained interned, Jews persecuted, and collaborationists in place." For his part, Giraud seemed little different from Darlan on many key issues, even telling Macmillan that the Allies only cared about Vichy's human rights record because the Jews "owned so many of our newspapers."[38] If the Americans could not show that their backing of Giraud differed from the German backing of Henri-Philippe Pétain and Pierre Laval, then the French people might refuse to accept Allied ideas for the postwar French government. Only de Gaulle, Macmillan and other British officials argued, could provide the new blood necessary to show that the Allies wanted to help France move forward, not backward. Giraud, he feared, wanted an authoritarian government or even a junta of generals to rule France.

The Americans, however, continued to distrust de Gaulle enough to justify their continued support of Giraud. Backing the latter as Darlan's replacement had the virtue, in American eyes, of undercutting the former's claims to rule. As Eisenhower wrote, with Giraud in control, "General de Gaulle's political aspirations would be relegated to a secondary place and the entire political situation would be clarified."[39] Murphy invited scores of anti-Gaullist Frenchmen to Algeria; they came, in Macmillan's observation, "like flies to a honeypot" to make de Gaulle's political situation as difficult as possible and hopefully force him to remain in London. Macmillan complained that Murphy was "inclined to emotional relapses on the subject of General de Gaulle and was stimulated by the rather poisonous telegrams emanating from the American Embassy in London, where antipathy to General de Gaulle amounted to a phobia."[40]

The British saw American plans to back Giraud as nothing more than a continuation of their failed attempts to back Darlan or, for that matter, Pétain. The British therefore continued to back de Gaulle, "with all his faults," as Alexander Cadogan wrote. They certainly recognized his flaws more clearly than the Americans saw Giraud's. Macmillan colorfully wrote that de Gaulle was "one of those horses which either refuses to come to the starting gate at all, or insist in careering down the course before the signal is given, or suddenly elect to run on a course different from the one appointed by the stewards of the Jockey Club." The British acknowledged his arrogance and inflexibility, but they much preferred him to Giraud as a replacement for Darlan. They also showed themselves more open to compromise solutions than the Americans. In a note written during the firestorm that Hull's letter created, Cadogan admitted that he and other British diplomats had hoped that "the result of 'Torch' might well be that other figures would emerge that would balance de Gaulle."[41] But the distasteful American decision to back Darlan and then Giraud forced the British to rely almost exclusively on de Gaulle.

Eden told Halifax that the British and Americans would have to find a compromise way for de Gaulle and Giraud to share power or risk a serious rupture in the Anglo-American alliance. "It is, we believe, common sense that some form of union between Fighting French [de Gaulle] and the French in North Africa [Giraud] should be our first aim. If all Frenchmen could be persuaded to combine under one authority, however it was labelled, we might have relative peace among them. We shall not get it in any other way." Eden might well have added that the Allies needed a compromise approach on France in order to get peace between the British and Americans just before the start of a contentious conference on grand strategy. Churchill wrote "Good" in the margin of the telegram, an indication of the desire among senior British leaders to find a compromise.[42]

Most American leaders still backed Giraud, but some at lower levels had begun to warm to at least the idea (if not the person) of de Gaulle, leaving open the possibility of the United States backing a compromise as well. The OSS recognized the need to undo the harm done to America's image as a result of the "dangerous" and "harmful" decision to give Darlan nearly dictatorial powers in North Africa.[43] With Darlan now dead, the OSS wanted the United States to switch its support to de Gaulle as a way of atoning for previous American support for Pétain and Darlan. Despite his flaws, de Gaulle had a "clear program" to eliminate all traces of Vichy from French political life and could see well beyond the military problems to the fundamental political problem of unifying France after the war. Both of these traits gave him advantages over Giraud and his clear lack of political acumen. Despite the distaste that many Americans still felt for him, de Gaulle also had an increasingly loyal following of people, especially young people, across France and its empire who saw him as "the incarnation of their country."[44] Had the American leadership taken the OSS's advice, they might have saved themselves a lot of headaches and disagreements with their British allies.

Darlan had correctly assessed Giraud as a soldier without much political sense. Virtually all the Americans in North Africa who worked directly with Giraud grew disenchanted with him. On meeting new people, he bored them with a well-rehearsed and increasingly fantastic story of his escape from prison, then soon ran out of other topics of conversation. He could not contribute meaningfully to discussions about the important topics of the day, nor did he seem to have any knowledge of areas outside of France and its empire. His American sponsors could live with his limited range of cocktail party chatter, but the most astute among them, including the OSS officials noted above, soon realized that they could not build wartime and postwar France on his weak understanding of politics. After meeting with Giraud in Casablanca, Roosevelt said, "As an administrator he is appalling and will be appalling as a leader."[45] Harold Macmillan noted that the Americans at long last saw "the ass behind the lion's skin."[46]

For his part, de Gaulle had come to that conclusion months, or maybe even years, before and moved quickly to outmaneuver his old commanding officer every chance he got. At a lunch in Casablanca, Giraud regaled French officers with his old tale of escape, after which de Gaulle remarked, "Now, general, perhaps you could recount to us the circumstances in which you were taken prisoner."[47] More practically, de Gaulle built a network of political and military allies across the French political spectrum and inside the French Resistance that showed the political skill that would serve him, and France, so well in the coming months and years. Shortly after the assassination of Darlan, he convinced the BBC to broadcast a direct appeal to Giraud to discuss the "laws of the Republic" and the form of government France would have after the final destruction of the illegal Vichy regime.[48] Doing so gave de Gaulle both the imprimatur of British backing and made it clear that only he and Giraud would participate in the discussions over France's future.

DE GAULLE'S STRATAGEM ALMOST BACKFIRED. Churchill and Roosevelt urged the two Frenchmen to come to the Casablanca conference to discuss the future of France. De Gaulle wanted to isolate Giraud, not share the inner circle of Allied leadership with him. He told Macmillan that the British would "be doing a disservice to France by compromising with Giraud and the Vichy men surrounding him."[49] But the Americans and the British still hoped for a compromise—or maybe a wedding. As Roosevelt told Churchill, "We'll call Giraud the bridegroom, and I'll produce him from Algiers, and you get the bride, de Gaulle, down from London, and we'll have a shotgun wedding." Still, de Gaulle resisted, leading Churchill to warn him that the invitation came directly from the president of the United States and that to turn it down would mean remaining a pariah in Washington. "If, with your eyes open," Churchill told de Gaulle through Eden, "you reject this unique opportunity, we shall endeavor to get on as well as we can without you."

As de Gaulle soon discovered, the British needed the Americans far more than they needed him. Churchill thought that de Gaulle "must be mad to jeopardize the whole future of his Movement" by snubbing the Americans. If he insisted on giving in to what the prime minister described as his "fantasy of egotism," then Eden could tell him that the British might cut him loose.[50] In the end, the bride and groom did not exactly kiss and drive off into the sunset, but under intense pressure from their American and British sponsors, they did shake hands for the cameras and agree on enough anodyne principles (such as their joint declaration in favor of the "triumph of human liberties") to project a minimal image of French unity.[51] The unity did not last, however.

De Gaulle left Casablanca in a much stronger position than when he arrived, and he knew it. Roosevelt had seen with his own eyes that Giraud was, in Murphy's assessment, "a rather simple-minded soldier." De Gaulle, by contrast, "stole the show," projecting a clear vision for France, a charisma that attracted more and more Frenchmen to his cause, and a sense of determination that Giraud lacked. De Gaulle could, however, be tough and

Charles de Gaulle and Henri Giraud share an awkward handshake to please Roosevelt and Churchill. Churchill warned Roosevelt that the pleasantries would not last. The United States and Britain "cannot each have a pet Frenchman," he warned.

maddeningly sensitive on issues of French pride. At one point, he complained about the insufficient number of French flags for a conference held on French soil. He also showed little gratitude to the Americans and British who had done the actual fighting to liberate North Africa. Nevertheless, he demonstrated political thinking that even Murphy described as "two jumps ahead of everyone else's," and he could articulate a vision for France's postwar future that impressed his critics.[52] For these reasons, experienced and talented French leaders like Generals Philippe Leclerc and Alphonse Juin, economist Jean Monnet, and diplomat René Massigli rallied to de Gaulle, even though some of them did not like or trust him. Their help in the political battles to come proved central to de Gaulle's eventual triumph as well as the maturation of his vision.

De Gaulle and Giraud left Casablanca having agreed to share power, at least on paper, to keep their American and British matchmakers happy. In the early spring, it seemed for a time that the marriage might last. "Union is now the *mot d'ordre*," noted British diplomat Roger Makins.[53] There remained a war to win against the Germans, and as part of that war, Free French leaders needed to show a common face if they hoped to play a major role in the liberation of their own country. Discussions had already begun over the creation of an Allied Military Government for Occupied Territories (AMGOT), effectively an American military occupation of France at the end of the war. Much as they hated each other, neither de Gaulle nor Giraud wanted to see anything on the model of AMGOT. They wanted the Allies to treat France as a liberated country like the Netherlands or Norway, not a conquered one like Germany or Italy. Unity served that goal more than mutual hatred.

The British agreed. They, too, disliked the idea of AMGOT, arguing instead for elections in liberated France as soon as possible. Control over civil affairs would become the responsibility of that newly elected government while the Allied armies completed the defeat of Germany. The British knew, of course, that their candidate, de Gaulle, had the best chance of coming out of those elections the winner. They also knew that any unelected French leader who appeared imposed from the outside and backed by Allied military power might seem illegitimate in the eyes of the French people.

Lurking behind all of these discussions lay the real fear of a civil war in France once the Germans left. France certainly had enough scores to settle, enough ideological differences, and enough weapons lying around to create a volatile mix. Both Giraud and de Gaulle had generally anti-communist political orientations, but no one knew if either had enough strength to stop a French communist group from taking advantage of the chaos. Jean Monnet worried that de Gaulle might "find himself the Kerensky," a reference to the Russian leader who tried to lead a provisional government after the fall of the czar in 1917. Unable to contain the revolution, he ended up deposed by the Bolsheviks.[54]

Monnet, Murphy, Macmillan, and others did their best to broker a compromise, but given the gravity of the moment, emotions ran high. Neither French leader showed much interest in giving the other any power with the future of France at stake. Monnet and General Georges Catroux, the highest-ranking military officer to declare his loyalty to de Gaulle, saw the need not just to choose a person to lead France but also to create a stable and efficient system around that person to, in Monnet's words, imprison him in a cabinet. Building a fully functional bureaucratic administration might limit the dictatorial tendencies of the two larger-than-life Frenchmen while simultaneously building the foundations for a democratic French government. All of Catroux's efforts, however, failed. Despite his loyalty to Gaullism as a political movement, he found de Gaulle's "antics" and Giraud's incompetence too frustrating. He stormed out of one meeting screaming, "The whole thing is insane. I can stand it no longer." He told Harold Macmillan that he could not help France as long as he sat trapped "between a madman and an ass."[55]

OVER TIME, GIRAUD, PRESUMABLY THE ASS, proved no match for de Gaulle, presumably the madman, in the high-stakes games of politics. Although some American officials, like Eisenhower and George Marshall, still maintained a residual level of faith in Giraud, most who knew him well, like Murphy, had begun as early as the Casablanca conference to see that he had no hope of effectively unifying diverse elements and leading France. Still, they backed Giraud out of their intense hatred of de Gaulle's grandstanding and unwillingness to see him gain control. Planning for AMGOT continued apace, even though almost everyone involved in it realized its many risks. Still, to many Americans, almost any future for France seemed better than one with de Gaulle at the helm.

De Gaulle also had a habit of making grand offensive gestures. In one egregious case, he promoted a diplomat who had so offended Roosevelt that the White House staff had banned him from ever returning.[56] In April, Roger Makins wrote to a friend that the American hatred of de Gaulle was "so violent as to be almost pathological."[57] From the American embassy in

London came all kinds of invective against de Gaulle. Jacob Beam, a future ambassador to the Soviet Union, accused de Gaulle of setting up his own SS squad and indoctrinating its members with virulent anti-American and anti-British feeling. The squad, he alleged, was training to assassinate Giraud. In a letter to H. Freeman Matthews, who had worked in Vichy with Leahy, then became head of the State Department's European division, Beam compared de Gaulle to Adolf Hitler or Joseph Goebbels four times. If the United States did not distance itself from de Gaulle, Beam and Matthews both warned, one of two outcomes was likely. In the first, the communists, whom Beam said "do not trust de Gaulle but are willing to use him for their purposes," would execute a successful coup once de Gaulle, backed by the Allies, had liberated France from the Germans. In the second, the French people would find that "instead of having Adolf across the Rhine, they will have an Adolf of their own in Paris." If the United States backed de Gaulle and his tactics, which were "so reminiscent of the early days of Adolf and his boys," Matthews warned, then all pro-American feeling in France would disappear.[58]

De Gaulle's behavior did little to change American suspicions. On May 4, with tensions between him and Giraud especially high, he gave a combative and sarcastic speech in London that Jean Monnet described as "Hitlerian" in its tone. Rather than offer Giraud a compromise or an olive branch, de Gaulle's speech signaled his willingness to risk a complete rupture between the two movements. The Americans were furious and the British perplexed. After hearing the speech, Makins wrote to a friend about de Gaulle: "Not only does our horse refuse to come to the right racecourse but shows signs of ill-breeding! What are we to do with him[?]"[59]

The United States did what it could to help Giraud the general even as the weaknesses of Giraud the politician became increasingly obvious. Shortly after the Casablanca conference, the United States agreed to equip as many as eleven divisions of French troops under Giraud's command and to provide them with more than 1,000 airplanes. The United States also pledged to refurbish French warships in American shipyards and set a favorable franc-to-the-dollar exchange rate of fifty to one. The success of Free French forces under his command in training and fighting gave the Americans enough positive results to justify sticking with Giraud.[60] Maybe if he proved himself a conquering hero on the battlefield, he could build enough prestige to challenge de Gaulle and force him into a postwar power-sharing arrangement.

The long-awaited capture of Tunis on May 8, 1943, led to some hope. De Gaulle and Giraud together took the salute of some of the first Free French units supplied with American weapons, demonstrating a return of French military power; fortuitously for Allied public affairs officers, May 8 is also Joan of Arc Day. In retrospect, Macmillan thought that this moment marked the high point of Giraud's powers and of the French unity the Allies had tried to construct. Behind the scenes, de Gaulle had begun to outmaneuver him. Macmillan observed that Giraud had turned into de Gaulle's "queen consort," always near him on the stage but never shining in the spotlight.[61]

The United States refused to recognize de Gaulle as the head of a government, holding to its officially stated policy of not recognizing any political body not chosen by the French people through free and fair elections. The policy had the benefit of sounding high-minded and democratic. It had the additional benefit of stalling for time, giving the Americans a chance to hope that Giraud could mature, de Gaulle would fade, or some moderate politician could peacefully take power from them both once normal political processes resumed.

For the time being, however, French politics remained in limbo, run in exile by a committee in which no one had confidence. Macmillan complained after one tense meeting that "the committee of any English village darts club would have put up a better show."[62] Even in its provisional state, however, it gave the Americans and British fits. Both groups, de Gaulle's and Giraud's, had competing but expansive visions for France and its place in the postwar world. Even when they agreed more than they disagreed, they ended up arguing. In thinking about the shape of the postwar government in France that such leaders would run, Makins wrote, "I sometimes wonder as I contemplate the parents (and the accoucheurs) whether the child will not turn out to be a Frankenstein."[63]

IT CERTAINLY MUST HAVE SEEMED as though the Americans and British had become the midwives at the birth of a strange and temperamental child.

The French government in North Africa seemed to operate under norms completely alien to the British political mind. Roger Makins wrote of an elegant dinner he attended in honor of the "slippery character" and former Vichy governor of Morocco, Charles Noguès. At the end of the night, a guest whispered to Makins that the event was a farewell dinner, a comment that made little sense to him until Noguès fled in the middle of the night to Portugal to escape arrest from the same people who had feted him the night before.[64] Macmillan wrote to Eden that in the makeshift French system in North Africa, "if you do not like a chap . . . you don't turn him out of the party or anything like that [as one would do in England]. You just say he is a Monarchist, or has plotted to kill [Robert] Murphy, and you shoot him off into prison or a Saharan concentration camp. Then a week or two later you let him out and make him Minister for something or other. It's really very exhilarating." It also caused a great deal of instability. Under such chaos, Macmillan warned, "Civil war in France is anyway a possibility."[65]

In June, as the Allies finalized their preparations for an invasion of Sicily, de Gaulle and Giraud came to Algiers to try another round of negotiations. In this atmosphere of confusion and recrimination, Giraud became convinced that de Gaulle had come to lead a coup. He accused de Gaulle of trying to "introduce into France a political system on the Nazi model" and de Gaulle refused to continue the discussions until Giraud apologized.[66] Giraud responded by calling out soldiers of the elite Moroccan Goumiers, increasing the tensions on the ground. The two leaders and their staffs acted in a manner well beneath them, with Giraud insisting that de Gaulle only use the pronoun "we," not "I," and de Gaulle thanking only the British in his public speeches. The two stubborn Frenchmen stopped meeting face-to-face, instead exchanging angry letters from nearby hotels while their subordinates yelled and screamed at one another. Makins and Murphy tried to calm everyone down, and in the end, Makins felt that the French themselves felt shame at their own childish behavior at a time when the future of their country hung precariously in the balance. Instead of working together to help liberate their country, they bickered over wording in speeches. They eventually embraced for the cameras and made public statements of support for one another, but no one expected the honeymoon to last for long.

The chaos in Algeria only underscored in American minds their frustrations with the French in general and de Gaulle in particular. Especially with the invasion of Italy about to begin, the sparring and spatting between the two Frenchmen seemed petty and unnecessarily distracting. Roosevelt informed Eisenhower that he need not deal with de Gaulle any further and could, if he wished, treat all of North Africa as occupied territory. Macmillan thought that the president had "made up his mind to break de Gaulle if he possibly could do so." He could most easily and directly accomplish that feat by dealing with France and the French Empire in parts rather than as a unified whole. Macmillan suspected that Roosevelt wanted to place much of Senegal, including Dakar, inside an American sphere of influence and perhaps seek independence for the French colonies in North America. Macmillan also suspected that Roosevelt might send American troops to occupy Dakar if de Gaulle tried to remove the pro-American governor there, an old nemesis of de Gaulle's named Pierre Boisson.[67]

In late June, the French leaders decided on a bit of separation. Giraud took command of French military personnel in northwest Africa, while de Gaulle took command of French military personnel in the rest of the empire and those training in Britain. They also created an organization, the Comité français de la libération nationale (CFLN) with Giraud and de Gaulle as copresidents. The CFLN saw itself as a kind of nascent government in exile with its senior members serving as a de facto cabinet and parliament, but the United States, already bitten by Vichy and Darlan, refused to give it the elevated status of a government in exile, treating it instead as nothing more than a gathering of unelected French leaders.

The formation of the CFLN eased tensions somewhat but did not solve the underlying problems or the contest between the two French leaders. Makins worried not only about the future of France but also the future of the Anglo-American relationship as long as the two allies continued to back such intense rivals. He and Murphy both knew that if de Gaulle and Giraud could not learn to share power somehow, "an intolerable strain would have been put upon Anglo-American relations, and we should have been faced with the disagreeable necessity of either supporting de Gaulle-against American wishes or of throwing him over with all the lamentable consequences which that would have had in France and in Europe." Indeed, soon after he wrote this letter, the tentative deal that Makins and Murphy had helped to broker fell apart as the verbal agreements between de Gaulle and Giraud unraveled. By mid-July, Makins could foresee a full break between the two French rivals, with unpredictable consequences to come. If they could not find an answer, Makins warned, "all the King's horses and all the King's men" would not put France back together again.[68] Macmillan solemnly observed that the French were so difficult an ally because of the curious mixture of pride and humiliation they displayed. "I have often felt that the solutions here could not be dealt with by politicians," he wrote. "They are rather problems for the professional psychiatrist."[69]

The Americans still thought that Giraud offered them their best chance to resurrect France and to redeem the failures of their own Vichy and Darlan policies. His conservative politics, anti-Soviet attitude, and desire to focus on military matters such as the operations in Sicily suited the Americans more than de Gaulle's constant politicking and attempts to build a broad coalition of support that included prominent socialists and communists.[70] The Americans hoped that if Giraud could lead a Free French army to glory, he could eventually build his own base of support. Maybe under American tutelage, he could also learn over time how to handle his political responsibilities as well.

American support for Giraud proved no more popular than America's support for Pétain and Darlan, owing largely to the high number of Vichy officials who rallied to him. *Time* described American dealings with Giraud "as politically disheartening [and] as morally threatening to the United Nations cause" as the deal with the "turncoat" Darlan had been. They wanted the United States to awaken to the reality that the French people themselves had begun to embrace de Gaulle in no uncertain terms.[71]

Giraud, moreover, proved hopeless at the task of administering French North Africa. His refusal to use his authority to abrogate Vichy's anti-Semitic laws in Algeria led to widespread speculation that Giraud harbored anti-Semitic tendencies of his own.[72] He also welcomed into his government some of the most notorious Vichy collaborators, including, most controversially, Marcel Peyrouton, whom *Newsweek* blasted for his "ruthless record" as Vichy's interior minister and his enforcement of anti-Semitic legislation.[73] The French people themselves showed their preference for de Gaulle, as evidenced by the far larger number of young men joining de Gaulle's Free French units as opposed to Giraud's. The more conservative and anti-republican Giraud looked, moreover, the easier it became for de

Gaulle to depict himself as a champion of the people and distance his movement from Vichy, Darlan, and Giraud alike.

THE AMERICANS TRIED TO BOOST Giraud's standing by sending him on a three-week tour of North America in June and July 1943. The trip proved disastrous in every sense. To underscore Giraud's role as a military head only, no civilians met his plane in Washington, hardly the kind of reception to help establish his political bona fides. To keep the conversations on topics he could handle, the White House told the press corps that "not a word of politics will be discussed. This is strictly military." Giraud felt uncomfortable in the limelight and stumbled when answering even simple questions from Canadian and American reporters. At one point in Ottawa, he suggested that the Nazis had done much good before the war, leading to a rash of critical headlines that further convinced his American backers of his political naivete. Walter Lippmann, who had always disliked America's policy for France, wrote that "it is time to stop the official propaganda campaign for Giraud and against de Gaulle."[74] Even on military topics, Giraud proved helpless. Word came back to Macmillan that Giraud's "lectures [to American generals] on military strategy fatigued them." Eisenhower's influential chief of staff, Lt. General Walter Bedell Smith, especially lost faith in Giraud.[75]

De Gaulle, meanwhile, took advantage of Giraud's trip by giving a stirring Bastille Day speech on the greatness of France to an enormous crowd in Giraud's own base of operations in Algiers.[76] The decision of the United States to recognize the post-Mussolini government in Italy under Marshal Pietro Badoglio frightened de Gaulle into believing that the United States might still do the same for a France led by Pétain or even Laval. He therefore came to Algiers to solidify his relationship with men like General Juin and to consolidate his power. He built his military forces by linking the Free French and the North African French forces under the CFLN. By midsummer 1943, he claimed to have 1.2 million men under his command.

The Americans saw de Gaulle's increasing power as a threat. An American intelligence report given to President Roosevelt argued that de Gaulle "no longer had confidence in the Anglo-Saxons and that in the future he would base his power solely on Russia and perhaps on Germany (repeat

Henri Giraud meeting with President Roosevelt, Admiral Leahy, and General Marshall during his disastrous 1943 trip to Washington. Giraud's limitations helped convince American leaders to jettison Giraud, though they had not yet warmed to Britain's choice, Charles de Gaulle.

Germany)." De Gaulle continued to claim falsely that the United States recognized his government, while at the same time displaying a "well-nigh intolerable attitude toward Washington." A cable from Algiers reported that de Gaulle "made derogatory references to the United States in effect as the power against which the French must join forces," a comment that only underscored the general sense of de Gaulle as ungrateful and unreliable. "The conduct of the BRIDE continues to be more and more aggravated," Roosevelt wrote to Churchill. The president accused de Gaulle of planning a putsch, of being too cozy with the Soviets, and delivering speeches that sounded like "pages out of Mein Kamph [sic]."[77]

Although everyone saw Giraud's North American trip as a complete failure, Giraud himself came back to Algeria in what Macmillan described as "one of his most majestic moods." Seemingly unaware of how others viewed him, he had convinced himself that he had American backing and therefore "spoil[ed] for a row with de Gaulle." The trip had "evidently tickled his vanity" and convinced him of the intense anti–de Gaulle sentiments of American leaders. To Macmillan, this level of self-delusion only proved the "political incomprehension" from which Giraud suffered. A late July deal named de Gaulle and Giraud copresidents of an eighteen-member CFLN, but insiders saw that the arrangement could never last because it left France too weak to have a voice "when matters of primary interest to France were being discussed and decided."[78]

Perhaps in an effort to assert his position at the head of this bizarre political arrangement, in September 1943, Giraud reacted to an anti-Axis uprising in Corsica by dispatching a military expedition without informing the other members of the CFLN or his American allies. He wanted French forces, not British or American ones, to accept the Italian and German surrender on the French island. But by the time the operation got underway, the Italians had switched sides and the Germans had nearly completed an evacuation through the port of Bastia while fighting their erstwhile Italian allies. Giraud's plan for basking in the glory of liberating part of France turned into another comic opera and a further French distraction from the campaign underway against Italy.

The whole sordid episode, according to Macmillan, showed Giraud's "inane vanities" on display. De Gaulle soon learned that Giraud had also run his own intelligence network independent of the CFLN. "He has been exploded by mines of his own making," Macmillan wrote. By launching a bid for Corsica that distracted from larger and more important Allied operations, Giraud had angered the members of the CFLN, the Americans, and the British. All assumed that he had dreamed up the plan not to help win the war but as part of a clumsy attempt to gain a leg up on de Gaulle. He had failed all around. To make matters even worse, crowds on the island chanted "Vive de Gaulle!" when they saw Giraud and his entourage. "Corsica was a test of strength," Macmillan concluded, "and Giraud lost as he deserved to lose."[79] His most important remaining ally, General Alphonse Georges, turned on him after the Corsica fiasco, saying that Giraud was "eaten slowly up, leaf by leaf, like an artichoke. And when at last the core is reached, it is cold and sodden."[80] Giraud himself seemed to recognize his own limits, lamenting after the operation failed, "I am a soldier. This is only too true."[81]

Cordell Hull tried to rescue yet another failed policy, but he, too, at least seemed to have come to the realization that Giraud's time on the stage had come to an end. Hull came to North Africa in October, "flitting about," in Macmillan's words, "like a Monsignor in a Papal Palace."[82] The British and Americans discussed the future of France, and de Gaulle continued to present as difficult a problem for the Allies as ever. In his meetings with high-level American and British officials, Hull gave no indication that the Americans would continue to back Giraud. Macmillan and the British rightly interpreted Hull's behavior as sending a signal that although the Americans did not yet want to throw their support behind de Gaulle, they might be ready to cut Giraud loose. Macmillan perceptively recognized that Hull and Murphy were "inexorably caught in the meshes of a past which everyone now wished to forget."[83] Giraud represented that past, aristocratic, reactionary, and now clearly on the wrong side of history. Reflecting on how far he had fallen since his courageous escape from a German prison and his embrace by the Americans, Macmillan wrote of Giraud, "I would suppose that never in the whole history of politics has any man frittered away so large a capital in so short a time." By November, he had left the CFLN and had his post of copresident eliminated. Wags inside the Gaullist camp noted that he went away without anyone even noticing that he had gone.[84]

EVEN WITHOUT GIRAUD ON THE SCENE, the tensions and bitter legacies of American relations with Vichy remained an issue of deep tension and complicated American policy for many months. In late December 1943 and January 1944, Hull publicly denied rumors that the Americans had kept a back channel open to Vichy and that Laval used that channel to try to broker a compromise peace between the Allies and the Nazis. Even as planning for the liberation of France continued apace, some senior British officials remained unconvinced that the United States had fully abandoned Vichy. A note from Lord Halifax to the Foreign Office in February 1944 warned that "within the last week Admiral Leahy had advised the President that when Allied troops enter France, the most reliable person to whom we could look for help in rallying the French was, in his view, Pétain." A handwritten note in the margin, presumably from Eden, reads, "We have always suspected Admiral Leahy of this."[85] A notation in the William Donovan files indicates that as late as December 1943, people representing Giraud and Pétain had indeed had discussions about the latter remaining head of a post-liberation French state, suggesting that at least an indirect link may have existed between the Americans and Pétain. A rumor also reached Donovan that "someone claiming to be a go-between of the United States approached [François] Piétri, the [Vichy] French ambassador in Madrid, around the middle of January 1944 in order to effect contact between France and the United States."[86]

But even if Leahy and a few Americans still thought the magic name of Pétain had some life left in it, the broader image of Vichy itself had finally become too toxic even for Leahy and Hull. By the end of 1943, the Germans had forced Pétain and Laval to accept into government some true fascist ideologues and thugs like the new secretary-general for the maintenance of order, Joseph Darnand, and the commissioner-general for Jewish affairs, Louis Darquier de Pellepoix. These new appointments marked a turn, in Robert Paxton's phrasing, from "professionalism to vigilantism in police work" and "the final paroxysm of a moribund dictatorship."[87] Under their rule, the deportation of Jews and the crackdown on anyone suspected of communist or Gaullist sympathies greatly increased. Nor could anyone any longer pretend that Vichy had any authority independent of German beneficence.

The Americans therefore had little choice but to turn to de Gaulle as all other options faded and as he himself rose to the occasion. In a letter to President Roosevelt that captured American feelings more generally, New York congressman and French Legion of Honor winner Joseph C. Baldwin wrote, "I don't believe I have ever met or talked with a more unattractive and 'constipated' man. But I am convinced that to the majority of the French both within and without he stands as a symbol of resistance." After meeting him in Algiers, Baldwin concluded that "General de Gaulle is too dangerous a man not to have somehow or other in our pocket, or openly and fully disavowed and out of the picture."[88] The latter option no longer being possible because of de Gaulle's popularity among the French people, the Americans belatedly accepted the necessity of the former. De Gaulle would move into the Allied house, however difficult a lodger he might remain.

Although the Americans had finally decided to shift their support to de Gaulle, they still did not trust him. Planning for AMGOT, the post-invasion American government of occupation, continued, although most

American officials from Eisenhower on down saw it as an emergency contingency they would only use to prevent civil war. The British distanced themselves from the idea, with Macmillan arguing that France differed from Italy, a declared enemy of the Allies, or "a colonial territory of backward and uncivilized people" like "Somaliland, Libya, Cyrenaica, and similar territories which anyway are accustomed to be governed by foreigners," he wrote in typical imperial style. Macmillan worried that any attempt by the Allies to occupy and govern France could result in violence. "I do want to save England and America from the consequences of a policy towards France which may easily leave us even more hated than Germany in the years to come."[89]

For his own reasons, of course, de Gaulle agreed. As the date for the cross-Channel liberation of France approached, de Gaulle felt ever more confident and the Americans recognized his growing strength. On June 2, 1944, just days before the launching of Operation OVERLORD, the CFLN reformed itself as the GPRF, the Provisional Government of the French Republic, with de Gaulle at its head. "It must not be said that France was absent from the Allied Headquarters at the moment of the assault on Europe," he proclaimed.[90] The Allies knew that they needed his help and his networks for OVERLORD to succeed. The day after the creation of GPRF and just two days from the start of the liberation of France, Eisenhower wrote that "de Gaulle is now controlling the only French military forces that can take part in this operation. Consequently, from the purely military viewpoint we must . . . deal with him alone."[91]

Eisenhower already knew that dealing with de Gaulle meant recognizing the GPRF and de Gaulle as its sole head. Incredibly enough, Roosevelt did not. He seemed to believe that the Americans could still find a way to rid themselves of de Gaulle. He told Secretary of War Henry Stimson that de Gaulle would become a "very little figure" as the Allies moved across liberated France. Other political forces would naturally emerge and give the Americans options other than the GPRF or AMGOT. Fair and free elections would give the French people their own opportunity to select their leaders. Roosevelt believed that they would choose someone other than de Gaulle to lead them. Stimson hoped that his boss was right, but he wrote that the president's assessment "is contrary to everything I hear. . . . [De Gaulle] has become the symbol of deliverance to the French people."[92]

Still, American policy remained so hostile to de Gaulle that senior British officials suspected the Americans of planning a trick. They thought that maybe the Americans still hoped, even at this late date, to work with Vichy leaders or some other like-minded French officials after the liberation. Murphy's close links to prominent far-right French figures like Jacques Lemaigre-Dubreuil did little to dispel those fears. Macmillan saw Lemaigre-Dubreuil as a "crook" and worried about how easily such disreputable men could flatter and influence the Americans simply because they too disliked de Gaulle.[93] Lemaigre-Dubreuil had served under Giraud in the prewar French army, then had been a senior leader of the Cagoule in the 1930s. The OSS suspected him of using the information he had obtained about TORCH to help German-backed bankers spirit tens of millions of francs out of North Africa in exchange for a cut of the proceeds. American behavior struck Cadogan as so odd that he assumed that Roosevelt "must have made a secret agreement with Pétain and/or Laval" that he hid from his British allies. He could find no other explanation for American behavior.[94]

AS ALLIED FORCES, including a small but symbolic contingent of Free French commandos, steamed toward Normandy, the stage was set for de Gaulle. He had full control of the GPRF and had pledged himself to the total restoration of France and the complete elimination of Vichy. He had in fact proved as difficult an ally before OVERLORD as Giraud had before TORCH. Touchy and intransigent, de Gaulle added to the stress of the already tense atmosphere surrounding the operation. He gave a speech denouncing the AMGOT plan's provision for an American-backed military scrip and another on D-Day itself in which he dropped the word *provisional* in describing the new French government. Stimson called de Gaulle's behavior "as bad as if he were trying to steal our ammunition on the battlefield or turn our guns against us."[95] Cadogan noted that "we always start by putting ourselves in the wrong, and then de Gaulle puts himself *more* in the wrong."[96]

As usual, however, when it came to France, de Gaulle thought two steps ahead of almost everyone else. While Allied forces crawled toward the critical transportation hub of Caen, de Gaulle came to the beautiful medieval town of Bayeux, liberated quickly and thus largely unharmed. De Gaulle arrived on June 14, with the British and Americans hoping that he would set foot on French soil, pose for a few pictures, shake a few hands, then quickly return to London. But if they truly believed de Gaulle would let this opportunity pass, then they did not know him as well as they thought they did. They did know, however, that he came to France, as Murphy described him to Hull, "in a very bitter state of mind" for what he considered the vastly insufficient role the Allies had given him in the liberation of France.[97]

Towering over the crowd in a pressed, crisp French uniform, the six-foot, four-inch tall de Gaulle came to Bayeux's central square and gave a speech recorded by a French camera crew and distributed across France.[98] The acclaim he received everywhere he went proved beyond a shadow of a doubt that the French people supported him. He had really come to Bayeux to cement his control over this small slice of liberated France as his own kind of bridgehead. On his way out of town, he told the British that one of his representatives would stay behind to run Bayeux in the name of the Republic of France. The two Vichy administrators that the Americans had left in power disappeared as quickly as the portrait of Pétain that had hung in the city hall for a full week after the landings.[99]

The Americans responded with fury at what they saw as nothing less than an attempted coup. Cordell Hull complained that "General de Gaulle must realize that the 15,000 casualties on the beachhead of Normandy were not suffered by the U.S. people just for . . . letting some French politician come to the invasion area in the heat of battle and play politics behind General Eisenhower's back."[100] His behavior in Bayeux, however heroic it appeared to the French people, struck Americans as more proof that de Gaulle did not share the basic strategic aims of his sponsors. In a memorandum written in August 1944, the War Department argued that de Gaulle "has indicated very little interest in the defeat of the Axis. He has shown great zeal, however, in scheming to increase his own power, to eliminate rival Frenchmen, and to force the world to recognize him as the ruler of the French empire."[101]

De Gaulle may have angered a lot of people in Washington and London, but his performance in Bayeux undoubtedly let him steal a march on the Americans, the British, and his French rivals. On hearing of the events in Bayeux, Henry Stimson wrote in his diary that "de Gaulle was bad, but not to deal with him was worse." He could give the Americans what they wanted: order in France and promises of fair elections. If de Gaulle lost those elections, so much the better. But if he won them, then the United States would need to patch up its differences with him as soon as possible. "Personally, I have great distrust of de Gaulle," Stimson wrote, but America's policy of either isolating him or hoping he would somehow magically fade away no longer struck him as "realistic." The longer the Americans held to an anti–de Gaulle position, moreover, the greater the opportunity for him to cause friction inside the alliance.[102] Eisenhower still mistrusted him but saw him as the lone viable alternative to the "Vichy gang" Allied forces now had no choice but to eliminate.[103]

Accordingly, Roosevelt invited de Gaulle to visit Washington July 5–12, shortly after de Gaulle met with Pope Pius XII in a recently liberated Rome. Hull warned that the invitation was "not to plan the future of any one man, but the future of the French Republic, for whose freedom and independence U.S. and Canadian and British soldiers and sailors are making such a magnificent fight today."[104] Hull's omission of the contribution of Free French soldiers and sailors would have been hard for de Gaulle to miss. Still, that the visit happened at all spoke volumes about de Gaulle's growing influence. Unlike the visit of Giraud the previous year, this one came with all the pomp and circumstance of a state visit. Stimson came away with a grudging admiration, noting that de Gaulle managed to pull off the visit "without any particular outrages."[105] He spoke cordially and intelligently to a wide variety of Americans, although he did say that Cordell Hull remained "handicapped by his limited knowledge of everything that was not America." Still, de Gaulle's performance sufficed. Although Roosevelt derisively told his wife, Eleanor, that de Gaulle did not lead a state, merely "some French committee," the United States confirmed its recognition of the GPRF as the de facto authority in France and named veteran diplomat Jefferson Caffrey as ambassador.[106]

With those decisions came the final nail in the coffin of Washington's failed Vichy policy. Eisenhower called the plan to drop AMGOT in favor of giving full sovereignty to de Gaulle's GPRF "a splendid idea." *Time* magazine called it "common sense" and "one of the great decisions of the war." The head of Army Civil Affairs announced that "the business of civil administration belongs to the French. Our job is merely to help them cope with an emergency." Backing a single source for French power in liberated areas would create the basis for national unity and reduce the possibility of civil violence as the American and British armies moved east. A cynic might well have observed that the deal looked suspiciously like the one the Americans had cut with Darlan, but in this case, de Gaulle had greater claim on the loyalty of the French people. "There is no question about this fact in Normandy. It is completely accepted by French and military alike," wrote American reporter Joseph Jones from Cherbourg.[107]

NORMANDY GAVE DE GAULLE A firm foundation on which to build, but it did not represent all of France. In order to solidify his hold on the rest of the country and secure the American agreement to leave civil affairs to the French, de Gaulle would need to do more. He ensured his control with a triumphal entry into Paris just hours after its liberation in late August. He marched at the head of an enormous and jubilant column down the avenue des Champs Élysées, flanked by the men who would form a generation of future military and civilian leaders of France. He visited Notre Dame Cathedral, barring the pro-Vichy cardinal of Paris from joining him and not flinching when a sniper fired two shots at him inside. He then gave a stirring speech at the Hôtel de Ville before setting up his office and getting to work reestablishing the authority of the French state over liberated France.

Just before the liberation of Paris, a Vichy admiral and cabinet official sent a message to Leahy to inform him that Pétain wanted to go to the capital to seek de Gaulle's affirmation of the legality of Vichy in exchange for Pétain's support for de Gaulle as France's provisional leader.[108] Under this plan, the two men would then await the Americans together in order to forestall a communist coup d'état. Laval, too, wanted to go to Paris, even though he knew there was an excellent chance of his being arrested or assassinated by the French Resistance in the city.[109] By this point, he and Pétain despised each other and Laval likely believed that only the Americans could save his skin. One OSS agent reported that "both Pétain and Laval had entertained the illusion until the last that the Americans would greet them with open arms" because of their shared hatred of de Gaulle and fear of the communists.[110]

Leahy never bothered to respond to Pétain's indirect overtures. Neither did de Gaulle. Instead, de Gaulle's triumph sent the leaders of Vichy on the run. To forestall the possibility of Pétain or Laval welcoming the Americans or issuing an order for French forces to join the Anglo-American alliance, the Germans moved them and many other collaborators to the Sigmaringen Castle in Baden-Württemberg. There, they formed a bizarre and surreal Vichy French state in exile, complete with the headquarters of the Bank of France, various mistresses and hangers-on, and representatives of most major French media outlets. The morbid and bizarre scene of the French government that the United States had once recognized being a virtual prisoner of the Nazis in a castle run by the Gestapo revealed what a broken reed America's Vichy policy had been all along. Although Cordell Hull and his historian William Langer continued to defend the policy as the best of a bad set of choices, the events of 1944 revealed the leadership of Vichy France as the German prisoners they had been all along.

The echoes of America's dealings with Vichy, both real and rumored, lingered. At the end of 1944, rumors persisted that the United States Army had continued to work with and through Vichy officials in liberated France, leading Washington to issue public orders to Eisenhower that he "should have no dealings with the Vichy regime except for the purpose of liquidating it."[111] Evidently, the orders, issued for public consumption much more than for Eisenhower's, did not achieve their goal. The United States government reissued them a month later, adding that it "has no intention of dealing with any individual in France who is known to have willfully collaborated with the enemy."[112] With those orders came the belated official acknowledgment that Vichy was in fact what most Americans had known all along—an enemy of the United States, its people, its values, and its interests.

CONCLUSION

AS TIME GOES BY

IN A CASE ON A WALL at the United States Army War College where I work, in a well-trod hallway between the main entrance and the cafeteria, hangs an American flag. There is nothing unusual about an American flag at a military installation, of course, but few passersby bother to look closely at this one. A letter in the display case explains that it flew for a time over the grave of the Marquis de Lafayette in Picpus cemetery in eastern Paris. Since his death in 1834, Lafayette's grave, complete with earth from the United States, has almost always had an American flag fly over it. Every July 4, American dignitaries attend a ceremony for replacing the flag. General Alexander Haig, then serving as Supreme Allied Commander, Europe placed the one in the display case in my building over Lafayette's grave in 1977. The flag is therefore a special and rare gift. The letter accompanying it bears the signature of the president of the French branch of the Sons of the American Revolution, René de Chambrun, the same René de Chambrun who had hurried to Washington in 1940 to spend a weekend on the presidential yacht with his distant cousin by marriage, Franklin Roosevelt.

Chambrun became a celebrity lawyer after the war, with high-profile clients such as the exiled King Peter II of Yugoslavia and the collaborationist fashion magnate Coco Chanel. His real passions, however, were defending

the reputation of his father-in-law and protecting the Franco-American relationship. He and his wife went to Montparnasse cemetery in southern
Paris to lay flowers on Pierre Laval's grave every year on the anniversary of
Laval's execution (see below). They may have been the only people in the
world who still grieved over Laval. Ever the lawyer, Chambrun wrote books
and articles trying to exculpate or absolve Laval for his wartime behavior
at the head of the Vichy government. He also created a foundation dedicated to collecting materials that allegedly proved Laval's good intentions
as a shield between the murderous Nazis and a virtuous France.

Chambrun was not alone in trying to change the past. After the war
ended, almost everyone involved in Vichy had an incentive to forget,
modify, or selectively remember its history. The United States, now led by
a new president and senior advisers, wanted to focus on the narrative of
triumph and victory solidified by the events of 1944 and 1945. In the new
postwar order, France would emerge as a key partner in the occupation of
Germany, a member of the United Nations Security Council, and a cornerstone of stability in Europe. France also became an ally in deterring the
Soviet Union and a founding member of the North Atlantic Treaty Organization. Keeping the Vichy skeletons firmly in the closet made the most
sense for all concerned.

Great Britain, too, made a political change with Clement Attlee and Ernest Bevin replacing Winston Churchill and Anthony Eden. They wanted
to focus on economic recovery, restructuring the empire, and resisting Soviet expansion. They needed a strong, stable, noncommunist France to help
promote stability on the continent. Although Attlee had held the wartime
title of deputy prime minister, he had little influence on foreign policy
during the war itself and could easily separate himself from the policies of
his predecessor on a wide variety of topics, including France. The new
Labour leadership conveniently reimagined the history of 1940–1945 as a
shared Anglo-French struggle in the common interest of creating the
Western European military alliance that Bevin saw as essential to British
security.

For France, of course, the problem ran much deeper. For most Frenchmen
and Frenchwomen, the Second World War was as much a civil war as a
war against the invading Germans. In 1945, the Nazis went home, but
thousands of French collaborators remained, often in their same jobs, and
sometimes supported by the money and power of the US government.[1] The

trials of Pierre Laval and Henri-Philippe Pétain, like the Nuremberg trials in neighboring Germany, singled out a small number of villains so that the majority could go on with their lives, even if they themselves had blood on their hands. Dozens of senior Vichy officials who definitely had blood on their hands, including Marcel Peyrouton and Louis Darquier de Pellepoix, avoided meaningful punishment, lived long comfortable lives, and died peaceful deaths.[2] France, like Germany, wanted to look forward, not backward.

French historian Henry Rousso described a "Vichy syndrome" that has plagued France as a result of the need to bury the history of Vichy deep within the collective psyche.[3] Despite this national amnesia, the ghosts of the past returned with a depressing regularity, as in the trial of long-serving French government official and postwar prefect of the Paris police Maurice Papon in 1997–1998 on charges of helping Vichy deport more than 1,600 French Jews to death camps. His conviction on charges of crimes against humanity reignited bitter acrimony over both Vichy and its memory in France. So, too, did the futile attempts of France to extradite men like Darquier from their self-imposed exiles in countries like Spain.

As recently as 2018, French president Emmanuel Macron provoked controversy for saying that it was "legitimate" for his government to honor Marshal Pétain on the centennial of the end of the First World War. "You can be a great soldier during World War I and then go on to make disastrous choices during World War II," Macron said while standing on one of the last battlefields of the earlier war. His comments caused a firestorm of criticism in France, where most believe that Pétain's leadership of the Vichy state should, in effect, erase any public commemoration of his contributions to French victory in 1918.[4] The controversy caused some quick backpedaling and a promise from Macron not to include Pétain's name in the ceremonies.

PRECISELY BECAUSE OF THESE CONTROVERSIES, we must take a deep and critical look at the Second World War in all of its complexity and all of its dark undersides. Writing Vichy, and the Anglo-American relationship to it, out of the history of the Second World War only helps us tell the story we wish to tell ourselves. When we mislead ourselves about our past, we not only fail to learn, but we sometimes learn exactly the wrong lessons. Sometimes, as with the Papon case and Macron's praise for Pétain's First World War service, the tensions in historical memory refuse to remain buried.

I began this book project with the hypothesis that the relationship of the United States with Vichy was a case of "dirty hands," of a state temporarily doing what it had to do in a time of war. If the United States could ally with dictatorships worldwide (most notably the murderous and tyrannical Soviet Union), then surely it could work with Vichy in the pursuit of the greater goal of defeating the Nazis. If that meant dealing with opportunists like Pierre Laval and Jean-François Darlan, and if it meant temporarily denying the French people their freedom and liberty, then such was the unfortunate price the United States knew it would have to pay in the pursuit of the greater good of ensuring the final defeat of the Nazis.[5] Like the decision not to bomb the rail lines leading to Auschwitz, such decisions may appear flawed in retrospect but could be justified by the limited information available to decision makers and the desperate need for victory in the context of a total war.

But my initial hypothesis placed far too much emphasis on the rational weighing of good versus bad, interest versus values. The "dirty hands" argument, advanced after the war by William Langer, provided cover for a policy based as much on fear, confusion, and misguided faith as anything else. American leaders had for so long avoided serious thinking about national defense that when the strategic situation radically changed in 1940, they had no idea what to do. They had unintentionally depended so much on French strength to delay having to rearm that when France for all intents and purposes disappeared, they feared that they could not meet the first requirement of a government, the defense of its citizens. Working together with Vichy, with which the United States did share some interests, seemed the right policy to frightened officials from Washington to Algeria.

Our collective memory of the Second World War as a period of American strength clouds the real trepidation that drove policy from 1940 to 1943. The fall of France led to an unprecedented opening of the American treasury for spending on defense, new laws to conscript men into military service in peacetime, paranoia over potential fifth columnists, secret wiretaps, new alliances, and much more, all driven by a terrifying awareness of the myriad dangers of the post-1940 environment. We sometimes associate these sentiments with the Japanese attack on Pearl Harbor, but they entered the American consciousness a year and a half earlier.

To buy time and reduce strategic uncertainty, the United States reached out to a Vichy French state that it knew all along had pro-Nazi tendencies. American leaders naively believed that they could pursue a politics of personality, wooing men like Pétain with American money, influence, and diplomatic recognition to prevent France from becoming a formal German ally or giving the Germans access to French warships. Any Vichy acquiescence to German demands along these lines would have multiplied America's defense problems. Hull, Langer, and a few others pointed to these successes to argue that the American approach had been the correct one, notwithstanding the intense criticism of it from prominent Americans and from the British, and also notwithstanding a lack of evidence that recognition and money from the United States had had any positive influence at all on Vichy policy.

It does not take too much imagination to see how this policy could have gone disastrously wrong. American officials were much too slow to recognize the powerless of Pétain and Vichy's craven subservience to Nazi Germany. They also took too long to recognize the political skills of Charles de Gaulle as he rose from an obscure voice on the BBC in 1940 to the undisputed leader of France by 1944. American officials at least saw the evil that Laval represented, but they deceived themselves into thinking that they could turn men like Giraud and Darlan into reliable American allies despite their manifest flaws.

That America's flirtation with Vichy did not go disastrously wrong had little to do with any wise decisions made inside the United States. The United States was fortunate that the Germans did not really want Vichy as an active partner or ally.[6] They wanted the western front calm and France to serve mainly as a provider of money, food, labor, and industrial goods. The German invasion first of the Balkans, then of the Soviet Union in June 1941 fortuitously drew German attention east and away from French issues just at the time that the United States and Britain had begun to think more and more about the importance of North Africa.

America's Vichy policy had long-term legacies. As early as January 1945, with the war still not yet won, the new American ambassador to France complained to the new secretary of state that anti-American bitterness pervaded France because of America's past association with Vichy. Less than

Darlan and Clark shake hands on the deal to make Darlan high commissioner for French North Africa. Despite intense criticism over its terms, the deal might have cemented Darlan's place as the leader of France for years to come. Note the portrait of Pétain staring down over Clark's shoulder.

a month into his new job, Jefferson Caffrey warned Edward Stettinius of persistent rumors in France "that America was surreptitiously supporting Pétain and Laval" even while they sat in captivity in Sigmaringen Castle. Caffrey also saw evidence of the deep negative impact that four years of Vichy's anti-American propaganda had had on the French people. The French welcomed individual Americans with open arms, but, he believed, France suffered from a "post-liberation neurosis," and America's policy toward the Vichy regime sat at the center of it.[7] Either the French believed Vichy's propaganda that the United States had only liberated them in order to impose its own concept of economic imperialism on France, or they resented the United States for having backed Vichy for so long. The destruction and damage caused by even well-intentioned GIs as they moved through France only added to the bitterness.[8] Even in triumph, the United States had a lot of work in front of it to rebuild faith among the French people.

The end of the war in Europe should have marked a great moment of triumph in the French relationship with the British and the Americans.

Largely with Allied help, the French had rid themselves of their German occupiers and soon began the process of rebuilding one of Europe's great republics. France became a charter member of the United Nations and acquired a permanent security council seat even before the writing of a constitution for the Fourth Republic. Disagreements over the empire and France's place in the world more generally remained, but together, the three allies had achieved much. Strategically, they shared many crucial interests, including rebuilding the European economy, limiting Soviet influence in Central and Western Europe, and occupying Germany to prevent its resurgence.[9]

Nevertheless, much anger remained and most of it traced back to Vichy. Few Gaullists would forget that the United States had dealt with the likes of Pétain, Laval, Darlan, and Giraud before belatedly and grudgingly accepting de Gaulle as the leader of France. Nor would Americans forgive what they saw as de Gaulle's arrogance and what Henry Stimson called "the constant series of gratuitous obstructions and unilateral actions with which the general plagued American leaders, civil and military." As a result, the great triumph of 1945 left a bad taste once the celebrations began to die down. "What might have been a truly warm—and emotionally strong—relationship in the Lafayette tradition," wrote Stimson's coauthor and later John F. Kennedy's national security adviser McGeorge Bundy, "was on both sides marked by coolness."[10]

Bundy was too smart and too experienced by the time he wrote these lines in 1947 not to have known that states, no matter how close, do not base their relationships on tradition but on shared interests. In 1918–1919, France and the United States had also emerged triumphant but had disagreed strongly over existential matters such as the future of Germany, the long-term relationship between the two states, and the future of the French Empire. The disagreements had changed somewhat in the ensuing generation, but the tone and the power dynamic had experienced revolutionary change. Now the Americans held the unquestioned military and economic leadership role in the West, and no amount of de Gaulle's political skill could change that fundamental fact.

THE END OF THE WAR proved beyond a shadow of a doubt the strength of the United States. At least for a few more months, the French did not fully control their own destiny. They needed food, fuel, and loans from the Americans, who did not offer them without strings. The Americans also designed some snubs and slights to avenge what they saw as de Gaulle's coarse behavior during the war. The Americans and British consciously excluded de Gaulle and France from the conference at Potsdam in part because the new president, Harry Truman, remained angry at the way that de Gaulle, whom he called an SOB, had treated Roosevelt. Truman told his secretary of state, the former South Carolina senator James Byrnes, that if he wanted to talk to de Gaulle at the conference, he would send for him, just as he would send for the head of any other minor power.[11] Similarly, Winston Churchill took a pre-Potsdam vacation at Hendaye in southwestern France but intentionally did not meet with de Gaulle before, during, or after the trip.

By that point, Truman's was not the only new face in America's relationship with France. Robert Murphy had moved, at his own request, away from North Africa to Italy, where he became the president's personal representative there. After eleven years in the high-stress job of secretary of state, Cordell Hull retired in late November 1944. Mark Clark spent most of 1944 and 1945 in Italy, where he controversially captured Rome instead of destroying the German Tenth Army. Because of that mistake, the Germans escaped and lived to fight on, holding on to northern Italy until the end of the war. For all of them, the experiences of Vichy and North Africa faded into memory.

The United States and its new team in France distanced themselves from the failed policies of their predecessors. They raised no finger to help Pétain, who returned to France to face charges of treason in July and August 1945.[12] A French court found him guilty, sentenced him to death, and stripped him of all military honors except that of marshal of France, given to him during the First World War. No American official pled his case on his behalf or tried to save his life.[13] The French government, directed by de Gaulle personally, eventually granted Pétain clemency from his death sentence. He spent the next six years of his life in declining health on the Île d'Yeu off the western coast of France, a place even more isolated than Vichy had been.[14]

Pierre Laval tried to escape to Portugal via Spain, but to his surprise, the Spanish government sent him back to Paris, where he stood trial in October. Laval and Chambrun tried to put up a defense, but Laval knew it would not work. Even many of Laval's most strident opponents criticized the speed and show trial-like feel of the proceedings, although few shed a tear for him when a firing squad executed him on October 15 in the notorious Fresnes prison, where Vichy police had frequently tortured members of the French Resistance and the Special Operations Executive.[15] Laval's arguments that he had acted as a screen between the Germans and the French people to spare them the worst of the occupation failed to convince his countrymen, who saw Laval as nothing more than an opportunist and collaborationist who deserved to pay with his life.

As for de Gaulle, he outlasted them all, forming a new cabinet and helping to usher in the Fourth Republic in October 1946. Of course, few people in 1946 (to say nothing of 1940) could have imagined just how long de Gaulle would remain a central figure in French politics and a thorn in the side of his American and British allies. After abruptly resigning over disagreements about the limits to executive authority in the Fourth Republic constitution, he came back to politics as president of the Fifth Republic (which contains far fewer constraints on the executive) from 1959 to 1969. He remained in power long enough to complicate American and British policy for European recovery, oversee the end of the French Empire in North Africa, launch an independent French nuclear weapons program, withdraw France from the North Atlantic Treaty Organization's integrated military command structure, criticize America's war in the former French colony of Indochina (Vietnam), and stir up trouble on the American border by calling for Quebec to secede from Canada. He also vetoed the entry into the European Economic Community of Great Britain, then led by the former British minister resident in wartime Algeria, Harold Macmillan.[16]

It is fascinating to speculate on the future of France and Europe if Ferdinand Bonnier de la Chapelle had missed his target or gotten cold feet on Christmas Eve, 1942. Some American officials believed that Darlan, who hated Algeria but could not safely return to metropolitan France as long as Vichy remained in control, sincerely wanted to retire from politics and hand the reins of power to a civilian politician.[17] Darlan had spoken to Murphy about relocating to Warm Springs, Georgia, so that Darlan's son, Alain, could get treatment for his polio. The Allies might also have found a way to, in Alexander Cadogan's words, push Darlan down a well once he had outlived his utility.

But had Bonnier failed, it does not require much imagination to see Darlan, just sixty-one years old and in good health, hanging on to the power

British prime minister Harold Macmillan, American president Dwight Eisenhower, and French president Charles de Gaulle at a summit meeting in Paris in 1959. Their relationship began in French North Africa a decade and a half earlier.

he had worked so hard to acquire and using it to consolidate his hold on North Africa. Doing so would have blocked the ascent of Giraud and de Gaulle, both of whom Darlan viewed as traitors to France. Keeping them both away from the levers of government might have provided Darlan with sufficient incentive to remain in office until someone else emerged to govern France. Darlan and most of the people with whom he surrounded himself deeply mistrusted parliamentary democracy and much preferred authoritarian models of government.

By the time of the assassination, moreover, the Americans had gotten over their initial revulsion toward him. "I am convinced," Eisenhower told the War Department in late November 1942, "that Darlan is bending every effort to cooperate and facilitate what we are trying to do."[18] Through that cooperation, Darlan had formed an effective working relationship with the United States that could have kept him in power indefinitely. The Americans might well have leveraged that relationship and turned to Darlan instead of de Gaulle for help in planning and executing their cross-Channel attack and subsequent campaign through Normandy. They might have accepted him as leader of postwar France just as they acquiesced in António de Oliveira Salazar's continued rule over Portugal and Francisco Franco's over Spain. How different the rest of the war, the liberation, and the postwar period might have turned out if Darlan, rather than de Gaulle, had emerged as the leader of France.

But through a combination of guile, political acumen, and Bonnier's handling of a pistol, de Gaulle did emerge as that leader. He quickly put a firm hand on the governance of France. In doing so, he made sure that France did not descend into civil war and that the United States threw away its plans for the Allied Military Government for Occupied Territories. True to his vision of June 1940, France had played its role in winning a world war and had emerged from the war strong and independent. De Gaulle also began the process of influencing what his fellow Frenchmen and Frenchwomen would remember—and forget—about the Vichy years. In de Gaulle's reconstruction of the past, the liberation of the country had happened not just because of the French army or the Resistance, but because of the efforts of an entire French nation and empire worldwide, just as he had prophesied in June 1940.[19] With Pétain in seclusion and both Darlan and Laval dead, de Gaulle could sell to the French people exactly what they wanted to hear: that Vichy had been a terrible parenthesis in an otherwise glorious French history. Moreover, they could remember Vichy as having been illegally and forcibly imposed from the outside by the Germans. Although that reconstruction of recent history left a lot to be desired, it offered something to nearly everyone, including the British and the Americans. This book has been an attempt to bring that history back to life in the interests of giving us a fuller and more complete picture of the epic global tragedy that was the Second World War.

NOTES

ABBREVIATIONS

AD   Archives Diplomatique, La Courneuve, France

AGWAR   Adjutant General's Office, War Department (USA)

ANP   Archives Nationales, Pierrefitte, France

BNF   Bibliothèque Nationale François Mitterrand, Paris

CAC   Churchill Archives Centre, Cambridge University

FDRL   Franklin Roosevelt Presidential Library, Hyde Park, NY

FRUS   Foreign Relations of the United States Series

IWM   Imperial War Museum, London

LCMD   Library of Congress Manuscripts Division, Washington, DC

NYPL   New York Public Library Manuscripts Division

TNA   The National Archives, Kew, United Kingdom

USAHEC United States Army Heritage and Education Center, Carlisle, PA

YODL   York University Online Digital Library

INTRODUCTION: A FIGHT FOR LOVE AND GLORY

1. Henry L. Stimson and McGeorge Bundy, *On Active Service in Peace and War* (New York: Hippocrene Books, 1971), 541.

2. A. J. Liebling, "Paris Postscript," in *Reporting World War II, Part One* (New York: Library of America, 1995), 33. See his *The Road Back to Paris* (New York: Paragon, 1988) for more of his Second World War writings.

3. Robert Murphy, *Diplomat among Warriors: The Unique World of a Foreign Service Official* (New York: Pyramid, 1965), 39.

4. William Langer Papers, Folder 2, USAHEC.

5. Harold Ickes, *The Secret Diary of Harold L. Ickes, Volume Three, The Lowering Clouds, 1939–1941* (New York: Simon and Schuster, 1954), 188.

6. Robert Doughty, *The Breaking Point: Sedan and the Fall of France* (Mechanics-burg, PA: Stackpole Books, 2014), 2.

7. Diary of Lord Halifax A7 / 8 / 4, YODL, www.dlib.york.ac.uk/yodl, entry for May 25, 1940.

8. Hans J. Morgenthau, *Politics among Nations: The Struggle for Power and Peace,* 2nd ed. (New York: Norton, 1956), 161; Winston Churchill, *The Gathering Storm* (London: Cassell, 1948), 13. See also Jean-Baptiste Duroselle, *Politique étrangère de la France. La décadence, 1932–1939* (Paris: Imprimerie Nationale, 1979). Of course, the British had their empire and its troops as well.

9. See, among many other excellent analyses, Andrew Roberts, *Masters and Commanders: How Four Titans Won the War in the West, 1941–1945* (New York: Harper Perennial, 2008), Mark Stoler, *Allies and Adversaries: The Joint Chiefs of Staff, the Grand Alliance, and U.S. Strategy in World War II* (Chapel Hill: University of North Carolina Press, 2000), and William Johnsen, *The Origins of the Grand Alliance: Anglo-American Collaboration from the Panay Incident to Pearl Harbor* (Lexington: University Press of Kentucky, 2016).

10. For a recent treatment, see Charles Kupchan, *Isolationism: A History of America's Efforts to Shield Itself from the World* (New York: Oxford University Press, 2020).

11. Marc Bloch's *Strange Defeat: A Statement of Evidence Written in 1940* (New York: Oxford University Press, 1946, 1949) helped to solidify in postwar American minds the notion of a French Third Republic sick in body, mind, and soul. My thanks to Leonard Smith for a discussion of Bloch's importance to postwar American constructions of France in this period. Bloch was a well-known Jewish historian and veteran of the First World War. Vichy police arrested him and handed him to the Germans. The Gestapo executed him in June 1944.

12. Murphy, *Diplomat among Warriors,* 28, 34.

13. Murphy, *Diplomat among Warriors,* 36. See also Ernest May, *Strange Victory: Hitler's Conquest of France* (New York: Hill and Wang, 2001).

14. A 2019 final question on the popular game show *Jeopardy!* asked contestants to identify the name of the wartime government of France. None of the three former champions on that night's show could answer it correctly.

15. The words are on metal placards attached to many French public buildings.

16. See https://avalon.law.yale.edu/wwii/atlantic.asp.

17. Isolation as a concept is complex and multilayered. As I use the term here, it means not ignoring the outside world but avoiding coalitions, alliances, and multilateralism. For more on the term and its uses over time, see Kupchan, *Isolationism,* chap. 2.

18. For a refreshingly positive view of this process, see Oona A. Hathaway and Scott J. Shapiro, *The Internationalists and Their Plan to Outlaw War* (London: Penguin, 2017).

19. Cable N. 401, December 12, 1940, 4-JO-4101, France, Présidence de la Conseil, Information Presse Censuré, BNF.

20. https://history.state.gov/milestones/1921-1936/naval-conference. The United States and Great Britain each agreed to limit itself to 500,000 tons, and France to 175,000 tons. The treaty did have a few loopholes that complicate calculating exact naval tonnage.

21. George E. Melton, *Darlan: Admiral and Statesman of France, 1881–1942* (Westport, CT: Praeger, 1998), 46.

22. Trevor Dupuy, *Encyclopedia of Military History,* 2nd rev. ed. (London: Jane's, 1986), 1052, 1127.

23. Paul Kennedy, *The Rise and Fall of the Great Powers: Economic Change and Military Power from 1500 to 2000* (New York: Random House, 1987), 332.

24. David Kennedy provides a concise summary in *Freedom from Fear: The American People in Depression and War, 1929–1945* (New York: Oxford University Press, 1999), 393–399.

25. For more, see chap. 17 of https://www.e-ir.info/publications/.5.

26. Murphy, *Diplomat among Warriors,* 34.

27. William Bullitt to Cordell Hull, July 1, 1940, FRUS II 1940, p. 463.

28. Lynne Olson, *Those Angry Days: Roosevelt, Lindbergh, and America's Fight over World War II* (New York: Random House, 2013), 54, 201.

29. Allen W. Dulles, Rapporteur, Memorandum on Western Hemisphere Security, November 25, 1940, "Studies of American Interests in the War and Peace" Folder, Matthew Ridgway Papers, Series 3, War Plans Division, 1939–1942, Box 57, USAHEC. Emphasis in original.

30. James Byrnes, *Speaking Frankly* (New York: Harper, 1947), 9.

1. WE'LL ALWAYS HAVE PARIS

1. A. J. Liebling, *The Road Back to Paris* (New York: Paragon House, 1988), 34 and 45.

2. On May 4, 1939, the French neosocialist and future collaborator Marcel Déat published the pro-appeasement "Mourir pour Danzig?" [Why die for Danzig?] in the Paris daily *L'Oeuvre.*

3. For a recent treatment of the Polish campaign, see Roger Moorhouse, *Poland 1939: The Outbreak of World War II* (New York: Basic Books, 2020).

4. Quoted in Fredrik Logevall, *JFK: Coming of Age in the American Century* (New York: Random House, 2020), 248.

5. Quoted in David Kennedy, *Freedom from Fear: The American People in Depression and War, 1929–1945* (New York: Oxford University Press, 1999), 435.

6. Stephen Wertheim, *Tomorrow, the World: The Growth of U.S. Global Supremacy* (Cambridge, MA: Harvard University Press, 2020), 41–44. For an early example of this kind of thinking, see Edwin D. Schoonmaker, *Our Genial Enemy, France* (New York: Ray Long, 1932). See also chapter 1 of Frank Costigliola, *France and the United States: The Cold War Alliance since World War II* (New York: Twayne's, 1992).

7. For more, see François Kersaudy, *Norway 1940* (London: Arrow, 1990).

8. "France Girds against War," *Sunday Evening Star* (Washington), April 9, 1939, 4.

9. Marie-Louise Dilkes, *Remembering World War Two: Through the Door to the American Embassy* (self-published, 1955), entry for September 5, 1939. In author's possession thanks to the generosity of her great-niece Virginia Dilkes. Marie-Louise was from Philadelphia and first came to France in 1917 as a volunteer. She began working in the embassy in 1934. My thanks to Monique Seefried for putting Virginia and me in touch.

10. William Shirer, *The Collapse of the Third Republic: An Inquiry into the Fall of France in 1940* (New York: Simon and Schuster, 1969), 525.

11. James Byrnes, *Speaking Frankly* (New York: Harper, 1947), 8.

12. For a perspective on German views of France before Sedan, see Gerhard L. Weinberg, *The Foreign Policy of Hitler's Germany* (Chicago: University of Chicago Press, 1980), chap. 3.

13. See Ernest R. May, *Strange Victory: Hitler's Conquest of France* (New York: Hill and Wang, 2001), Robert Doughty, *The Breaking Point: Sedan and the Fall of France, 1940* (Hamden, CT: Archon Books, 1990), 99–100, and Robert M. Citino, *Quest for Decisive Victory: From Stalemate to Blitzkrieg in Europe, 1899–1940* (Lawrence: University Press of Kansas, 2002), chap. 8.

14. William Langer Papers, Folder 3, USAHEC.

15. Doughty, *Breaking Point*, 1.

16. Harold Ickes, *The Secret Diary of Harold L. Ickes, Volume Three, The Lowering Clouds, 1939–1941* (New York: Simon and Schuster, 1954), 178. Although a Republican, Knox had supported Roosevelt's foreign policy and the idea of preparedness more generally.

17. These were the headlines of the *Evening Star* (Washington) for May 12 and 13.

18. Dilkes, *Remembering World War Two*, entry for May 16, 1940.

19. Robert Murphy, *Diplomat among Warriors: The Unique World of a Foreign Service Official* (New York: Pyramid, 1965), 39.

20. Shirer, *Collapse of the Third Republic*, 24.

21. Operation DYNAMO evacuated 366,162 men from Dunkirk. Operation AERIAL evacuated 191,870 more from western France. See Lionel Ellis, *The*

War in France and Flanders, 1939–1940 (London: Her Majesty's Stationery Office, 1953). The memorial to the Dunkirk operation celebrates the heroism of the French "and their allies." It makes no specific reference to the British.

22. Ickes, *Secret Diary,* 3:208.

23. Langer Papers, Folder 3, USAHEC.

24. Langer Papers, Folder 4, USAHEC.

25. Ickes, *Secret Diary,* 3:183.

26. Ickes, *Secret Diary,* 3:179–182.

27. Dilkes, *Remembering World War Two,* entry for May 18, 1940.

28. Ickes, *Secret Diary,* 3:209.

29. Shirer, *Collapse of the Third Republic,* 25.

30. Virginia Cowles, "The Beginning of the End," in *Reporting World War II, Part One: American Journalism, 1938–1944* (New York: Library of America, 1995), 53–54. Irène Némirovsky famously captured the sense of panic in her *Suite française,* the English translation of which appeared in 2006 (New York: Knopf).

31. Sonia Tomara, "French Conceal Despair; Move as Automatons," *New York Herald-Tribune,* June 19, 1940.

32. *Life,* July 8, 1940, 22 and July 22, 1940, 18.

33. William Bullitt to Cordell Hull, May 28, 1940, FRUS II, p. 453.

34. Ralph Delany Payne Jr. in *Life,* July 8, 1940, 75.

35. Langer Papers, Folder 4, USAHEC.

36. Richard de Rochemont, "Vichy vs. France: A Government of Fine Words and Cheap Intrigues Draws the Scorn of Its People," *Life,* September 1, 1941, 66. My thanks to my good friend William J. Astore for passing this article to me. Bill, here is your footnote.

37. René de Chambrun, *I Saw France Fall. Will She Rise Again?* (New York: Morrow, 1940), 178.

38. See Nicolas Atkin, *Pétain* (Harlow, UK: Longman, 1998), and, in French, Marc Ferro, *Pétain* (Paris: Fayard, 1987), and Michèle Cointet, *Pétain et les français, 1940–1951* (Paris: Perrin, 2002).

39. Robert Paxton, "The Last King of France," *New York Review of Books,* February 14, 1985, 17.

40. Rochemont, "Vichy vs. France," 61.

41. For an English-language account that gives a sense of the Pétain myth, see Alistair Horne, *The Price of Glory: Verdun 1916* (New York St. Martin's, 1962),

as well as his *To Lose a Battle: France 1940* (London: Macmillan, 1969). For a more rounded view of the battle and its legacy, see Paul Jankowksi, *Verdun: The Longest Battle of the Great War* (New York: Oxford University Press, 2014).

42. *Life,* July 22, 1940, 16.

43. Patrice Higonnet, "The Inevitability of Vichy," *Times Literary Supplement,* March 13, 1981, 287–288.

44. Robert Paxton, "Exposing a Nation's *Secret de Famille,*" *Times Literary Supplement,* November 13, 1987, 1257.

45. Paxton, "The Last King of France," 17.

46. Rochemont, "Vichy vs. France," 66.

47. Militärgeschichtliches Forschungsamt, *Germany and the Second World War* (Oxford: Clarendon, 1991), 2:303.

48. Two important French studies are Michèle Cointet, *Nouvelle histoire de Vichy, 1940–1945* (Paris: Fayard, 2011), and Jean-Pierre Azéma and Olivier Wieviorka, *Vichy, 1940–1944* (Paris: Perrin, 2004).

49. SS troops destroyed the carriage in 1945 to keep it from falling into Allied hands.

50. *Vichy et ses environs: Guides bleus illustrés* (Paris: Hachette, 1937), 5–6, 13.

51. Dilkes, *Remembering World War Two,* entry for September 14, 1939.

52. See also Michèle Cointet, *Vichy capitale, 1940–1944* (Paris: Perrin, 1992).

53. See Eugen Weber, *The Hollow Years: France in the 1930s* (New York: Norton, 1994).

54. Robert Paxton, *Vichy France: Old Guard and New Order, 1940–1944* (New York: Columbia University Press, 1972), 34; *Life,* July 8, 1940, 20.

55. Paxton, *Vichy France,* 33 and 37; Herman Lebovics, *True France: The Wars over Cultural Identity, 1900–1945* (Ithaca, NY: Cornell University Press, 1992). Benoist-Méchin was condemned to death in 1947 for collaboration but received an amnesty and later published a historical account of these events favorable to Vichy in *Soixante jours qui ebranlèrent l'occident* [Six days that shook the West] (Paris: Albin Michel, 1956). He died in 1983.

56. Kittredge Memo regarding Conditions in France, Report of André Philip, August 5, 1942, Tracy Barrett Kittredge Papers, Record Number 60017.93, Hoover Library Digital Collections, Stanford University.

57. Yves Bouthillier, *Le drame de Vichy: Face à l'ennemi, face à l'allié* (Paris: Plon, 1950), 11.

58. Rochemont, "Vichy vs. France," 67 and 69.

59. The words belong to the influential far-right French nationalist Charles Maurras. See Chris Millington, *A History of Fascism in France from the First World War to the National Front* (London: Bloomsbury, 2020), 113.

60. Julian Jackson, *France: The Dark Years, 1940–1944* (New York: Oxford University Press, 2001), 140.

61. Charles de Gaulle, *Vers l'armée de métier* [Toward a professional army] (Paris: Berger-Levrault, 1934).

62. Julian Jackson, *De Gaulle* (Cambridge, MA: Harvard University Press, 2018), chap. 5.

63. Quoted in Jackson, *De Gaulle,* 120.

64. For more, see Rachel Chin, "Who Speaks for France? Vichy, Free France and the Battle over French Legitimacy: 1940–1942," *British Journal for Military History* 6, no. 3 (November 2020): 2–22.

65. https://www.bbc.com/news/10339678.

66. See Martin Blumenson, *The Vildé Affair: Beginnings of the French Resistance* (Boston: Houghton Mifflin, 1977), and Agnès Humbert, *Notre guerre* (Paris: Tallandier, 2004).

67. Chin, "Who Speaks for France?" 3.

68. Pétain had been de Gaulle's first commanding officer in 1913 and the two remained close until 1925. De Gaulle even served as Pétain's ghostwriter when the latter was angling for a seat in the Académie française. It is, however, a myth that de Gaulle named his eldest son Philippe in Pétain's honor. By the mid-1930s the two were barely on speaking terms. Their wives, moreover, cordially disliked each other.

69. William C. Bullitt to Cordell Hull, July 1, 1940, FRUS II, 1940, p. 462.

70. Matthews to Hull, December 27, 1940, FRUS II, 1940, p. 430.

71. For more context on the evolution of Vichy foreign policy, see Peter Jackson and Simon Kitson, "The Paradoxes of Vichy Foreign Policy, 1940–1942," in *Hitler and His Allies in World War II,* ed. Jonathan R. Adelman (London: Routledge, 2007), 79–115.

72. George E. Melton, *Darlan: Admiral and Statesman of France, 1881–1942* (Westport, CT: Praeger, 1998), 72.

73. In Ottawa in December 1941, Churchill famously quipped, "Some chicken! Some neck!" See https://blogs.fcdo.gov.uk/corinrobertson/2012/03/29/some-chicken-some-neck/.

74. Bullitt to Hull, July 1, 1940, FRUS II, pp. 465–467.

75. Bullitt to Hull, July 1, 1940.

76. Document 10, France, Présidence de la conseil information presse censuré, July 13, 1940, 4-JO-4101, BNF.

77. Murphy, *Diplomat among Warriors,* 48.

78. Wertheim, *Tomorrow, the World,* 47 and 61.

79. Alexander Sachs, "Summary of Study of French Colonial Empire and Application for Present Phase of War and American Security," William Donovan Papers, Box 69A, Files Number 405–410, USAHEC.

80. Consul General in Algiers Felix Cole to Cordell Hull, June 27, 1940, and Consul General in Casablanca Herbert Goold to Cordell Hull, June 26, 1940, FRUS II, pp. 570–572.

81. "Mr. Bullitt in New York," *Times* (London), July 22, 1940, and "US and Pétain Government," *Times* (London), July 16, 1940, ANP, F60/1726, Dossier Vichy et les États-Unis.

82. For more, see Jean-Paul Cointet, *Pierre Laval* (Paris: Fayard, 1993), and Fred Kupperman, *Laval* (Paris: Balland, 1987).

83. For more on French fascism in these years, see Millington, *History of Fascism in France.*

84. Jackson, *France,* 139.

85. Paxton, *Vichy France,* 33.

86. For much more, see Michael Marrus and Robert Paxton, *Vichy France and the Jews* (Stanford, CA: Stanford University Press, 1995), chap. 5, and Jackson, *France,* 217–219, who argues that Laval was motivated primarily by a desire not to have France pay for their care.

87. Murphy, *Diplomat among Warriors,* 56.

88. Matthews to Hull, November 12, 1940, FRUS II, 1940, p. 451.

89. Chambrun, *I Saw France Fall,* 174.

90. René de Chambrun, *Mission and Betrayal: Working with Franklin Roosevelt to Help Save France and Britain* (Palo Alto, CA: Stanford University Press, 1993), 81 and 138–143. Alice Roosevelt Longworth hated her cousins in the White House so much that Chambrun watched her train her new puppy to urinate on newspaper and magazine photographs of the president.

91. Robert Murphy to Cordell Hull, July 29, 1940, FRUS II, pp. 378–379.

92. See Yves Durand, "Collaboration French-Style: A European Perspective," in *France at War: Vichy France and the Historians,* ed. Leonard V. Smith, Laura Lee Downes, Sarah Fishman, Robert Zaretsky, and Ioannis Sinanoglou (Oxford: Berg, 2000), 61–76.

93. Rochemont, "Vichy vs. France," 68.

94. J. R. M. Butler, *Grand Strategy, Volume II: September 1939–June 1941* (London: His Majesty's Stationery Office, 1957), 189. Butler went on to become the Regis Professor of History at Cambridge.

95. See Bernard Costagliola, *Darlan: La collaboration à tout prix* (Paris: CNRS Éditions, 2015).

96. Rochemont, "Vichy vs. France," 68. Side boys are the honor guard who line up to greet a VIP when he or she embarks or disembarks from a navy ship.

97. Melton, *Darlan*, 86, and Bouthillier, *Le drame de Vichy*, 105.

98. António Costa Pinto, "Le salazarisme et le fascisme européen," *Vingtième siècle* 62 (1999): 15–22.

99. Millington, *History of French Fascism*, 114.

100. In December 1940, the French government made plans to move from Vichy to Versailles. Pétain planned to move into the Palace of Trianon. Paxton, *Vichy France*, 19 and 79.

101. Lynne Olson, *Those Angry Days: Roosevelt, Lindbergh, and America's Fight over World War II, 1939–1941* (New York: Random House, 2013), 100 and 130.

102. Matthew Ridgway, War Plans Division, National Strategic Decisions, May 22, 1940, Matthew B. Ridgway Papers, Series 3, War Plans Division, 1939–1942, Box 57, Folder "Memoranda by Ridgway and Others on Army Organization and on Possible American Involvement in World War II," USAHEC. Emphases in original.

103. Matthew Ridgway, Aide Memoire, May 23, 1940, Matthew B. Ridgway Papers, Series 3, War Plans Division, 1939–1942, Box 57, Folder "Memoranda by Ridgway and Others on Army Organization and on Possible American Involvement in World War II," USAHEC.

104. Wertheim, *Tomorrow, the World*, 55.

105. Ickes, *Secret Diary*, 3:187–188.

106. Ickes, *Secret Diary*, 3:210.

107. *Life* reproduced the map in its September 16, 1940, issue on p. 81.

2. A HILL OF BEANS IN THIS CRAZY WORLD

1. *Confessions of a Nazi Spy*, directed by Anatole Litvak (Warner Brothers, 1939).

2. For more, see Rhodri Jeffreys-Jones, *The Nazi Spy Ring in America: Hitler's Agents, the FBI, and the Case that Stirred a Nation* (Washington, DC: Georgetown University Press, 2020).

3. George Britt, *The Fifth Column Is Here* (New York: Wilfred Funk, 1940). My thanks to Fredrik Logevall for sharing with me the Kennedy anecdote. For more, see Logevall's *JFK: Coming of Age in the American Century, 1917–1956* (New York: Random House, 2020), 269–274.

4. For the 1917 comparison, see Michael S. Neiberg, *The Path to War: How the First World War Created Modern America* (New York: Oxford University Press, 2016), chap. 8.

5. For two recent studies of this period, see Stephen Wertheim, *Tomorrow, the World: The Birth of U.S. Global Supremacy* (Cambridge, MA: Harvard University Press, 2020), chap. 2, and Charles Kupchan, *Isolationism: A History of America's Efforts to Shield Itself from the World* (New York: Oxford University Press, 2020), chap. 7.

6. J. R. M. Butler, *Lord Lothian: Philip Kerr, 1882–1940* (New York: St. Martin's, 1960), 120.

7. Marie-Louise Dilkes, *Remembering World War Two: Through the Door to the American Embassy* (self-published, 1955), entry for August 24, 1940.

8. Wertheim, *Tomorrow the World,* chap. 2.

9. Jean Edward Smith, *FDR* (New York: Random House, 2007), 449.

10. Cable N. 366, October 28, 1940, 4-JO-4101, France, Présidence de la Conseil, Information Presse Censuré, BNF. For more on Joseph Kennedy's defeatism, see Logevall, *JFK,* 232–239.

11. Sir John Wheeler-Bennett, *Special Relationships: America in Peace and War* (London: Macmillan, 1975), 82. John Kennedy was among the undergraduates Wheeler-Bennett deeply influenced.

12. Harold Nicolson, *The Diaries and Letters of Harold Nicolson, Volume II, The War Years, 1939–1945* (New York: Atheneum, 1967), 122.

13. https://www.presidency.ucsb.edu/documents/republican-party-platform-1940.

14. For more, see Samuel Zipp, *The Idealist: Wendell Willkie's Wartime Quest to Build One World* (Cambridge, MA: Belknap, 2020); David Levering Lewis, *The Improbable Wendell Willkie: The Businessman Who Saved the Republican Party and His Country and Conceived a New World Order* (New York: Liveright, 2018), chaps. 6, 7; Olson, *Those Angry Days,* 170.

15. Smith, *FDR,* 448–449.

16. Olson, *Those Angry Days,* 185.

17. Harold Ickes, *The Secret Diary of Harold L. Ickes, Volume Three, The Lowering Clouds, 1939–1941* (New York: Simon and Schuster, 1954), 184.

18. Ickes, *Secret Diary,* 3:180; Smith, *FDR,* 417.

19. Henry Stimson and McGeorge Bundy, *On Active Service in Peace and War* (New York: Harper, 1948), 323.

20. Freya Stark, *Dust in the Lion's Paw: Autobiography, 1939–1946* (New York: Harcourt, Brace, and World, 1961), 185.

21. Roosevelt had been assistant secretary of the navy from 1913 to 1920.

22. Stimson, *On Active Service,* 325.

23. https://www.mtholyoke.edu/acad/intrel/WorldWar2/fdr16.htm.

24. Ickes, *Secret Diary,* 3:178–179.

25. "Les évènements de juin [1940] vus par la presse américaine," Dossier 21, Presse, 5 novembre 1939 à 16 juillet 1942, AD.

26. For more, see David Kennedy, *Freedom from Fear: The American People in Depression and War, 1929–1945* (New York: Oxford University Press, 1999), chaps. 13, 14.

27. "Senate Debates Conscription," *Life,* August 19, 1940, 28.

28. William Johnsen, *The Origins of the Grand Alliance: Anglo-American Collaboration from the Panay Incident to Pearl Harbor* (Lexington: University Press of Kentucky, 2016), 83–85; Mark Skinner Watson, *The War Department: Chief of Staff Prewar Plans and Preparations* (Washington, DC: US Army Historical Division, 1950), 105–106, 168–180. Historians sometimes claim that the Burke-Wadsworth Act passed by a single vote, but they are conflating the act itself with a controversial extension passed in August 1941 that forced the first draft of men to stay beyond their original twelve-month term of service to thirty months.

29. Olson, *Those Angry Days,* 212.

30. For more, see David L. Roll, *The Hopkins Touch: Harry Hopkins and the Forging of the Alliance to Defeat Hitler* (New York: Oxford University Press, 2013), 60.

31. "Destroyers for Bases," *Life,* September 16, 1940, 19.

32. Olson, *Those Angry Days,* 191.

33. J. R. M. Butler, *Grand Strategy, Volume II: September 1939–June 1941* (London: His Majesty's Stationery Office, 1957), 244–245. The bases were located in Newfoundland (then not yet a part of Canada), eastern Bahamas, southern Jamaica, western Saint Lucia, western Trinidad, Antigua, and British Guiana. The British also ceded to the Americans air bases in Newfoundland and Bermuda.

34. Cable No. 389, November 21, 1940, 4-JO-4101, France, Présidence de la Conseil, Information Presse Censuré, BNF.

35. Cable No. 389.

36. "L'aide américain à la Grande-Bretagne," Cable N. 406, December 8, 1940, 4-JO-4101, France, Présidence de la Conseil, Information Presse Censuré, BNF.

37. For some context, see Theresa L. Kraus, "Planning the Defense of the South Atlantic, 1939–1941: Securing Brazil," in *To Die Gallantly: The Battle of the*

Atlantic, ed. Timothy Runyan and Jan M. Copes (Boulder, CO: Westview, 1994), 55–66.

38. St. Quentin, Télégramme no. 1286, Washington, July 6, 1940, Dossier 30, États-Unis, Relations avec la France, 30 mai–31 août 1940, AD.

39. For more on Latin America in this period, see Jorge Rodríguez Beruff, *Strategy as Politics: Puerto Rico on the Eve of the Second World War* (San Juan: La Editorial Universidad de Puerto Rico, 2007), and Thomas M. Leonard and John F. Bratzel, *Latin America during World War II* (New York: Rowman and Littlefield, 2007).

40. https://avalon.law.yale.edu/20th_century/decad058.asp#b2.

41. Cable N. 369, October 31, 1940, 4-JO-4191, BNF.

42. Cables N. 21 and 22, July 25 and 26, 1940, 4-JO-4101, BNF; "Note: Question des Antilles," January 3, 1941, ANP 3W284/A/III2A2.

43. See David G. Haglund, *Latin America and the Transformation of US Strategic Thought, 1936–1940* (Albuquerque: University of New Mexico Press, 1984), and Fitzroy André Baptiste, *War, Cooperation, and Conflict: The European Possessions in the Caribbean, 1939–1945* (Westport, CT: Praeger, 1988).

44. René de Chambrun, *Mission and Betrayal: Working with Franklin Roosevelt to Help Save France and Britain* (Palo Alto, CA: Stanford University Press, 1993), 74; George E. Melton, *Darlan: Admiral and Statesman of France, 1881–1942* (Westport, CT: Praeger, 1998), 73.

45. Cordell Hull to Waterman (United States Consul at Bordeaux), June 17, 1940, FRUS II, p. 456.

46. https://www.mtholyoke.edu/acad/intrel/WorldWar2/fdr16.htm.

47. William Shirer, *The Collapse of the Third Republic: An Inquiry into the Fall of France in 1940* (New York: Simon and Schuster, 1969), 681–682. For more on the atmosphere of 1940, see Glyn Prysor, "The 'Fifth Column' and the British Experience of Retreat, 1940," *War in History* 12, no. 4 (2005): 418–447.

48. Pierre Lazareff, editor of *Paris-Soir,* writing in *Life,* August 19, 1940, 69.

49. William Donovan and Edgar Mowrer, "Donovan Bares 5th Column Acts in Europe and Warns America," [June 1940] William J. Donovan Papers, Box 1B, Folder 8, US Army Heritage and Education Center.

50. "5th Column in Action: How It Worked in Fall of Paris," *New York Post,* September 17, 1940, 1. The term comes from the Spanish Civil War. Ernest Hemingway popularized it in the United States in a 1938 play, the only one he ever wrote.

51. Olson, *Those Angry Days,* 123.

52. Olson, *Those Angry Days,* 100–104.

53. Olson, *Those Angry Days,* 104.

54. Ickes, *Secret Diary,* 3:188–189, 197.

55. Eleanor Roosevelt, "My Day, June 21, 1940," *The Eleanor Roosevelt Papers Digital Edition,* accessed October 1, 2019, https:www2.gwu.edu/~erpapers /myday/displaydoc.cfm?_y=1940&f=md055612.

56. The cases are known today as Nardone I and Nardone II. For more, see https://www.justice.gov/file/20886/download. The Nardone cases give us the phrase "fruit of the poisonous tree."

57. *Warrantless Wiretapping: Hearings before the Subcommittee on Administrative Practice and Procedure, Ninety-Second Congress* (Washington, DC: Government Printing Office, 1973), 90.

58. Diary of Lord Halifax A7/8/4, YODL, www.dlib.york.ac.uk/yodl, entries for June 25, July 1, and July 4, 1940.

59. Diary of Lord Halifax A7/8/4, YODL, www.dlib.york.ac.uk/yodl, entry for July 3, 1940.

60. Martin Gilbert, ed., *The Churchill War Papers* (New York: Norton, 1995), June 22, 1940, CAB 65/13, Confidential Annex, TNA.

61. R. T. Thomas, *Britain and Vichy: The Dilemma of Anglo-French Relations, 1940–1942* (New York: St. Martin's, 1979), 45.

62. He nevertheless supported the attack as necessary to British defense. See Harold Macmillan, *The Blast of War, 1939–1945* (New York: Harper and Row, 1968), 152. Parts of the French fleet peacefully surrendered in Alexandria at the same time.

63. Diary of Lord Halifax A7/8/4, YODL, www.dlib.york.ac.uk/yodl, entry for July 5, 1940.

64. Matthews to Hull, October 14, 1940, FRUS II, p. 393.

65. In June, Italy had initially demanded all metropolitan French territory east of the Rhône river, Corsica, Tunisia, French Somaliland (Djibouti), Casablanca, Mers-el-Kébir, and Algiers. The Germans rebuffed them for fear that the French would not sign an armistice under such terms, but the Italian government maintained hopes that it could acquire significant French territory at the final peace conference. Norman J. W. Goda, *Tomorrow the World: Hitler, Northwest Africa, and the Path toward America* (Chapel Hill: University of North Carolina Press, 1998), 5.

66. Dilkes, *Remembering World War Two,* entry for July 7, 1940.

67. Robert Paxton, *Vichy France: Old Guard and New Order, 1940–1944* (New York: Columbia University Press, 1972), 84, 112.

68. Matthews to Hull, November 14, 1940, FRUS II, p. 405.

69. https://avalon.law.yale.edu/wwii/frgearm.asp; Goda, *Tomorrow the World,* 18.

70. Goda, *Tomorrow the World,* 21.

71. Télégramme no. 1272 and Télégramme Secret, both July 9, 1940, Dossier 30, États-Unis, Relations avec la France, 30 mai–31 août 1940, AD. On the many problems the French ambassador had in the United States, see "La position de l'ambassade de France à Washington," July 6, 1941, ANP 3W284/A/III2A2. In September 1940, St. Quentin returned to Vichy. Later in the war, he joined forces with Henri Giraud, then with de Gaulle.

72. "America Condemns Pétain France," *Times* (London), September 25, 1940, ANP, F60/1726, Dossier Vichy et les États-Unis.

73. Paul Baudoin to "Tous les postes," July 8, 1940, Dossier 30, États-Unis, Relations avec la France, 30 mai–31 août 1940, AD.

74. Alistair Horne, "Mers-el-Kébir Was a Bizarre and Melancholy Action," *Smithsonian* 16, no. 4 (July 1985): 128. The British commander of the operation called it "an absolutely bloody business" and "the biggest political blunder of modern times."

75. No. 186, Most Secret, COG West Africa to Charles de Gaulle, August 9, 1940, "Vichy French Colonies: Intelligence," Vichy WO 208/52, TNA.

76. Jean-Pierre Azéma and Olivier Wieviorka, *Vichy, 1940–1944* (Paris: Perrin, 2004), 71–74.

77. See, for example, Edward R. Murrow, "Can They Take It?" in *Reporting World War II, Part One: American Journalism, 1938–1944* (New York: Library of America, 1995), 77–103.

78. See Kori Shacke, *Safe Passage: The Transition from British to American Hegemony* (Cambridge, MA: Harvard University Press, 2017), chap. 11.

79. David Dutton, *Anthony Eden: A Life and Reputation* (London: Arnold, 1997), 151. Notably, the entire discussion of British relations with Vichy France appears in the book's chapter on Eden and his relationship with the United States. Eden was appointed foreign secretary in December 1940.

80. Dutton, *Anthony Eden,* 151.

81. Julian Jackson, *De Gaulle* (Cambridge, MA: Harvard University Press, 2018), 114.

82. The Aljazeera documentary *Blood and Tears: French Decolonization, Part One* has some terrific footage of France and the French Empire during the Second World War that features de Gaulle, Éboué, Pétain, and others: https://www.aljazeera.com/program/featured-documentaries/2020/11/24/blood-and-tears-french-decolonisation/.

83. New Caledonia and Gabon soon declared for de Gaulle as well. Martin Thomas, *The French Empire at War* (Manchester, UK: Manchester University

Press, 1998), 53–60; Géraud Létang, "Traque impériale et repression impossible? Vichy face aux Français Libres du Tchad," *Revue européenne d'histoire* 25, no. 2 (2018); Eric Jennings and Jacques Cantier, eds., *L'empire colonial sous Vichy* (Paris: Odile Jacob, 2004).

84. See Andrew Stewart, *The First Victory: The Second World War and the East Africa Campaign* (New Haven, CT: Yale University Press, 2016).

85. Goda, *Tomorrow the World,* 41.

86. See François Kersaudy, *Churchill and de Gaulle* (New York: HarperCollins, 1990).

87. Sir Llewellyn Woodward, *British Foreign Policy in the Second World War* (London: Her Majesty's Stationery Office, 1962), 1:92.

88. Dutton, *Anthony Eden,* 151–152.

89. Nicolson, *Diaries and Letters,* 2:19.

90. Quoted in Woodward, *British Foreign Policy,* 1:77.

91. "Greek and French Ballyhoo Is Cogent but Contained," *Life,* January 6, 1941, 17.

92. Quoted in Milton Viorst, *Hostile Allies: FDR and Charles de Gaulle* (New York: Macmillan, 1965), 68.

93. William Bullitt to Cordell Hull, July 5, 1940, FRUS II, p. 470.

94. Sumner Welles, Memorandum of Conversation, July 8, 1940, FRUS II, pp. 506–507.

95. Cordell Hull, Memorandums of Conversation, July 16 and July 18, 1940, FRUS II, pp. 508–509.

96. Cordell Hull, Memorandum of Conversation, September 30, 1940, FRUS II, p. 523.

97. Butler, *Grand Strategy,* 2:428, and Langer Papers, chap. 4, Folder 1, USAHEC. Macmillan wrote that Churchill "never lost hope of the French" and always tried to "promote a kind of collusive conspiracy in the Vichy government." Macmillan, *Blast of War,* 153.

98. John Colville, *The Fringes of Power: 10 Downing Street Diaries, 1939–1945* (New York: Norton, 1985), 276.

99. David Dilks, ed., *The Diaries of Sir Alexander Cadogan, 1938–1945* (London: Cassell, 1971), 337.

100. Macmillan, *Blast of War,* 154.

101. Woodward, *British Foreign Policy,* 1:96.

102. Olson, *Those Angry Days,* 261.

3. NO GOOD AT BEING NOBLE

1. He remains the only American to have been awarded the Medal of Honor, the Distinguished Service Cross, the Distinguished Service Medal, and the National Security Medal. He also won the French Croix de Guerre. For more on him and his fascinating life, see Douglas Waller, *Wild Bill Donovan: The Spymaster Who Created the OSS and Modern American Espionage* (New York: Free Press, 2011). My thanks to my friend and Donovan descendent Peter Crean for help with Donovan's papers.

2. He probably lost that appointment in no small part because of opposition from his archenemy, J. Edgar Hoover. The two had hated each other since their time in the Justice Department together in the 1920s. Hoover had a detailed file on Donovan, which undoubtedly contained information on his many extramarital affairs, including one with Rebecca Hamilton, the wife of a scion of the J. P. Morgan dynasty, Pierpont Hamilton. A descendant of Alexander Hamilton, Pierpont Hamilton later won one of the first Medals of Honor for Operation TORCH.

3. Cable N. 425, December 27, 1940, BNF, 4-JO-4101, France, Présidence de la Conseil, Information Presse Censuré.

4. "Flying Rumors Make Donovan Washington's Man of Mystery," *Buffalo Evening News,* December 6, 1940.

5. Délégation Française à Wiesbaden à D[irection des] S[ervices d'] A[rmistice] [n.d.], AD, Series 1GMII, Folder Colonel Donovan.

6. "Heading: Chronology," November 1940, William J. Donovan Papers, Box 1B, Folder 8, USAHEC.

7. For some background, see Andrew Buchanan, *American Grand Strategy in the Mediterranean during World War II* (Cambridge: Cambridge University Press, 2014).

8. For more, see Johnathan Fennell, *Fighting the People's War: The British and Commonwealth Armies in the Second World War* (Cambridge: Cambridge University Press, 2019), 125–129.

9. The Minister in Greece (MacVeagh) to the Secretary of State, Athens, January 18, 1941, FRUS, II, document 28.

10. Vichy Foreign Ministry to French Ministers in Athens, Belgrade, Sofia, and Cairo, February 11, 1941, AD, Series 1GMII, Dossier 20.

11. Lend-Lease passed in March 1941, but it did the Balkans little good. The Germans invaded Yugoslavia and Greece in April, conquering both. Bulgaria, as Donovan predicted, joined the Axis the same month. See the Minister in Bulgaria (Earle) to the Secretary of State, Sofia, January 21, 1941, and

January 23, 1941, FRUS, 1941, General, The Soviet Union, Volume I, documents 27 and 31.

12. Cable nos. 73 and 74, January 23, 1941, AD, Series 1GMII, Dossier 20.

13. Drew Pearson, "Washington Daily Merry-Go-Round," *Washington Daily Herald,* December 12, 1940. It is, of course, entirely possible, even highly likely, that Pearson got his information from Donovan himself.

14. Weygand and de Gaulle had known each other since both participated in operations in support of the new Polish army against the Soviet Union in 1920. For more on him, see Max Schiavon, *Weygand: L'intransigeant* (Paris: Tallandier, 2018), and Bernard Destremau, *Weygand* (Paris: Perrin, 2001). For an English-language biography, see Barnett Singer, *Maxime Weygand: A Biography of the French General in Two World Wars* (London: McFarland, 2008).

15. Robert Murphy, *Diplomat among Warriors: The Unique World of a Foreign Service Official* (New York: Pyramid, 1965), 59.

16. H. Freeman Matthews to Cordell Hull, November 8, 1940, FRUS II, p. 615.

17. "The Situation in Northern Africa," May 1940, Box 69A, William Donovan Papers, USAHEC, Files Number 405–410.

18. Singer, *Maxime Weygand,* 110.

19. *Life,* December 23, 1940, 19. Gaullist forces, backed by the British, tried and failed to seize the port of Dakar in September 1940. Vichy forces did not, as de Gaulle had boldly predicted, rally to him. They remained loyal to Pétain instead. For more, see Julian Jackson, *De Gaulle* (Cambridge, MA: Harvard University Press, 2018), 78–81.

20. Leo Amery to Sir John Dill, October 28, 1940, CAC, AMEL 2/3/14. Dill was soon named the British head of the combined chiefs of staff.

21. *Life,* December 23, 1940, 19.

22. Weygand was arrested after the war, released in 1946, and had his name cleared in 1948. Nevertheless, in the eyes of many of his countrymen, he remained associated with Vichy and its collaboration with Germany for the rest of his long life. He died in 1965 at age ninety-eight.

23. Weygand Cable 5, Algiers, February 3, 1941, AD, Series 1GMII, Folder Colonel Donovan.

24. The Ambassador in Spain (Weddell) to the Secretary of State, March 1, 1941, FRUS, 1941, Europe, Volume II, document 162.

25. The Minister to Ireland (Gray) to the Secretary of State, Dublin, March 10, 1941, FRUS, 1941, The British Commonwealth; The Near East and Africa, Volume III, document 27.

26. Memorandum of Conversation with Comte de St. Quentin, July 16, 1940, Cordell Hull Papers, Box 58, Reel 29, LCMD. He used the same phrase in another conversation with St. Quentin on June 27.

27. For more on Gibraltar, see Norman J. W. Goda, *Tomorrow the World: Hitler, Northwest Africa, and the Path toward America* (Chapel Hill: University of North Carolina Press, 1998), chap. 5.

28. See Chapter 4 for more. For the situation in Tangier itself, see Goda, *Tomorrow the World,* 57–58.

29. Murphy, *Diplomat among Warriors,* 62. See Chapter 6 for more.

30. "French Evacuate France," *Life,* September 30, 1940, 69.

31. Diary of Lord Halifax A7/8/6, YODL, www.dlib.york.ac.uk/yodl, entries for October 11 and October 24, 1940.

32. Frank Norris, "Free France, Poor and Paralyzed, Waits for Germany to Finish War," *Life,* September 23, 1940, 78–79.

33. Robert Paxton, *Vichy France: Old Guard and New Order, 1940–1944* (New York: Columbia University Press, 1972), 77. Paxton argues that the Vichy government offered collaboration to the Germans, but the Germans saw little from the French that they wanted other than a benevolent neutrality.

34. Langer Papers, Folder 7, Chapter 3 (2 of 2), USAHEC.

35. Matthews to Hull, October 26 and 27, 1940, FRUS II, pp. 397–398.

36. Paxton, *Vichy France,* 67. Fonck evidently did not know that Laval planned to offer him and his pilots to the Nazis for a war against Britain. Stunned by Laval's duplicity, Fonck tried to warn Pétain against meeting Hitler at Montoire. A postwar commission cleared Fonck of charges of collaboration and even awarded him a Resistance medal.

37. Ambassade de France, Washington, AD, November 1, 1940, Series 1GMII, Dossier 21.

38. Matthews to Hull, October 14, 1940, FRUS II, p. 392.

39. André Maurois, "The Case for France," *Life,* January 6, 1941, 62, 66. He was born Émile Salomon Herzog into a prominent Alsatian Jewish family.

40. Letter to the editor, *Life,* January 27, 1941, 7.

41. The Lehmans and the Roosevelts were New York State Democratic powerhouses. Herbert Lehman was Roosevelt's lieutenant governor from 1928 to 1932.

42. http://www.fdrlibrary.marist.edu/archives/pdfs/docsworldwar.pdf.

43. Alexander Sachs, "Significance of African and Far Eastern Events for the War and US Defense with a Study of the French Colonial Empire," September 26–30, 1940, Donovan Papers, Box 69A, Files Number 405–410, USAHEC.

44. Alexander Sachs, "Summary of Study of French Colonial Empire and Application for Present Phase of War and American Security," [September 1940], p. 34, Donovan Papers, Box 69A, Files Number 405–410, USAHEC.

45. The gold, loaded onto the cruiser *Émile Bertin,* had been destined for safekeeping in Halifax, but while it was at sea, Vichy officials changed the orders and sent it to Martinique. Olivier Courteaux, *Canada between Vichy and Free France, 1940–1945* (Toronto: University of Toronto Press, 2013), 35.

46. Vice-Consul at Martinique to Secretary of State, August 7, 1940, FRUS II, p. 515.

47. Admiral Robert to Secretary of State for the Navy, Vichy, November 5, 1940, Donovan Papers, Box 69A, Files Number 405–410, USAHEC. The admiral, John Greenslade, later became a leading advocate of the removal of Japanese Americans from the West Coast.

48. P. Benech to French Admiralty, November 6, 1940, Donovan Papers, Box 69A, Files Number 405–410, USAHEC.

49. For more on Leahy, see Phillips Payson O'Brien, *The Second Most Powerful Man in the World: The Life of Admiral William D. Leahy, Roosevelt's Chief of Staff* (New York: Dutton, 2019).

50. My thanks to Jacqueline Travisano and Enrique Vila del Corral for giving me the chance to stand on that same terrace.

51. Roosevelt to Leahy, November 17, 1940, James Gavin Papers, Box 14, Folder 3, USAHEC. Leahy's papers are in the Gavin archives because Gavin, named US ambassador to France in 1961, wanted to understand how another military man had handled the job.

52. Pershing to Leahy, November 27, 1940, James Gavin Papers, Box 14, Folder 3, USAHEC.

53. He came back to Washington in July 1942 and established the job that became chairman of the Joint Chiefs of Staff. He was the first admiral in American history to wear five stars in the rank of fleet admiral.

54. "America's Ambassador to Vichy Sails to His Post on a Cruiser," *Life,* January 6, 1941, 25.

55. Langer Papers, Folder 2, USAHEC.

56. OSS Confidential Report, "The Fall of France," [1942], TNA FO 371 / 36007; Ambassador René St. Quentin, Télégramme no. 1278, July 8, 1940, Dossier 30, Series 1GMII, AD.

57. See Fredrik Logevall, *Embers of War: The Fall of an Empire and the Making of America's Vietnam* (New York: Random House, 2013), 29–34.

58. William Langer Papers, Folder 6, USAHEC. The use of the word *sin* in connection with the Third Republic and the Popular Front was common.

59. William Langer, *Our Vichy Gamble* (New York: Knopf, 1947), chap. 3.

60. "Roosevelt and de Gaulle," Arthur M. Schlesinger Papers, MSSCOL 17775, Box 467, Folder Vichy, NYPL.

61. Murphy, *Diplomat among Warriors,* 64.

62. Adrienne Doris Hytier, *Two Years of French Foreign Policy: Vichy 1940–1942* (Westport, CT: Greenwood Press, 1974), 202; Washington to Leahy, November 18, 1940, ANP 3W284/A/III2A2.

63. "French Food Ships," *Times* (London), March 11, 1941, and "A French View of Ambassador's New Task," *Times* (London), January 9, 1941, ANP, F60/1726, Dossier Vichy et les États-Unis.

64. Committee on French Resistance Draft Minutes, August 8, 1940, and Colonial Matters, August 12, 1940, "Vichy French Colonies: Intelligence" Folder, TNA Vichy WO 208/52; Sir Geoffrey Shakespeare, Report on Blockade in French West and North African Territories, February 5, 1941, IWM, Box No. P. 79, Documents 10910, Folder GHS 3; ANP, F60/1726, Dossier Vichy et les États-Unis; "No American Food for French Relief," *Times* (London), September 12, 1940, ANP, F60/1726, Dossier Vichy et les États-Unis.

65. Richard de Rochemont, "Vichy vs. France: A Government of Fine Words and Cheap Intrigues Draws the Scorn of Its People," *Life,* September 1, 1941, 70.

66. J. R. M. Butler, *Grand Strategy, Volume II: September 1939–June 1941* (London: His Majesty's Stationery Office, 1957), 406–407.

67. Fabian Ware to Leo Amery, March 11, 1941, CAC, AMEL 2/3/14.

68. "L'opinion américaine et l'envoie de secours à l'Europe," N. 415, December 17, 1940, BNF, 4-JO-4101, France, Présidence de la Conseil, Information Presse Censuré.

69. Note sur Relations Commerciales, August 17, 1940, Dossier 30, Series 1GMII, AD.

70. Marie-Louise Dilkes, *Remembering World War Two: Through the Door to the American Embassy* (self-published, 1955), entry for March 16, 1941.

71. Langer Papers, Chapter 4, Folder 1, USAHEC.

72. "Oil for French North Africa," *Times* (London), June 30, 1941, and "US Warns Vichy," *Times* (London), August 4, 1941, ANP, F60/1726, Dossier Vichy et les États-Unis.

73. Saint-Quentin, Telegram no. 1535, August 23, 1940, Dossier 30, Series 1GMII, AD.

74. Vidkun Quisling was the collaborationist leader of Norway after the German victory there. The word *quisling* became a common term for puppet and collaborationist regimes throughout Europe during and after the war.

75. Quoted in Murphy, *Diplomat among Warriors,* 64.

76. Mark Stoler, *Allies and Adversaries: The Joint Chiefs of Staff, the Grand Alliance, and U.S. Strategy in World War II* (Chapel Hill: University of North Carolina Press, 2000), 24; Langer Papers, Folder 2, USAHEC.

77. Paxton, *Vichy France,* 111–113. Paxton makes clear that the Germans were more interested in Vichy remaining in a pro-German state of neutrality than becoming an active belligerent. The Germans did not want Vichy actions in sub-Saharan Africa to force them to worry about their southern flank at a time when they were planning major operations to their east against the Soviet Union.

78. Memorandum of Conversation with Henry-Haye, July 16, 1940, Cordell Hull Papers, Box 58, Reel 29, LCMD.

79. Memorandum of Conversation with Henry-Haye, September 11, 1940, Cordell Hull Papers, Box 58, Reel 29, LCMD.

80. Memorandum of Conversation with Henry-Haye, November 4, 1940, and Matthews to Hull, November 14, 1940, in FRUS II, pp. 400, 405.

81. They also had a dish called Oysters Foch. My thanks to Augustine Meaher for sharing the anecdote about Antoine's.

82. Matthews to Hull, November 16, 1940, FRUS II, pp. 413–414.

83. Roosevelt to "My Dear Leahy," December 20, 1940, FRUS II, p. 426.

84. Quoted in Hytier, *Two Years of French Foreign Policy,* 190–192.

85. William Mortimer Moore, *Free France's Lion: The Life of Philippe Leclerc, De Gaulle's Greatest General* (Philadelphia: Casemate, 2011), 85. There remains a large memorial to mark Leclerc's landing in Douala in August 1940.

86. For more on the rhetorical battle, see Rachel Chin, "Who Speaks for France? Vichy, Free France and the Battle over French Legitimacy: 1940–1942," *British Journal for Military History* 6, no. 3 (November 2020): 2–22.

87. Paxton describes the firing as a "palace coup." Paxton, *Vichy France,* 92–93.

88. The duke (sometimes known as Napoleon II) was the son of the Habsburg Marie Louise, the Duchess of Parma, thus his remains were in the Habsburg imperial crypt until 1940. His heart and intestines are still there.

89. Murphy, *Diplomat among Warriors,* 59.

90. The Chargé in France (Murphy) to the Secretary of State, Vichy, December 9, 1940, FRUS, 1940 General and Europe Papers, Volume II, pp. 414–417.

91. Matthews to Hull, December 18, 1940, FRUS II, pp. 423–424.

92. Matthews to Hull, December 18, 1940, and Hull to Murphy, December 13, 1940, FRUS II, 420–422.

93. Leahy to Roosevelt, January 25, 1941, Gavin Papers, Box 14, Folder 3, USAHEC; the pro-Vichy Canadian diplomat Pierre Dupuy found that he could only wake Pétain up in meetings by "loudly repeating the name of General de Gaulle." Courteaux, *Canada between Vichy and Free France,* 61.

4. WE MUSTN'T UNDERESTIMATE AMERICAN BLUNDERING

1. Robert Murphy, *Diplomat among Warriors: The Unique World of a Foreign Service Expert* (Garden City, NY: Doubleday, 1964), 66–68.

2. Cordell Hull, *The Memoirs of Cordell Hull* (New York: Macmillan, 1948), 2:951. It appears that the reports of German agents in North Africa were greatly exaggerated and maybe even spread by the British to undermine the American aid plan.

3. Hillenkoetter was in Pearl Harbor on December 7, 1941, and was wounded in action on board the USS *West Virginia.* For more on him, see https://www.cia .gov/library/center-for-the-study-of-intelligence/csi-publications/csi-studies /studies/vol-60-no-1/pdfs/Schroeder-Forged-by-Fire-Hillenkoetter.pdf.

4. John C. Beam, "The Intelligence Background of Operation TORCH," 1983, AD-A, 129–136, p. 3, USAHEC.

5. Murphy, *Diplomat among Warriors,* 68.

6. "Weygand Begs His Army to Back Pétain: Maintain Order Is Commander's Plea to Troops," *Washington Evening Star,* February 1, 1942, 1. CBS Radio in the United States obtained a recording of the speech and broadcast an English-language version of it to an American audience nationwide.

7. "Compte rendu des entrevues de M. Murphy avec le général Weygand et le gouverneur-général Boisson," December 22, 1940, ANP, 3W284/A/III/2A2.

8. Memorandum of Conversation between Robert D. Murphy, American Counselor of Embassy in France, and Maxime Weygand, French Delegate General in North Africa, Initialed by General Weygand at Algiers February 26, 1941, FRUS II, p. 1059.

9. Hull, *Memoirs,* 2:949.

10. Hull, *Memoirs,* 2:948.

11. Langer Papers, Chapter 4, Folder 1, USAHEC.

12. Robert Paxton, *Vichy France: Old Guard and New Order* (New York: Knopf, 1973), 97. Wasson died at the hands of a sniper in Jerusalem in 1948 while serving as consul there. The identity of the sniper remains a mystery.

13. Churchill to Roosevelt, March 13, 1941, in Langer Papers, Chapter 4, Folder 1.

14. Robert Murphy had already warned Vichy officials in December 1940 that the United States would not allow Germany to take control of Dakar. "Compte rendu des entrevues de M. Murphy avec le général Weygand et le gouverneur-général Boisson," December 22, 1940, ANP 3W284/A/III2A2. For much more on German ambitions in Gibraltar and the Atlantic, see Norman J. W. Goda, *Tomorrow the World: Hitler, Northwest Africa, and the Path toward America* (Chapel Hill: University of North Carolina Press, 1998). He argues that the Germans wanted the Canaries more than they wanted Gibraltar because the former put them in a better position to threaten the United States.

15. Langer Papers, Chapter 4, Folder 2, USAHEC.

16. See Hal Vaughan, *FDR's Twelve Apostles: The Spies Who Paved the Way for the Invasion of North Africa* (New York: Lyons, 2006).

17. Murphy, *Diplomat among Warriors,* 90.

18. Eddy later translated for Roosevelt and King Ibn Saud after the Yalta Conference of 1945, became an ambassador to Saudi Arabia, then resigned when President Harry Truman recognized the State of Israel.

19. "SOE and Operation TORCH," Colonel Sir A D Dodds-Parker Papers 10/18/1, IWM. Dodds-Parker was the Special Operations Executive station chief for France. Fleming named the Jamaica estate where he wrote many of his James Bond novels Goldeneye. My thanks to my friend Simon Read, who is currently at work on a biography of Fleming.

20. Beam, "Intelligence Background of Operation TORCH," 8–9.

21. For more, see Christian Destremau, *Le moyen-orient pendant la seconde guerre mondiale* (Paris: Tempus, 2011), chap. 2, and Ashley Jackson, *The British Empire and the Second World War* (London: Continuum, 2006), chap. 8.

22. Freya Stark, *Dust in the Lion's Paw* (New York: Harcourt, Brace, and World, 1961), 75. Chapter 7 gives an excellent description of life under siege in Baghdad.

23. Stark, *Dust in the Lion's Paw,* 77.

24. In late 1941, al-Husseini made his way to Rome, then Berlin, where he met with Hitler and tried to raise a pro-Axis Arab Legion. He also toured concentration camps with Heinrich Himmler.

25. For India, see Sugata Bose, *His Majesty's Opponent: Subhas Chandra Bose and India's Struggle against Empire* (Cambridge, MA: Harvard University Press, 2011).

26. Derounian wrote under many pen names. See John Roy Carlson, *Cairo to Damascus* (New York: Knopf, 1951), 170.

27. Historian Douglas Porch offers a brief recap of the campaign in http://www .ccc.nps.navy.mil/rsepResources/si/dec02/middleEast.asp.

28. Harold Nicolson, *The War Years, 1939–1945* (New York: Atheneum, 1967), 162.

29. His Majesty's Minister, Kabul, to the Secretary of State for Foreign Affairs, India Office, 30th May 1941, British Library IOR: L / PS / 12 / 413, Activities of Vichy Officials, 1940–1941.

30. Leahy to Roosevelt, April 21, 1941, Arthur Schlesinger Papers, Mss Coll 17775, Box 467, Vichy, NYPL. Schlesinger used shorthand—for example, "poss / y" for "possibility" and "Demcies" for "democracies." I have taken the liberty of rendering his shorthand into conventional English for clarity.

31. Paxton, *Vichy France,* 117–118. Alphonse Juin, a future hero of the Free French, was among the prisoners released.

32. Langer Papers, Chapter 4, Folder 2, USAHEC. Pétain never put the Paris Protocols into effect, and the German invasion of the Soviet Union soon distracted German attention from them.

33. "America's Dossier against Vichy," *Times* (London), June 11, 1941; "Laval Lectures Americans," *Times* (London), May 27, 1941; "Un malentendu existe entre la France et les États-Unis," *Paris-Soir,* May 28, 1941, ANP, F60 / 1726, Dossier Vichy et les États-Unis.

34. Hull, *Memoirs,* 2:949.

35. Langer Papers, Chapter 4, Folder 2, USAHEC.

36. Hull, *Memoirs,* 2:958.

37. Hull, *Memoirs,* 2:958–959.

38. Cordell Hull to Franklin Roosevelt, May 13, 1941, and Roosevelt to Hull, May 14, 1941, in Arthur Schlesinger Papers, Mss Coll 17775, Box 467, Folder Vichy, NYPL.

39. Hull, *Memoirs,* 2:960.

40. Langer Papers, Chapter 4, Folder 2, USAHEC.

41. Hull, *Memoirs,* 2:961–962.

42. "Vichy: A Turning Point," *Times* (London), May 17, 1941, ANP, F60 / 1726, Dossier Vichy et les États-Unis.

43. Hull, *Memoirs,* 2:965.

44. Cable N. 431, January 2, 1941, N. 445, January 16, 1941, and N. 457, January 28, 1941, 4-JO-4101, France, Présidence de la Conseil, Information Presse Censuré, BNF. Cable N. 431 did, however, warn that if the United States ever did get involved in the war, "nothing will stop the machine of war in its movement."

45. GOC [General Officer Commanding] Palestine and Transjordan to War Office, July 10, 1941, British Library, Coll 6 / 93; Syria Situation after the Capitulation of France 1940, 9 / 1003. See also Destremau, *Le moyen-orient,* chap. 3. De Gaulle reacted to the events in Syria with such unrestrained anger that many senior British officials thought he might be insane. For more, see Julian Jackson, *De Gaulle* (Cambridge, MA: Harvard University Press, 2018), 173–180. Sir Edward Spears, who tried to hide the existence of Jewish ancestry in his family by displaying virulent anti-Semitism, was an important witness to these events.

46. Moshe Dayan lost an eye fighting with an Australian unit that crossed into Syria in June 1941.

47. N. 459, January 30, 1941, 4-JO-4101, France, Présidence de la Conseil, Information Presse Censuré, BNF.

48. Paxton, *Vichy France,* 174–175.

49. For much more, see Rebecca Erbelding, *Rescue Board: The Untold Story of America's Efforts to Save the Jews of Europe* (New York: Doubleday, 2018). See also Laurent Jolly, *L'état contre les juifs: Vichy, les Nazis, et la persécution antisémite* (Paris: Grasset, 2018).

50. Leahy to Hull, June 16, 1941, FRUS II, p. 509.

51. Acting Secretary of State to Leahy, June 27, 1941, FRUS II, pp. 509–510.

52. https://encyclopedia.ushmm.org/content/en/article/wannsee-conference-and -the-final-solution.

53. N. 459, January 30, 1941, 4-JO-4101, France, Présidence de la Conseil, Information Presse Censuré, BNF.

54. Anthony Biddle to President Roosevelt, June 16, 1941, James Gavin Papers, Box 14, Folder 1, USAHEC.

55. Murphy, *Diplomat among Warriors,* 85–86.

56. Jackson, *De Gaulle,* chap. 8.

57. Anthony Biddle to President Roosevelt, June 9, 1941, James Gavin Papers, Box 14, Folder 1, USAHEC.

58. William Leahy to Sumner Welles, April 1, 1941, James Gavin Papers, Box 14, Folder 2, USAEHC.

59. Hull, *Memoirs,* 2:963.

60. William Leahy to President Roosevelt, July 18, 1941, James Gavin Papers, Box 14, Folder 2, USAHEC.

61. Leahy to Roosevelt, July 18.

62. Langer Papers, Chapter 5, Folder 1, USAHEC.

63. "French Colonies and US Intentions," James Gavin Papers, Box 14, Folder 2, USAHEC. The notation appeared in Leahy's diary for July 21, 1941.

64. See Fredrik Logevall, *Embers of War: The Fall of an Empire and the Making of America's Vietnam* (New York: Random House, 2013), 36–41.

65. Hull, *Memoirs,* 2:1039.

66. William Langer Papers, Folder 5.

67. Some of the cartoons are reproduced in Richard Minear, ed., *Dr. Seuss Goes to War: The World War II Cartoons of Theodore Seuss Geisel* (New York: New Press, 2001). See especially pp. 132 and 155–160.

68. Quoted in Langer Papers, Chapter 5, Folder 1, USAHEC.

69. The Consul-General at Algiers to Secretary of State, August 2, 1941, FRUS II, p. 406.

70. Secretary of State to the Consul General at Casablanca, August 6, 1941, FRUS II, p. 408.

71. Donald Reed, *Admiral Leahy at Vichy France* (Chicago: Adams Press, 1968), 32.

72. Langer Papers, Chapter 5, Folder 2, USAHEC.

73. "Aide-memoire du Maréchal Pétain pour son entrevue avec Goering, 1 décembre 1941," AN, 415AP4, dossier 14. The memo is a pathetic, groveling document unlikely to have inspired much respect in the eyes of any German who read it or heard a discussion based on it.

74. George E. Melton, *Darlan: Admiral and Statesman of France, 1881–1942* (Westport, CT: Praeger, 1998), 138.

75. Hull, *Memoirs,* 2:1043.

76. Barnett Singer, *Maxime Weygand: A Biography of the French General in Two World Wars* (London: McFarland, 2008), 163.

77. Melton, *Darlan,* 133.

78. Leahy Diary, entry for November 18, 1941, in James Gavin Papers, Box 14, Folder 2, USAHEC.

79. Reed, *Leahy at Vichy,* 35.

80. Leahy Diary, entry for November 18, 1941.

81. Hull, *Memoirs,* 2:1044–1045.

82. Melton, *Darlan,* 127–128.

83. Murphy, *Diplomat among Warriors,* 96.

84. Melton, *Darlan,* 139.

85. Leahy Diary, entries for December 10 and 12, 1941.

86. Roosevelt created the Coordinator of Information (COI) office in July 1941 with Donovan as its head. The COI officially became the Office of Strategic Services (OSS) in June 1942 and moved from the White House to the Joint Chiefs of Staff.

87. Coordinator of Information, Office of Strategic Services, The War This Week, reports of December 11–18, December 18–24, and December 24–31, 1941, William J. Donovan Papers, Box 103A, USAHEC.

88. "New Danger to America," *Times* (London), May 19, 1941, "Vichy Protests to America," *Times* (London), May 21, 1941, and "New Pressure on Vichy," *Times* (London), August 14, 1941, ANP, F60 / 1726, Dossier Vichy et les États-Unis.

89. The War This Week, December 18–24, USAHEC.

90. The Me 264, first commissioned in 1937, flew for the first time in December 1942. It had the range to fly from Martinique to New York City and back. Limits on German resources meant that the Germans eventually used the few models they built mostly for long-range reconnaissance.

91. For a view from the German side, see Goda, *Tomorrow the World,* 171–173.

92. For a basic timeline, see https://winstonchurchill.org/publications/finest-hour /finest-hour-136/when-mice-roared-the-thirty-minute-invasion-of-st-pierre -and-miquelon/. The referendum offered residents the choice of de Gaulle or collaboration. It did not specifically list Pétain as an option, so many people crossed out both options or abstained from voting.

93. Olivier Courteaux, *Canada between Vichy and Free France, 1940–1945* (Toronto: University of Toronto Press, 2013), 134. For more background, see Martin F. Auger, "'A Tempest in a Teapot': Canadian Military Planning and the St. Pierre and Miquelon Affair, 1940–1942," *Acadiensis* 33, no. 1 (Autumn 2003).

94. Winston Churchill, *The Second World War,* vol. 3, *The Grand Alliance* (London: Cassell, 1950), 591.

95. Charles de Gaulle, *The Call to Honor* (New York: Viking, 1955), 215.

96. War Department, Survey of Newfoundland and the Miquelon Islands, September 12, 1941, S30–615, Volume 1, USAHEC F1122.S97 1941, V. 1, C. 1, pp. 65–69.

97. J. W. Pickersgill, *The Mackenzie King Record* (Toronto: University of Toronto Press, 1960), 314.

98. Lester B. Pearson, *Mike: The Memoirs of the Rt Hon. Lester B. Pearson* (Toronto: University of Toronto Press, 1972), 1:200.

99. François Kersaudy, *Churchill and de Gaulle* (New York: Athenaeum, 1983), 174–175.

100. Diary of Lord Halifax A7 / 8 / 10, YODL, www.dlib.york.ac.uk/yodl, entry for January 5, 1942.

101. "Incident at St. Pierre," *Time,* January 5, 1942, 26.

102. "Free French Take St. Pierre and Miquelon," *Washington Evening Star,* December 25, 1941, 1.

103. Hull, *Memoirs,* 2:1130, 1137.

104. Hull, *Memoirs,* 2:1132.

105. Hull, *Memoirs,* 2:948.

106. Paxton, *Vichy France,* 387–390.

107. Langer Papers, Chapter 5, Folder 1, USAHEC.

108. Langer Papers, Chapter 5, Folder 2, USAHEC.

5. THEY'RE ASLEEP IN NEW YORK

1. The best biographical source on Giraud is probably Michèle Cointet, *De Gaulle et Giraud: l'affrontement, 1942–1944* (Paris: Perrin, 2005).

2. "Fighting Fronts: Giraud's Task," *Newsweek,* January 4, 1943, 18.

3. "Great German Embarrassment," *Time,* May 11, 1942, 34.

4. The cover of *Newsweek* for January 4, 1943, featured Giraud and the line "How Giraud Is Forging a New Army in North Africa."

5. Dwight Eisenhower, *Crusade in Europe* (Garden City, NY: Doubleday, 1948), 99.

6. Leahy Diary for January 27, 1942, James Gavin Papers, Box 14, Folder 2, USAHEC.

7. "Amy Elizabeth Thorpe: World War II's Mata Hari," https://www.historynet .com/amy-elizabeth-thorpe-wwiis-mata-hari.htm. Thorpe married Brousse and moved with him to France. She was also known under her married name Elizabeth Pack or by her wartime code name Cynthia.

8. Coordinator of Information, OSS, The War This Week, January 1–2, 1942, William Donovan Papers, Box 103a, USAHEC.

9. J. R. M. Butler, *Grand Strategy, Volume II: September 1939–June 1941* (London: His Majesty's Stationery Office, 1957), 232.

10. Robert Murphy, *Diplomat among Warriors: The Unique World of a Foreign Service Expert* (Garden City, NY: Doubleday, 1964), 66. See also Alfred Salinas, *Les américains en Algérie* (Paris: L'Harmattan, 2013).

11. Lord Halifax to Foreign Office, January 16, 1942, FO 892 / 127, "1942 American Policy towards Vichy," TNA.

12. Milton Viorst, *Hostile Allies: FDR and De Gaulle* (New York: Macmillan, 1965), 88. The Bir Hakeim battle gives its name to the Métro station close to the Eiffel Tower.

13. Roosevelt to Leahy, February 1942 [no exact date] and Welles to Leahy, March 27, 1942, James Gavin Papers, Box 14, Folder 4, USAHEC.

14. Leahy Diary for February 7, 1942, James Gavin Papers, Box 14, Folder 2, USAHEC.

15. Eddy Florentin, *Quand les alliés bombardaient la France* (Paris: Tempus, 2008), chap. 4; "Not So Cozy," *Time,* March 16, 1942, 23–24. For more on Doriot, see Philippe Burrin, *La dérive fasciste: Doriot, Déat, Bergery, 1933–1945* (Paris: Seuil, 1986).

16. "Confiance: Ses amputations se poursuivent méthodiquement," British Library, Shelfmark Map CC.6.a.39.

17. "America and Vichy," *Times* (London), March 5, 1942, ANP, F60 / 1726, Dossier Vichy et les États-Unis.

18. Department of State Memorandum, April 30, 1942, James Gavin Papers, Box 14, Folder 4, USAHEC.

19. Coordinator of Information, OSS, The War This Week, April 9–16, 1942, William Donovan Papers, Box 103a, USAHEC.

20. Coordinator of Information, OSS, The War This Week, April 16–23, 1942, William Donovan Papers, Box 103a, USAHEC.

21. "France, We Are with You," *Time,* May 4, 1942, 24–25; "St. Pierre Laval," *Time,* May 25, 1942, 30; "To War Again?" *Time,* July 27, 1942, 27.

22. Transcript of WCBX Radio Broadcast, March 29, 1942, ANP, F60 / 1726, Dossier Vichy et les États-Unis.

23. "Laval Gets to Work," *Times* (London), April 16, 1942, and "US Ambassador in Vichy Summoned Home," *Times* (London), April 17, 1942.

24. American Survey, April 15, 1942, ANP, F60 / 1726, I 6800, Dossier Vichy et les États-Unis: Commentaires de Presse, Alliés.

25. Langer Papers, Chapter 6, Folder 2, USAHEC.

26. Stephen Trumbull, "Martinique No Sub Haven," *Miami Herald,* March 1, 1942.

27. "Seize Martinique," *Miami Herald,* April 24, 1942. My thanks to Augustine Meaher for passing these articles along.

28. "L'Amérique s'adresse au peuple français," August 2, 1942, ANP, F60 / 1759 / E101.

29. "Supine Nations Warned," *Daily Telegraph,* July 25, 1942, ANP, F60 / 1759 / Dossier États-Unis Divers.

30. For more, see Mark Stoler, *Allies and Adversaries: The Joint Chiefs of Staff, the Grand Alliance, and U.S. Strategy in World War II* (Chapel Hill: University of North Carolina Press, 2000), chap. 4.

31. The raid on Dieppe cost 900 dead and 2,000 prisoners of war, most of them Canadian. For more, see Robin Neillands, *The Dieppe Raid: The Story of the Disastrous 1942 Expedition* (Bloomington: Indiana University Press, 2005).

32. Murphy, *Diplomat among Warriors,* 101.

33. Michelier was so pro-German that he became known as Fritz, a play on his French nickname Frix.

34. Murphy, *Diplomat among Warriors,* 110–115.

35. Murphy, *Diplomat among Warriors,* 99–101.

36. Robert Paxton, *Vichy France: Old Guard and New Order* (New York: Columbia University Press, 1973), 305.

37. Coordinator of Information, OSS, The War This Week, June 18–25, 1942, William Donovan Papers, Box 103a, USAHEC.

38. Coordinator of Information, OSS, The War This Week, June 4–11, 1942, William Donovan Papers, Box 103a, USAHEC.

39. Quoted in Meredith Hindley, *Destination Casablanca: Exile, Espionage, and the Battle for North Africa in World War II* (Washington, DC: PublicAffairs, 2017), 172.

40. Coordinator of Information, OSS, The War This Week, May 21–28, 1942, William Donovan Papers, Box 103a, USAHEC.

41. Alexander Sachs, "Political-Economic Characteristics of the French Colonial Empire," September 30, 1940, in Donovan Papers, Box 69A, File Numbers 405–410. Unbelievable though it seems today, Algeria was once the world's single largest exporter of wine, shipping more than Spain, France, and Italy combined. See Owen White, *The Blood of the Colony: Wine and the Rise of French Algeria* (Cambridge, MA: Harvard University Press, 2021).

42. Albert Camus is probably the most famous *pied noir,* and he wrote beautifully about the contradictions of Algerian society. In English, see especially his *Algerian Chronicles,* translated by Arthur Goldhammer (Cambridge, MA: Harvard University Press, 2013). See also Jérôme Cotillon, "L'Empire français dans la révolution nationale: L'Exemple de la vision algérienne des entourages du maréchal Pétain," *Outre-Mers* 91, no. 343 (2004), and Jacques Cantier, *L'Algérie sous le régime de Vichy* (Paris: Odile Jacob, 2002).

43. Julian Jackson, *De Gaulle* (Cambridge, MA; Harvard University Press, 2018), xxxi.

44. Norman J. W. Goda, *Tomorrow the World: Hitler, Northwest Africa, and the Path toward America* (Chapel Hill: University of North Carolina Press, 1998), 21–29.

45. Murphy, *Diplomat among Warriors,* 112. See also Cantier, *L'Algérie.*

46. For much more on their relationship, see Cointet, *De Gaulle et Giraud.*

47. Julian Jackson, *France: The Dark Years, 1940–1944* (New York: Oxford University Press, 2001), 220; Paxton, *Vichy France,* 74.

48. Langer Papers, Chapter 7, Folder 2, USAHEC.

49. "Washington et Vichy," February 4, 1942, FO 892 / 127, "1942 American Policy towards Vichy," TNA.

50. On his arrival in North Africa, Harold Macmillan noted that revenge was a "genuine, if undesirable, emotion" motivating French politics there. "There is inevitably a still more cruel shadow overhanging liberated France." Harold Macmillan, "Recognition," January 5, 1944, CAC DUFC 4 / 8, Section IV.

51. Charles Lucet and André Baeyens, "The Fall of France," Office of Strategic Services, [April 1942], FO 371 / 36007, TNA.

52. Cadogan Minute, January 3, 1943, TNA FO 371 / 36007.

53. Bullitt to Roosevelt, January 29, 1943, William C. Bullitt Papers, MS 112, Series I, Box 73, Folder 1826, Yale University Libraries Special Collections. I am grateful to Robert Pennoyer for alerting me to the existence of this document. As the lawyer to Bullitt's daughter, Anne, Mr. Pennoyer arranged for Bullitt's extensive papers to find their way to Yale.

54. Langer Papers, Chapter 6, Folder 1, USAHEC.

55. "Washington et Vichy," February 4, 1942, FO 892 / 127, "1942 American Policy towards Vichy," TNA.

56. Duff Cooper, Despatch to the Secretary of State for Foreign Affairs, January 1945, CAC, DUFC 4 / 8.

57. Minute Sheet, R. E. Barclay, August 25, 1942, FO 371 / 32122, TNA.

58. Minute Sheet, M. P. Crawfurd, August 8, 1942, FO 371 / 32122, TNA.

59. "De Gaulle's Creed," *Time,* July 6, 1942, 32.

60. Jackson, *De Gaulle,* 95.

61. Matthews to Leahy, December 10, 1942, James Gavin Papers, Box 14, Folder 4.

62. "SOE and Operation TORCH."

63. Commander-in-Chief's Dispatch, p. 10, USAHEC. The Americans gave Mast the not-too-deceptive codename FLAGPOLE.

64. "SOE and Operation TORCH," December 1942, Colonel Sir A D Dodds-Parker, 10 / 18 / 1 Papers, IWM.

65. Those deputies were Lyman Lemnitzer, a future chairman of the Joint Chiefs of Staff and North Atlantic Treaty Organization (NATO) commander, and Jerauld Wright, a future commander of NATO naval forces. The pilot who flew

Clark from London to Gibraltar was Paul Tibbets, the man who later flew the *Enola Gay* over Hiroshima.

66. Murphy, *Diplomat among Warriors,* 119.

67. Major George Bare, Infantry, Advanced Infantry Officers Course, 1947–1948: The Algiers Operation, 8–11 November 1942, p. 10, USAHEC D766.99.A4 B37 1947a.

68. Other versions of the story say that the police were on an unrelated sweep for smugglers or that the servants were talking loudly in a café about some strange visitors at the villa.

69. Martin M. Philipsborn Papers, Box 2, Folder "Africa: Messages and Misc.," USAHEC.

70. Office of the United States Naval Attaché American Embassy London, England, 1939–1946, Tracy Barrett Kittredge Papers, Record Number 60017.262, Hoover Library Digital Collections, Stanford University.

71. Commander-in-Chief's Dispatch, p. 10, USAHEC.

72. Coordinator of Information, OSS, The War This Week, July 23–30, July 30–August 6, August 27–September 3, September 10–17, and September 17–14, 1942, William Donovan Papers, Box 103a, USAHEC.

73. Goda, *Tomorrow the World,* especially chap. 6.

74. "Growing Criticism of War Direction," *Times* (London), September 6, 1942, ANP, F60 / 1759 / Dossier États-Unis Divers.

75. "Willkie Assails Administration on Vichy Link," *Washington Post,* October 31, 1942. In Beirut, Willkie met de Gaulle. See also the account in Julia C. Tobey, *Captain McCrae's War: The World War II Memoir of Franklin D. Roosevelt's Naval Aide and USS* Iowa's *First Commanding Officer* (New York: Skyhorse, 2016), 123–124.

76. Daily Digest, October 31, 1942, ANP, F60 / 1759 / E105.

77. See Hindley, *Destination Casablanca,* 424–426.

78. *Divide and Conquer,* directed by Frank Capra (Office of War Information, 1943). Hollywood screenwriters completely reimagined Ernest Hemingway's Cuba-based novel *To Have and Have Not* (1944) in order to set the movie among French intrigue in Martinique.

79. "Should the United States Break Relations with Vichy?" *American Education Press* 8, no. 4 (May 25, 1942).

80. "Africa Is a Good Place for a Second Front," *PM,* October 26, 1942.

81. Henry Haye, Cable no. 1606 and 1607, April 20, 1942, Dossier 16, Corps Diplomatique Américain en France, 26 mai 1940–23 octobre 1942, AD.

82. Richard H. Minear, *Dr. Seuss Goes to War: The World War II Editorial Cartoons of Theodor Seuss Geisel* (New York: New Press, 1999), 157, 158.

83. N. 438, January 9, 1942, 4-JO-4101, France, Présidence de la Conseil, Information Presse Censuré, BNF.

84. "New Emblem of Fighting French Forces Seen Here," *New York Times,* October 26, 1942.

85. "Let's Get Those Ships," *Philadelphia Record,* October 31, 1942; "France's Shadow Empire," *New York Times,* October 24, 1942.

86. "The Conscience of Humanity Has Kept Silent for Too Long!" *New York Herald Tribune,* October 27, 1942.

87. Stoler, *Allies and Adversaries,* 90.

88. G-2 Intelligence Report Number 6, October 16, 1942, Martin M. Philipsborn Papers, Box 2, Africa, AFHQ II Corps, Intelligence folder, USAHEC.

89. "Report on Conditions and Opinion in France, January to July 1942," MISC 285, Item 3813, IWM.

90. "Mr. Hull's Warning to Vichy Envoy," *Times* (London), September 16, 1942, ANP, F60 / 1726, Dossier Vichy et les États-Unis.

91. Paxton, *Vichy France,* 281–282.

92. "France, We Are with You," *Time,* May 4, 1942, 24–25.

93. "France under Duress," *Times* (London), April 23, 1942, ANP, F60 / 1726, Dossier Vichy et les États-Unis.

94. The Dreyfus Affair was a tectonic scandal from 1894 to 1906 over false allegations of treason made against a Jewish French staff officer. The scandal grew as evidence emerged of a widespread cover-up by French officials.

95. "Report on Conditions and Opinion in France, January to July 1942," MISC 285, Item 3813, IWM; "Tidings of the Riviera," *Time,* November 9, 1942.

96. www.nationalarchives.gov.uk/education/resources/holocaust/riegner-telegram.

97. https://www.jewishvirtuallibrary.org/morgenthau-documents-state-department -inaction-january-1944.

98. "Vichy-US Break Is Near," *Daily Mail,* September 16, 1942, in Martin M. Philipsborn Papers, Box 3, Folder "Pre-Invasion Press Clippings," USAHEC. It also made the front page of the *Washington Evening Star,* September 15, 1942.

99. The Hull statement is the earliest of its kind I can find, yet it does not appear in any of the major secondary sources nor does it appear on the US Holocaust Museum's rather extensive web page on what Americans knew (https://exhibitions .ushmm.org/americans-and-the-holocaust/). Laurel Leff, *Buried by the Times: The Holocaust and America's Most Important Newspaper* (Cambridge: Cambridge

University Press, 2005), 149, notes the statement but only to say that the *Times* buried it on p. 5. Hull may have been trying to protect himself given his decision to recognize Vichy, or he may have been trying to get ahead of Wise, who, on November 24, 1942, announced to the American media that the Germans had already murdered 2,000,000 Jews. That story failed to make the front page of any American newspaper.

100. Diary of Lord Halifax A7/8/11, YODL, www.dlib.york.ac.uk/yodl, entries for September 4 and 23, 1942.

101. Coordinator of Information, OSS, The War This Week, July 16–23, July 23–30, and August 27–September 3, 1942, William Donovan Papers, Box 103a, USAHEC.

102. Deborah Lipstadt, *Beyond Belief: The American Press and the Coming of the Holocaust, 1933–1945* (New York: Free Press, 1986), 178–179. See also Robert Paxton, "Years of Shame," *New Republic,* November 18, 1981, 33–34. For more on the Holocaust in France, see Jacques Semelin, *La survie des juifs en France, 1940–1944* (Paris: CNRS, 2018), and Laurent Joly, *L'État contre les juifs: Vichy, les Nazis et la persécution antisémite* (Paris: Grasset, 2018).

103. Frank Brutto, "Nazi-Held Countries Ship Out Jews to 'Solve' Problem," *Washington Evening Star,* August 27, 1942, B-2.

104. "M. Cordell Hull et l'anti-sémitisme de Vichy," *France,* September 12, 1942, ANP, F60/1726, Dossier Vichy et les États-Unis.

105. Coordinator of Information, OSS, The War This Week, October 8–15, 1942, William Donovan Papers, Box 103a, USAHEC.

106. "Paris Press Orders Vichy: Let Hitler Defend Bases," *Daily Mail,* October 14, 1942, and "Vichy-US Break Is Near," in Martin M. Philipsborn Papers, Box 3, Folder "Pre-Invasion Press Clippings," USAHEC.

107. Intelligence Annexe, October 12, 1942, Martin M. Philipsborn Papers, Box 3, Folder "Africa Landing Orders and Annexes," USAHEC. The report nevertheless assumed the French would fight hard if so ordered by their chain of command.

108. Cole to Brigadier General J. E. Hull, October 20, 1942; Cole to Hull, October 19, 1942; Cole to Hull, October 21, 1942; London to AGWAR, October 28, 1942, all in FDRL, Map Room Files, Box 105, Folder 3. John E. Hull was the War Department's chief of the European Section of the General Staff. There is no relation to Cordell Hull.

109. Marshall to Eisenhower, October 16, 1942, FDRL, Map Room Files, Box 105, Folder 3.

110. "A New Crisis in France," *Trenton Evening Times,* October 26, 1942. The same themes appeared in William Philip Simms, "Crisis in France," *Washington Times,* October 27, 1942.

111. G-2 Intelligence Report Number 6, October 16, 1942, Martin M. Philipsborn Papers, Box 2, Africa, AFHQ II Corps, Intelligence folder, USAHEC. A naval intelligence report from 1942 noted that Laval had long feared that the Germans would replace him with Doriot. LTC Robert Solberg to William J. Donovan, July 20, 1942, Record Number 69085.125, Hoover Library Digital Collections, Stanford University.

112. "Vale Vichy," *Time*, November 30, 1942, 35.

113. "Dare We Ask the French to Defy Our 'Friends'?" *Philadelphia Record*, October 23, 1942.

114. William Philip Simms, "Axis Expecting Blow," *Washington News*, October 23, 1942, and Ernest Lindley, "Relations with France," *Washington Post*, October 24, 1942. The United States had, in fact, deployed several thousand men to Liberia throughout 1942.

115. "Open a Western Front CIO Conventions Urge," *UE News*, October 3, 1942.

116. Rick Atkinson, *An Army at Dawn* (New York: Holt, 2002), 23.

117. Eric Larrabee, *Commander in Chief: Franklin Delano Roosevelt, His Lieutenants, and Their War* (New York: Touchstone, 1987), 421.

118. Atkinson, *Army at Dawn*, 27, 33.

119. Larrabee, *Commander in Chief*, 422–424.

120. Colonel E. Lombard letter to Admiral Stark, with attachments, September 1, 1942, Tracy Barrett Kittredge Papers, Record Number 60017.98, Hoover Library Digital Collections, Stanford University.

121. W. A. Reitzel Intelligence Reports Concerning France, August 26, 1942, Tracy Barrett Kittredge Papers, Record Number 60017.145, Hoover Library Digital Collections, Stanford University.

122. G-2 Report, October 12, 1942, Box 3, Folder "Africa Intelligence," Martin M. Philipsborn Papers, USAHEC.

6. A BEAUTIFUL FRIENDSHIP?

1. The presidents were Calvin Coolidge and Herbert Hoover. Wright later became commander of the NATO Atlantic Fleet and ambassador to Taiwan. The *Seraph* was also the submarine used in Operation Mincemeat, an Allied plan to drop false planning documents on the body of "a man who never was."

2. "SOE and Operation TORCH," December 1942, Colonel Sir A D Dodds-Parker Papers, 10 / 81 / 1, IWM.

3. "SOE and Operation TORCH."

4. Harry Butcher, *My Three Years with Eisenhower* (New York: Simon and Schuster, 1946), 169. Butcher was Eisenhower's naval aide.

5. Rick Atkinson, *An Army at Dawn* (New York: Holt, 2002), 66, 115.

6. Eisenhower to Bedell Smith, November 9, 1942, in *The Papers of Dwight D. Eisenhower,* ed. Alfred D. Chandler (Baltimore: Johns Hopkins University Press, 1970), 677.

7. George Howe, *Northwest Africa: Seizing the Initiative in the West* (Washington, DC: Government Printing Office, 1957), 189.

8. Arthur Layton Funk, *The Politics of TORCH: The Allied Landings and the Algiers Putsch, 1942* (Lawrence: University Press of Kansas, 1974), 21.

9. The founder of the L'Oréal cosmetics empire, Eugène Scheuller, and the collaborationist automobile magnate Louis Renault provided the Cagoule with much of its funding. For more, see Valerie Deacon, *The Extreme Right in the French Resistance: Members of the Cagoule and Corvignolles in the Second World War* (Baton Rouge: Louisiana State University Press, 2016).

10. Funk, *Politics of TORCH,* 39.

11. War Department Cable Number 1284, August 31, 1942, FDLR, Map Room Files, Box 83, Folder 3.

12. G-2 Intelligence Report Number 6, October 16, 1942, Martin M. Philipsborn Papers, Bo2, Folder: Africa, AFHQ II Corps, Intelligence, USAHEC.

13. Naval officer and Roosevelt adviser George Elsey is the likely author of an unsent letter with Roosevelt's signature dated October 15, 1942. Flatteringly describing Pétain as "the venerated hero of Verdun," it has a friendly, almost deferential tone, excusing Pétain for any actions the Germans might have forced him to take and pledging American cooperation with him. Elsey probably prepared it in case Pétain showed signs of welcoming the American landings in North Africa. That Elsey or anyone else in the White House thought Pétain might do so is further proof of the faith that at least some Americans had in the Lafayette tradition. Roosevelt to "My Dear Old Friend," November 15, 1940, FDRL, George Elsey Papers, Series 1, Box 1. My thanks to Andrew Stewart for bringing this letter to my attention.

14. R. T. Thomas, *Britain and Vichy: The Dilemma of Anglo-French Relations, 1940–1942* (New York: St. Martin's, 1979), 139–140.

15. David W. King to Colonel Donovan, January 26, 1943, https://www.cia.gov /library/readingroom/docs/CIA-RDP13X00001R000100440008-8.pdf. My thanks to Betsy Rohaly Smoot, Kenneth Johnson, and Phil McCarty who helped me identify King, a Harvard student who joined the French Foreign Legion in 1914 and in 1940 became one of the American vice-consuls in Morocco linked to the OSS spy scheme.

16. Funk, *Politics of TORCH,* 46.

17. Langer Papers, Chapter 8, Folder 1, USAHEC.

18. War Department to State Department, February 25, 1943, FDRL, Map Room Files, Box 83, Folder 3.

19. "Paraphrase of Telegram Received from Algiers to AGWAR and USFOR," January 23, 1943, https://www.cia.gov/library/readingroom/docs/CIA -RDP13X00001R000100440008-8.pdf.

20. Office of Strategic Services, "The Fall of France," April 1942, FO 371/36007, TNA.

21. G-2 Intelligence Report Number 4, October 2, 1942, Martin M. Philipsborn Papers, Box 2, Folder: "Africa, AFHQ II Corps, Intelligence," USAHEC, pp. 2–3.

22. OSS, "The Fall of France."

23. Atkinson, *Army at Dawn,* 123.

24. William Eddy to Colonel Brien Clark, November 29, 1942, Colonel Sir A D Dodds-Parker Papers, 10/81/1, IWM.

25. OSS, "The Fall of France."

26. "Meeting Notes, Secret Session, Darlan and the North African Expedition," December 10, 1942, CAC, EADE 3/2, p. 26.

27. OSS, "The Fall of France."

28. Howe, *Northwest Africa,* 57.

29. Funk, *Politics of TORCH,* 121.

30. Commander-in-Chief's Dispatch, 1942–1943, p. 4, USAHEC.

31. JSM, Washington to Chiefs of Staff, July 20, 1942, WO 193/860 Vichy, TNA.

32. Chiefs of Staff, London, to JSM, Washington Secret Cypher, October 6, 1942, PREM 3/439/3, TNA.

33. Atkinson, *Army at Dawn,* 112.

34. Robert Murphy, *Diplomat among Warriors: The Unique World of a Foreign Service Expert* (Garden City, NY: Doubleday, 1964), 127.

35. Martin Thomas, *The French Empire at War, 1940–1945* (Manchester, UK: University of Manchester Press, 1998), 160, 163.

36. Commander-in-Chief's Dispatch, p. 15, USAHEC.

37. "Évaluation des Moyens Nécessaires pour le Transport et l'Entretien d'un Corps Expéditionnaire," September 19, 1942, Dossier 22, Guerre 1939–1945, Vichy, Amérique, USA, Series 1GMII, AD.

38. Major George Bare, Infantry, Advanced Infantry Officers Course, 1947–1948: The Algiers Operation, 8–11 November 1942, p. 9, USAHEC D766.99.A4 B37 1947a.

39. Funk, *Politics of TORCH,* 189.

40. "L'Amiral Leahy: Cerveau Militaire du Président," October 1, 1942, and Henry-Haye, Report No. 92, October 27, 1942, Dossier 22, Guerre 1939–1945, Vichy, Amérique, USA, Series 1GMII, AD.

41. Bare, "The Algiers Operation," p. 4.

42. "Draft of Commander-in-Chief's Dispatch"; "Memoir: Chapters Thirteen to Nineteen," p. 102, Oscar Reeder Papers, USAHEC.

43. Howe, *Northwest Africa,* 89–92.

44. Translation of Report from Commander of the Garrison at Safi to Commander of Marrakesh Division, November 14, 1942, Subject: Operations for November 8 and 9, 1942, Oscar W. Koch Collection, Series III, G-2, Third Army, Subseries 1, Box 3, Folder 12, USAHEC.

45. Robert Paxton, *Parades and Politics at Vichy* (Princeton, NJ: Princeton University Press, 1966), 352.

46. Ernie Pyle, *Here Is Your War* (New York: Holt, 1943), 52.

47. Martin Thomas, "The Discarded Leader: General Henri Giraud and the Foundation of the French Committee of National Liberation," *French History* 10, no. 1 (1996): 87.

48. Langer Papers, Chapter 8, Folder 2, USAHEC; Commander-in-Chief's Dispatch, p. 3, USAHEC.

49. Langer Papers, Chapter 8, Folder 2, USAHEC.

50. "Draft of Commander in Chief's Dispatch, North Africa Campaign," [n.d.], Arthur Nevins Papers, Box 6, Folder 9, USAHEC.

51. Aidan Crawley, *De Gaulle* (New York: Bobbs-Merrill, 1969), 188.

52. He remained so for the rest of his life. He opposed Moroccan independence and broke with de Gaulle when the latter proposed independence for Algeria.

53. Funk, *Politics of TORCH,* 206.

54. Clark had told Mast the same white lie in Cherchell.

55. Murphy, *Diplomat among Warriors,* 129.

56. George E. Melton, *Darlan: Admiral and Statesman of France, 1881–1942* (Westport, CT: Praeger, 1998), 171.

57. Murphy, *Diplomat among Warriors,* 131.

58. Julian Jackson, *France: The Dark Years, 1940–1944* (New York: Oxford University Press, 2001), 224.

59. Melton, *Darlan,* 172–173.

60. Funk, *Politics of TORCH,* 217.

61. Funk, *Politics of TORCH,* 218.

62. Howe, *Northwest Africa,* 123.

63. Bare, "The Algiers Operation," p. 20.

64. Langer Papers, Chapter 8, Folder 2.

65. "Draft of Commander in Chief's Dispatch, North Africa Campaign," Arthur Nevins Papers, Box 6, Folder 9, USAHEC.

66. Atkinson, *Army at Dawn,* 165.

67. Melton, *Darlan,* 174–175.

68. Langer Papers, Chapter 8, Folder 2.

69. Howe, *Northwest Africa,* 263.

70. Marshall to Eisenhower, November 11, 1942, FDRL, Map Room Files, Box 105.

71. Commander-in-Chief's Dispatch, p. 16, USAHEC.

72. "Draft of Commander in Chief's Dispatch, North Africa Campaign."

73. Henry Blumenthal, *Illusion and Reality in Franco-American Diplomacy, 1914–1945* (Baton Rouge: Louisiana State University Press, 1986), 297–298.

74. Melton, *Darlan,* 185.

75. Murphy, *Diplomat among Warriors,* 141.

76. Murphy, *Diplomat among Warriors,* 142.

77. Jean-Pierre Azéma and Olivier Wierviorka, *Vichy, 1940–1944* (Paris: Tempus, 2004), 94.

78. Commander-in-Chief's Dispatch, p. 16, USAHEC.

79. Robert Paxton, *Vichy France: Old Guard and New Order, 1940–1944* (New York: Knopf, 1972), 316.

80. Langer Papers, Chapter 8, Folder 2, USAHEC.

81. Meredith Hindley, *Destination Casablanca: Exile, Espionage, and the Battle for North Africa in World War II* (Washington, DC: PublicAffairs, 2017), 342–343.

82. Oscar Reeder Papers, "Memoir: Chapters Thirteen to Nineteen," USAHEC, pp. 93, 102–104.

83. Thomas, *The French Empire at War,* 165–171.

84. Martin Evans, *Algeria: France's Undeclared War* (New York: Oxford University Press, 2012), 77. Abbas issued his "Manifesto of the Algerian People" in February 1943.

85. "Relations between Moslems and Americans in North Africa," May 21, 1943, https://www.cia.gov/library/readingroom/docs/CIA-RDP13X00001R0001 00440008-8.pdf.

86. See Martin Thomas, "Defending a Lost Cause? France and the United States Vision of Imperial Rule in French North Africa, 1945–1956," *Diplomatic History* 26, no. 2 (2002): 215–247.

87. For more, see Yves C. Aouté, "La place de l'Algérie dans le projet antijuif de Vichy," *Revue française d'histoire d'outre mer* 301 (1993).

88. Murphy, *Diplomat among Warriors,* 160–161.

89. Commander-in-Chief's Dispatch, p. 17, USAHEC.

90. Christine Lévisse-Touzé, "L'Afrique du nord pendant la seconde guerre mondiale," *Relations Internationales* 77 (1994): 9–19. Giraud removed Moncref Bey by force in 1943.

91. Melton, *Darlan,* 189; Murphy, *Diplomat among Warriors,* 138.

92. London to AGWAR, November 11, 1942, FDRL, Map Room Files Box 105. Notably, Eisenhower made the pledge while praising the great French imperialist and long-term governor of Morocco, Marshal Hubert Lyautey, on Lyautey's birthday.

93. Melton, *Darlan,* 198–199, 208.

94. Barnett Singer, *Maxime Weygand: A Biography of the French General in Two World Wars* (Jefferson, NC: McFarland, 2008), 172.

95. Henry Stimson and McGeorge Bundy, *On Active Service in Peace and War* (New York: Harper, 1948), 542.

96. Melton, *Darlan,* 197.

97. Douglas Waller, *Wild Bill Donovan: The Spymaster Who Created the OSS and Modern American Espionage* (New York: Free Press, 2011), 141.

98. Eric Larrabee, *Commander in Chief: Franklin Delano Roosevelt, His Lieutenants, and Their War* (New York: Touchstone, 1987), 424.

99. Howe, *Northwest Africa,* 267.

100. Thomas, *Britain and Vichy,* 154.

101. Pyle, *Here Is Your War,* 58.

102. Funk, *Politics of TORCH,* 113–114.

103. Jackson, *France,* 150. Such professions included teaching, the press, and the cinema.

104. Olivier Courteaux, *Canada between Vichy and Free France, 1940–1945* (Toronto: University of Toronto Press, 2013), 161; Thomas, *Britain and Vichy,* 157.

105. Memorandum of Conversation with the Assistant Secretary (Berle), Washington, November 16, 1942, FRUS I, pp. 441–442.

106. Thomas, *Britain and Vichy,* 141, 147.

107. Hindley, *Destination Casablanca*, 317.

108. Memorandum for Colonel Donovan, December 21, 1942, https://www.cia.gov /library/readingroom/docs/CIA-RDP13X00001R000100440008-8.pdf.

109. David Dilks, ed., *The Diaries of Sir Alexander Cadogan, 1938–1945* (London: Cassell, 1971), 498.

110. Thomas, *Britain and Vichy*, 152.

111. Cole to Handy, Cable Number 768, November 5, 1942, FDRL, Map Room Files, Box 83, Folder 3.

112. Funk, *Politics of TORCH*, 108, 245.

113. The photograph is in Howe, *Northwest Africa: Seizing the Initiative in the West*, 266.

114. https://avalon.law.yale.edu/wwii/north-af.asp.

115. Combined Chiefs of Staff to Eisenhower, November 29, 1942, FDRL, Map Room Files, Box 105.

116. "Meeting Notes, Secret Session, Darlan and the North African Expedition," December 10, 1942, CAC EADE 3 / 2.

117. Office of Strategic Services, Coordinator of Information, The War This Week, December 17–24, William Donovan Papers, Box 103B, USAHEC; Thomas, *Britain and Vichy*, 156.

118. "Relations between Moslems and Americans in North Africa."

119. P. F. Pugliese to Major Doering, March 11, 1943, https://www.cia.gov/library /readingroom/docs/CIA-RDP13X00001R000100440008-8.pdf.

120. "Relations between Moslems and Americans" and "Paraphrase of Telegram Received from Algiers to AGWAR and USFOR."

121. "Meeting Notes, Secret Session, Darlan and the North African Expedition," December 10, 1942, CAC EADE 3 / 2.

122. Office of Strategic Services, Coordinator of Information, The War This Week, December 17–24, William Donovan Papers, Box 103B, USAHEC.

123. Langer Papers, Chapter 9, Folder 1, USAHEC.

124. Larrabee, *Commander in Chief*, 424.

125. Matthews to Leahy, December 10, 1942, James Gavin Papers, Box 14, Folder 4, USAHEC.

126. "Meeting Notes, Secret Session, Darlan and the North African Expedition," December 10, 1942, CAC EADE 3 / 2.

127. London to AGWAR, November 26, 1942, FDRL, Map Room Files, Box 105.

128. Eisenhower to AGWAR, November 20, 1942, FDRL, Map Room Files, Box 105.

129. London to AGWAR, November 22, 1942, FDRL, Map Room Files, Box 105.

130. Larrabee, *Commander in Chief,* 426.

131. Melton, *Darlan,* 216–217. Alain Darlan did come to Warm Springs in 1943 at Roosevelt's invitation.

7. ROUND UP THE USUAL SUSPECTS

1. George Howe, *Northwest Africa: Seizing the Initiative in the West* (Washington, DC: Government Printing Office, 1957), chaps. 15–17.

2. German forces surrendered Tunis in May 1943.

3. Mario Faivre, *We Killed Darlan: A Personal Account of the French Resistance in North Africa, 1940–1942* (Manhattan, KS: Sunflower University Press, 1975), 52. He is interviewed (in French) at https://collections.ushmm.org/search /catalog/irn81472.

4. Although descended from the rival house of Orléans, by ruling as Henri VI, the comte could honor the Comte de Chambord. Also known as the Bourbon Henri V, Chambord never officially ruled but was the Legitimist pretender from 1844 until his death in 1883. In this way, Henri VI would symbolically end the dispute between the two branches of the French royal family and clear the way for a unity government, at least among royalists. See Maurice Samuels, *The Betrayal of the Duchess: The Scandal That Unmade the Bourbon Monarchy and Made France Modern* (New York: Basic Books, 2020).

5. Faivre, *We Killed Darlan,* 103. See also Anthony Verrier, *Assassination in Algiers: Churchill, Roosevelt, de Gaulle, and the Murder of Darlan* (London: Macmillan, 1990).

6. George Melton, *Darlan: Admiral and Statesman of France, 1881–1942* (Westport, CT: Praeger, 1998), 211.

7. One person who did was George Patton, who called Darlan's death a "distinct loss." Martin Blumenson, ed., *The Patton Papers, 1940–1945* (Boston: Da Capo, 1996), 143.

8. Jon B. Mikolashek, *General Mark Clark: Commander of the U.S. Fifth Army and Liberator of Rome* (Philadelphia: Casemate, 2013), 43.

9. Rick Atkinson, *An Army at Dawn: The War in North Africa, 1942–1943* (New York: Holt, 2007), 256.

10. Atkinson, *Army at Dawn,* 253.

11. Mark Clark, *Calculated Risk* (New York: Enigma Books, 2007), 109.

12. David Dutton, *Anthony Eden: A Life and Reputation* (London: Arnold, 1997), 159.

13. Cadogan Diary, 1942, entries for December 25 and 26, CAC, ACAD 1/11.

14. Julian Jackson, *De Gaulle* (Cambridge, MA: Harvard University Press, 2018), 250.

15. Aidan Crawley, *De Gaulle* (New York: Bobbs-Merrill, 1969), 189–190. Crawley and Cowles were married.

16. Report of activities of T. B. Kittredge for week ending 9 January 1943, Tracy Barrett Kittredge Papers, Record Number 60017.280, Hoover Library Digital Collections, Stanford University.

17. Jackson, *De Gaulle,* 250.

18. Darlan is buried in the Mers-el-Kébir cemetery.

19. Jackson, *De Gaulle,* 250.

20. Robert Murphy, *Diplomat among Warriors: The Unique World of a Foreign Service Expert* (Garden City, NY: Doubleday, 1964), 143.

21. Faivre, *We Killed Darlan,* 130. Bonnier was posthumously exonerated in December 1945 by a tribunal that ruled his act an honorable one in the interests of the liberation of France.

22. Harold Macmillan, "North Africa New Deal," February 19 to March 23, 1943, Macmillan c887, Bodleian Library, Oxford.

23. Roger Makins [Lord Sherfield] to Frank Lee, April 13, 1943, MS. Sherfield 520, Bodleian Library, Oxford. See also Jackson, *De Gaulle,* chap. 11.

24. To be fair, there were assassination rumors floating around about almost anyone who was anyone in a position of authority in France and Algeria in 1942.

25. R. T. Thomas, *Britain and Vichy: The Dilemma of Anglo-French Relations, 1940–1942* (New York: St. Martin's, 1979), 160–165.

26. Murphy, *Diplomat among Warriors,* 143.

27. Harold Macmillan, "Situation in French North Africa," January 26, 1943, Macmillan c887, Bodleian Library, Oxford.

28. "The Record of General de Gaulle," [August 1944], emphasis in original; Roosevelt to de Gaulle (draft), August 31, 1944, both in FDRL, Map Room Files, Box 166.

29. London to AGWAR, November 9, 1942, FDRL, Map Room Files, Box 166.

30. Julia C. Tobey, *Captain McCrae's War: The World War II Memoir of Franklin D. Roosevelt's Naval Aide and USS Iowa's First Commanding Officer* (New York: Skyhorse, 2016), chaps. 14–15 provide an insider's account of some of the arrangements, though McCrae was not a party to the most important discussions on matters regarding France.

31. Lord Halifax to Foreign Office, FO 371/36007, TNA.

32. "United States Attitudes toward the French," June 21, 1943, FO 371/36007, TNA.

33. Harold Macmillan, "The Development of Local American Opinion," January 5, 1944, Macmillan c887, Bodleian Library, Oxford.

34. Churchill to Foreign Office, January 2, 1943, FO 371/36007, TNA.

35. "US Policy toward France," January 2, 1943, FO 371/36007, TNA.

36. Minute of January 5, 1943, FO 371/36007, TNA. Emphasis in original.

37. Macmillan, "Situation in French North Africa."

38. Macmillan, "North Africa New Deal."

39. The Conferences at Washington, 1941–1942, and Casablanca, 1943, FRUS (Washington, DC: Government Printing Office, 1941–1943), 812–813.

40. Harold Macmillan, "The Weeks Between," May 30, 1943, Macmillan c887, Bodleian Library, Oxford.

41. Macmillan, "The Weeks Between"; Cadogan Minute, January 3, 1943.

42. Draft Telegram to H[is] M[ajesty's] Ambassador, Washington, January 2, 1943, FO 371/36007, TNA.

43. Coordinator of Information, The War This Week, December 17–24, 1942, Donovan Papers, USAHEC.

44. Coordinator of Information, The War This Week, January 1–7, 1943, Donovan Papers, USAHEC.

45. Olivier Courteaux, Canada between Vichy and Free France, 1940–1945 (Toronto: University of Toronto Press, 2013), 163.

46. Harold Macmillan, "Recognition," January 5, 1944, CAC DUFC 4/8, Section VIII.

47. Jackson, De Gaulle, 253.

48. Jackson, De Gaulle, 252.

49. Harold Macmillan, "Unparaphrased Version of a Most Secret Cypher Telegram, Personal for the Prime Minister," January 17, 1943, Macmillan c887, Bodleian Library, Oxford.

50. Prime Minister to Foreign Secretary, January 18, 1943, Macmillan c887, Bodleian Library, Oxford.

51. Jackson, De Gaulle, 253–255.

52. Murphy, Diplomat among Warriors, 170, 174–177.

53. Roger Makins to "My Dear William," April 3, 1943, MS Sherfield 520, Bodleian Library, Oxford.

54. Harold Macmillan, "Memorandum of 13th May [1943]," Macmillan c887, Bodleian Library, Oxford.

55. Harold Macmillan, "Wednesday, 2nd June [1943]," Macmillan c887, Bodleian Library, Oxford; Makins to Strang, May 4, 1943, MS Sherfield 520, Bodleian Library, Oxford.

56. He was André Philip, a brilliant but brash socialist economist whom de Gaulle sent to Washington in November 1942.

57. Sherfield to Strang, April 7, 1943, MS Sherfield 520, Department of Special Collections, Bodleian Library, Oxford.

58. Jacob Beam to H. Freeman Matthews, March 4, 1943, and February 26, 1943; Matthews to Ray Atherton, June 25, 1943, Robert Murphy Correspondence, Record Number 78060.173, Hoover Library Digital Collections, Stanford University.

59. Roger Makins to William Strang, May 4, 1943, MS Sherfield 520, Bodleian Library, Oxford.

60. Howe, *Northwest Africa,* 361–362; Marcel Vigneras, *Rearming the French* (Washington, DC: Government Printing Office, 1957).

61. Macmillan, "The Weeks Between."

62. Harold Macmillan, "The Path to Union, May 7 to June 4, 1943," Macmillan c887, Bodleian Library, Oxford.

63. Sherfield to Strang, April 3, 1943, Sherfield 520, Bodleian Library, Oxford.

64. Roger Makins to Ernest Makins, June 4, 1943, Sherfield 520, Bodleian Library, Oxford.

65. Harold Macmillan to Anthony Eden, February 27, 1943, Macmillan c887, Bodleian Library, Oxford.

66. Macmillan, "The Path to Union."

67. Harold Macmillan, "The Début of the Committee," August 27, 1943, Macmillan c887, Bodleian Library, Oxford.

68. Makins (Lord Sherfield) to H. E. Philip Nichols, June 6, 1943, and Sherfield to Strang, June 15, 1943, Sherfield 520, Bodleian Library, Oxford.

69. Harold Macmillan, "General de Gaulle," January 5, 1944, Macmillan c887, Bodleian Library, Oxford.

70. De Gaulle had a productive conference with Stalin in December 1944, a move that American officials read as a hostile act. For more, see https://digitalarchive.wilsoncenter.org/document/123309.pdf?v=d41d8cd98f00b204e9800998ecf8427e.

71. "Expediency Again," *Time,* July 5, 1943, 30.

72. Murphy, *Diplomat among Warriors*, 160.

73. "Critical North Africa Muddle Up to Roosevelt and Churchill," *Newsweek*, January 25, 1943, 37.

74. "There Is No France," *Time*, July 19, 1943, 17.

75. Macmillan, "The Development of Local American Opinion."

76. Jackson, *De Gaulle*, 275.

77. "General Situation at the End of September 1943"; Ambassador Winant to Secretary Hull, May 17, 1943; John Wiley to Cordell Hull, May 6, 1943; and Roosevelt to Churchill, May 8, 1943, all from FDRL, Map Room Files, Box 166.

78. Macmillan, "Début of the Committee."

79. Harold Macmillan to Anthony Eden, October 4, 1943, Macmillan c285, Private Memoranda, The French Story, 1943, and Macmillan, "The Decline of General Giraud," January 5, 1944, Macmillan c887, Bodleian Library, Oxford.

80. Harold Macmillan, "Recognition," January 5, 1944, CAC DUFC 4/8, Section II.

81. "Report on Tunisia," *Newsweek*, January 18, 1943, 19.

82. Harold Macmillan, "Record of Conversation with Mr. Cordell Hull, Friday, 15th October 1943," Macmillan c285, Private Memoranda, The French Story, 1943, Bodleian Library, Oxford.

83. Eric Larrabee, *Commander in Chief: Franklin Delano Roosevelt, His Lieutenants, and Their War* (New York: Touchstone, 1987), 426.

84. Macmillan, "The Decline of General Giraud"; Harold Macmillan, "Final Report as Resident Minister, January 5, 1944," FO 371/42132, TNA.

85. J. Rives Child to Hull, December 29, 1943, and Halifax to Foreign Office, February 4, 1944, FO 371/41922, TNA.

86. Office of Strategic Services, "Further Views of Abetz on the French Situation," December 6, 1943, William Donovan Papers, Box 79A, Volume 15, USAHEC and "Piétri Approached by Intermediary for United States," Donovan Papers, Box 79A, Volume 15, USAHEC.

87. Robert Paxton, *Vichy France: Old Guard and New Order* (New York: Knopf, 1972), 297.

88. Baldwin to Roosevelt, May 18, 1944, Arthur M. Schlesinger Papers, Mss Col 17775, Box 467, Folder Vichy, NYPL.

89. Macmillan to Eden, October 4, 1943.

90. Jackson, *De Gaulle*, 309.

91. Alfred D. Chandler, ed., *Papers of Dwight Eisenhower* (Baltimore: Johns Hopkins University Press, 1971), 3:1904.

92. Henry L. Stimson and McGeorge Bundy, *On Active Service in Peace and War* (New York: Harper, 1948), 551.

93. Harold Macmillan to Anthony Eden, February 27, 1943, Macmillan c887, Bodleian Library, Oxford.

94. Thomas, *Britain and Vichy,* 175–177. Lemaigre made his fortune in the peanut oil business. The OSS code named him Peanuts.

95. Stimson and Bundy, *On Active Service,* 548.

96. Jackson, *De Gaulle,* 314. Emphasis in original.

97. Robert Murphy to Cordell Hull, June 10, 1944, FDRL, Map Room Files, Box 166.

98. Some of the footage is at https://www.youtube.com/watch?v=jnFnLxc4eMM.

99. Jackson, *De Gaulle,* 317–318.

100. Hull to Algiers, June 20, 1944, FDRL, Map Room Files, Box 166.

101. "The Record of General de Gaulle."

102. Stimson and Bundy, *On Active Service,* 549–550.

103. Chandler, *Papers of Dwight Eisenhower,* 3:1691.

104. Hull to Algiers, June 20, 1944.

105. Stimson and Bundy, *On Active Service,* 551.

106. Jackson, *De Gaulle,* 319.

107. "Common Sense in Normandy," *Time,* July 17, 1944, 38.

108. Vichy Secretary of State for Maritime Affairs Rear Admiral Gabriel Auphan to Leahy, cited in Leahy memo, February 27, 1945, FDRL, Map Room Files, Box 166. Auphan served nine years in hard labor for his service to Vichy. He was also the man who gave the order for the fleet in Toulon to scuttle itself in 1942.

109. "French Internal Political Situation," Second Week of August 1944, Donovan Papers, Box 79A, Folder 15, USAHEC.

110. "Portuguese Report on Conditions in France," Second Week of October 1944, Donovan Papers, Box 79A, Folder 15, USAHEC.

111. Foreign Office to British Embassy, Washington, December 8, 1943, TNA FO 371 / 36007.

112. Duff Cooper to Foreign Office, January 19, 1944, TNA 371 / 36007.

CONCLUSION: AS TIME GOES BY

1. For more on the end of the occupation in English, see Fabrice Virgili, *Shorn Women: Gender and Punishment in Liberation France* (Oxford: Berg, 2002); Antony Beevor and Artemis Cooper, *Paris after the Liberation, 1944–1949* (London: Penguin, 1994); and Herbert Lottman, *The People's Anger: Justice and Revenge in Post-Liberation France* (London: Hutchinson, 1986).

2. Both men lived into their nineties. A few, like Joseph Darnand, did pay for their crimes. He died by firing squad in October 1945.

3. Henry Rousso, *Le syndrome de Vichy: De 1944 à nos jours* (Paris: Seuil, 1987), published in English as *The Vichy Syndrome: History and Memory in France since 1944* (Cambridge, MA: Harvard University Press, 1991). See also Pierre Laborie, *Le chagrin et le venin. Occupation, résistance, idées reçues* (Paris: Gallimard, 2014).

4. James McAuley, "Under Intense Fire, Macron Insists France Won't Honor Its Most Famous Marshal—and Nazi Collaborator," *Washington Post,* November 8, 2018, https://www.washingtonpost.com/world/2018/11/07/why-is -frances-macron-honoring-nazi-collaborator/.

5. See, for example, David Schmitz, *Thank God They Are on Our Side: The United States and Right-Wing Dictatorships, 1921–1965* (Chapel Hill: University of North Carolina Press, 1999), and Benjamin L. Alpers, *Dictators, Democracy, and American Public Culture: Envisioning the Totalitarian Enemy, 1920s–1950s* (Chapel Hill: University of North Carolina Press, 2003).

6. Robert Paxton, *Vichy France: Old Guard and New Order, 1940–1944* (New York: Columbia University Press, 1972).

7. FRUS, 1945, Europe, Volume IV, 661. A similar sentiment is in "Propaganda Intelligence Highlights, Western Europe, France," September 1, 1945, Donovan Papers, Box 82A, Volume 11, USAHEC.

8. The dark side of the liberation of France is covered in William I. Hitchcock, *The Bitter Road to Freedom: The Human Cost of Allied Victory in World War II Europe* (New York: Free Press, 2008), and Mary Louise Roberts, *What Soldiers Do: Sex and the American GI in World War II France* (Chicago: University of Chicago Press, 2013).

9. See Richard F. Kuisel, *Seducing the French: The Dilemma of Americanization* (Berkeley: University of California Press, 1993); Victoria de Grazia, *Irresistible Empire: America's Advance through Twentieth-Century Europe* (Cambridge, MA: Belknap, 2006); and Christopher Endy, *Cold War Holidays: American Tourism in France* (Chapel Hill: University of North Carolina Press, 2004).

10. Henry L. Stimson and McGeorge Bundy, *On Active Service in Peace and War* (New York: Hippocrene Books, 1971), 551.

11. Walter J. Brown Papers, Journals, MSS 243, Box 8, Folder 13, Clemson University, Special Collections Library.

12. Julian Jackson, *De Gaulle* (Cambridge, MA: Harvard University Press, 2018).

13. Later, in June 1946, Truman did join an international movement to release the aged and obviously senile Pétain, even offering him asylum in the United States.

14. Despite occasional calls over the years to reinter his remains in the massive cemetery at Douaumont near Verdun, Pétain is still buried in the communal cemetery at Port-Joinville on the Île d'Yeu. In 1973, a right-wing group did in fact try to move the body (Clyde H. Farnsworth, "Body of Pétain Stolen from Island Grave off France," *New York Times,* February 20, 1973, https://www.nytimes.com/1973/02/20/archives/body-of-petain-stolen-from-island-grave-off-france-body-of-marshal.html). His tombstone was vandalized in 2017.

15. The jury was out for sixty-two minutes. Some American observers thought the quick trial, verdict, and execution were intended as a warning to other collaborators that they should remain quiet and not dare to interfere with the creation of a new government in France.

16. Jackson, *De Gaulle,* pt. 5.

17. George Howe, *Northwest Africa: Seizing the Initiative in the West* (Washington, DC: Government Printing Office, 1957), 355, 357.

18. London to AGWAR, November 19, 1942, FDRL, Map Room Files, Box 105.

19. Rousso, *Vichy Syndrome,* 14–18; Hugo Frey, "Rebuilding France: Gaullist Historiography, the Rise-Fall Myth and French Identity (1945–58)," in *Writing National Histories: Western Europe since 1800,* ed. Stefan Berger, Mark Donovan, and Kevin Passmore (London: Routledge, 1999), 205–216.

ACKNOWLEDGMENTS

I must start by thanking my friend Andrew Stewart, who encouraged me to write this book, read an earlier draft, provided expert feedback, and sent me scans of important material from the Bodleian Library. Thanks also to Rob Citino, Jeremy Collins, and Pete Crean of the National World War II Museum in New Orleans for offering me a chance to give a talk about this project in its early stages. Alexandra Richie and Sarah Kirksey have been encouraging me all the way. Alex even bought me a can of Vichy shaving cream so I'd remember to work on this project each and every day. The rainy day the three of us spent sipping coffee in Bayeux and talking about the Second World War in France remains a highlight of that wonderful trip.

Finding research material in these challenging times of shutdowns and quarantine has not always been easy. Vanda Wilcox, friend and historian extraordinaire, helped me track down some French sources with a big assist from archivist Meg Roussel. Virginia Dilkes and Monique Seefried shared with me Virginia's aunt's diary of her time in Paris. A big thanks to Sylvain Kast and Pierre-Samuel Nathanson for their help in obtaining some of the images. My thanks also to Jonathan Fennell and Dan Todman for alerting me to the digitized copy of the Halifax diary. Thanks also to the staffs at the US Army Heritage and Education Center; the Library of Congress; the French diplomatic archives at La Courneuve; the British National Archives; the Churchill Archives Centre at Cambridge; and the British Library, all of which I was able to visit before travel stopped. I was in fact enjoying lunch at the British Library when a message came in suggesting I come home as soon as possible, before the border closed.

I am, as always, blessed with friends who listen to ideas, give me critical feedback, and answer sometimes odd questions. Thanks to Jonathan Boff, Bill Astore, Bill Johnsen, Betsy Rohaly Smoot, Augustine Meaher, Genevieve Lester, Ed Kaplan, Annette Becker, Leonard V. Smith, Axel Hardt, Bob Hamilton, Darrell Driver, Tim Cook, Arnaud Goujon, Derek Varble, Kara and Jason Vuic, Fredrik Logevall, Wayne Lee, Tami Biddle, and Margaret Macmillan. The two anonymous readers provided excellent suggestions. I kept hearing the voice of my late friend Dennis Showalter in my head as I worked on parts of this manuscript. I am ever and always grateful to him for all that he taught me about the Second World War. Thanks to Jon Parshall for the excellent work on the maps and Jonathan Krause for the index and wise counsel. Thanks to Geri Thoma for her help and to Kathleen McDermott, with whom I am delighted to work once again. They both provided expert guidance when I needed it.

Closer to home, Jim Breckenridge, Ruth Collins, Michelle Ryan, Harry Leach, Mark Duckenfield, Jeff Wilson, and Kevin Dixon deserve thanks for providing me a wonderful place to work at the US Army War College.

My always supportive wife, Barbara, and our wonderful daughters, Claire and Maya, know what they mean to me. A few words here can never thank them for all that they do. Their idea to get a puppy may have delayed my finishing this book, but Rosie certainly livened up the house during the dark months of quarantine and she has been a faithful companion on many early mornings and weekends spent writing. Thanks to Melissa Barrick for hosting her on those days when I needed a few hours of quiet.

I dedicate this book to my friend Geoff Megargee, who eagerly volunteered to read this manuscript in an earlier form. Although he never had that chance, he proved a valuable sounding board for my early ideas. We lost Geoff far too soon. I miss him, his encouragement, and his kindness.

ILLUSTRATION CREDITS

Maps on pages viii and 179 by John Parshall.

Page 29
Reproduced from a copy of "La France nouvelle travaille." Vichy: Secretariat général de l'information, 1941, in the collection of Sylvain Kast

Page 34
Bibliothèques Clermont Metropole / BnF

Page 56
Library of Congress, Prints and Photographs Division, LC-DIG-hec-28864

Page 70
Gallica / BnF

Page 78
Library of Congress, Prints and Photographs Division, LC-H22-D-7006

Page 86
BnF

Page 107
US Naval History and Heritage Command

Page 122
BnF

Page 130
Archives Nationales, Paris

Page 134
Library of Congress, Prints and Photographs Division, LC-USZ62-102620

Page 144
Franklin Roosevelt Presidential Library

Page 150
Gallica / BnF

Page 187
National Archives

Page 192
National Archives

Page 203
National Archives

Page 209
Reproduced from a copy of "La France nouvelle travaille." Vichy: Secretariat général de l'information, 1941, in the collection of Sylvain Kast

Page 221
Franklin Roosevelt Presidential Library

Page 230
Library of Congress, Prints and Photographs Division, LC-USZ62-130362

Page 245
National Archives

Page 249
National Archives UK

INDEX